Praise for *Unstill Life*
by Gabrielle Selz

"Reading Gabrielle Selz's telling of the exhilarating twentieth-century decades when American art remade itself is like sitting to one side at a New York opening with someone who knows every story inside out. No one has died and all the living are here, too: Max Beckmann, Karel Appel, Carolee Schneeman, Alberto Giacometti, Mark Rothko and so many others whirl past, as at the center, the writer's complicated parents, the visionary and philandering MoMA curator Peter Selz and the beautiful writer Thalia Cheronis, hold our attention. Informed by the author's tenderness and longing, *Unstill Life* has the vitality of witness and the intimacy of memoir at its best."

—Honor Moore, author of *The Bishop's Daughter*

"This intimate look at the art world's movers and shakers is from the perspective of the younger daughter of Peter Selz, a major curator and museum director. . . . It's an exuberant tale of artists from Rothko to Christo that makes the reader marvel that neither the daughter nor her mother ever rejected the rascal who both animated and complicated their lives."

—Gail Levin, biographer of Edward Hopper, Judy Chicago and Lee Krasner

"Life inspires art inspires life—all of which inspire Gabrielle Selz's sparkling memoir of her brilliant but chaotic family. In *Unstill Life*, the art and people ricochet off each other, wreaking havoc but also encouraging everyone to live more intense, artistic lives."　　　　—Charlotte Rogan, author of *The Lifeboat*

Unstill Life

A DAUGHTER'S MEMOIR OF ART AND LOVE
IN THE AGE OF ABSTRACTION

GABRIELLE SELZ

W. W. Norton & Company

NEW YORK | LONDON

With the exception of a few minor characters whose personal details and names I have changed to protect their privacy, I have not altered any names or information concerning the people involved.

Copyright © 2014 by Gabrielle Selz

Since this page cannot legibly accommodate all the copyright notices, pages 349–51 constitute an extension of the copyright pages.

A portion of the prologue and chapter 19 originally appeared in *More* magazine in 2012.

For information about permission to reproduce selections from this book, write to Permissions, W. W. Norton & Company, Inc., 500 Fifth Avenue, New York, NY 10110

For information about special discounts for bulk purchases, please contact W. W. Norton Special Sales at specialsales@wwnorton.com or 800-233-4830

Manufacturing by RR Donnelley, Harrisonburg
Book design by Chris Welch
Production manager: Devon Zahn

Library of Congress Cataloging-in-Publication Data

Selz, Gabrielle.
Unstill life : a daughter's memoir of art and love in the age of abstraction/Gabrielle Selz.—First edition.
      pages cm
   Includes bibliographical references.
   ISBN 978-0-393-23917-1 (hardcover)
1. Selz, Peter, 1919–   2. Art historians—United States—Biography.   3. Art critics—United States—Biography.   4. Art museum curators—United States—Biography.   I. Title.
   N7483.S383S45 2014
   708.0092—dc23
   [B]   2013041177

W. W. Norton & Company, Inc.
500 Fifth Avenue,
New York, N.Y. 10110
www.wwnorton.com

W. W. Norton & Company Ltd.
Castle House, 75/76 Wells Street,
London W1T 3QT   1 2 3 4 5 6 7 8 9 0

To my parents

To paint a small picture is to place yourself outside your experience . . . However you paint the larger picture, you are in it. It isn't something you command.

—*Mark Rothko* ("I Paint Very Large Pictures"—*1941*)

The goal of art is the vital expression of self.

—*Alfred Stieglitz*

CONTENTS

Unstill Life

PROLOGUE

By the time my father's train pulled into the old brick station in Hartford, Connecticut, it was nearly ten, as black as Hades outside, my mother would have said. The platform was deserted save for me and a woman so deeply bundled in a long down coat she looked like a mummy. Still, when my eighty-six-year-old father descended from the passenger car, he waved and called out, "Hello!" like royalty on parade. His overcoat was buttoned up to his chin against the chill night air, a bright yellow scarf encircled his neck, a red beret sat at a jaunty angle on his head and tufts of white hair poked out above either ear.

Arrivals are his most perfect incarnation, I thought as I watched him swing his small shoulder bag carelessly. But instead of coming toward me, my father immediately made a beeline for the woman hidden in her big coat. In his excitement and fatigue, he'd mistaken the down-coated figure on the platform for my mother.

"Dad," I called out as the woman backed away. Hearing my

voice, my startled father turned toward me with such a look of confusion that I burst into tears.

"Oh," he said, catching me in his arms. "Tell your old man all about it."

It was the early spring of 2005, and my mother had just been diagnosed with midstage Alzheimer's. When I'd called my father with the news a week ago, to my surprise he'd volunteered to make the journey east to help me inventory her art collection. My father, the art critic and historian, the intellectual bon vivant, the infamous womanizer, had come to help me appraise and catalogue, to rally and reflect and bid his final goodbye to the woman who had remained the love of his life.

My mother was my father's first wife. They were married for seventeen years. During the 1950s and '60s they were central figures in the New York art world, when my father reigned as the chief curator of painting and sculpture at the Museum of Modern Art and the *New York Times* dubbed him *Mr. Modern Art*. Our home hosted the most celebrated artists of the day: charismatic Willem de Kooning, who invented Abstract Expressionism and then changed direction to merge gestural painting with human depiction and reinvent the face; somber-faced, bespectacled Mark Rothko, who painted great tablets of color and wanted his paintings to evoke the depth of emotion usually only felt through music and poetry; swarthy Franz Kline, with his thick black mustache, who was labeled one of the original "action" painters; Robert Motherwell, who painted iconic, geometric forms and was accompanied by his elegant wife, Helen Frankenthaler, whose paintings of thinned-down colors washed across the unprimed canvas; Ad Reinhardt, with a square head and broad shoulders, whom we called the black monk because of his dark monochromatic paintings; Philip Guston, a man with a huge slab of a face, a cigarette always dangling from his lips, who painted in soft pinks; and wild young Larry Rivers, who combined elements of Expressionism with early Pop art. Standing at the edge of the dining room of our Central Park West apartment, this was the world I watched: bright, saturated with art, glamorous but intimate, risqué and intellectual. At its center was my insatiable, animated father.

My elusive mother was his perfect contrast. She was a writer who liked stories more than people—with the exception of my father, whom she adored more than anything. She liked to sit still while "floating free." He liked to dart about and *do*. He was as full of turmoil as the art he championed. She was as contained and mysterious as a box by Joseph Cornell, her favorite artist. For a time he enlarged her world and she anchored his. Together they were two riddles that solved each other.

Then, abruptly in 1965, after seventeen years of marriage, the perfect design of their point-counterpoint fell apart. When I was seven, my father quit the Museum of Modern Art, abandoned my mother and our family and moved to California to direct his own museum. In less than ten years, he remarried four more times. My mother said wryly, "Your father has a gift for starting over." Though my mother had her share of boyfriends, she never remarried. She clung to the hope that they'd end up back together. Between each of his marriages—and often during them—my parents would briefly reunite. But the same problem recurred. My father was chronically, flagrantly unfaithful.

Still, art—far more so than their children—remained their passion and their glue.

THE MORNING AFTER my father's arrival, I found him wandering through my mother's house ogling the art. Stopping in front of the dining room table, he patted it like an old friend. He caressed the smooth surface of the elegant Biedermeier cabinet in the corner. Hands clasped behind his back, he smiled and nodded at the paintings on her walls, more than friends, some actually beloveds. Over against the couch he picked up a small Renaissance drawing of the madonna and child that I'd set aside. "I gave this to your mother when she was pregnant," he said excitedly. "Don't sell it, give it to me. Oh, wouldn't it be nice to have it again?"

I put my coffee cup down and pried the madonna from his grasp, remembering how my father had a special knack for getting what he wanted. "Mom told me to keep the Carracci. It's a mother and child. Besides, you took what you wanted when you left. What would you do with it now?"

"She's so beautiful." My father eyed the madonna with yearning, as if she were a fair damsel escaping his advances.

But I marched away, clutching the picture. I was going to put this beautiful lady high up on a shelf and out of his reach.

Over the next few hours we went through the house, room by room, wall by wall, painting by painting, first photographing each, then lifting them gently off their hooks, measuring and recording height by width—"Not width by height?" I asked.

No; my father shook his head. This was how it was done. It was essential to document where each piece had been created, shown, auctioned, catalogued, all this was imperative. Each work of art came from a place and had a history of relationships. Art breathed and had a life story.

While we inventoried, my father brought me up-to-date. He was finishing a book on the role of California art and artists in politics and culture since 1945, writing a catalogue for a show in South Korea on Egon Schiele, the Austrian figurative Expressionist who at the beginning of the twentieth century painted beautifully tortured nudes, and then he was to set off for Italy with his current wife so he could see Venice one last time. My father was like an old battleship that just kept cresting, dynamic and resilient. Sometimes his need to recite his latest list of accomplishments annoyed me. I'd feel envious and resentful, as if our family were just debris in his wake. Today, though, I felt sad. Among my mother's belongings I had just unearthed the broken Picasso plate. It pained me to realize how desperately she'd clung to a past, even a broken past. Leaning against the molded wooden doorframe, my father sighed. "We bought that plate when we were in Paris in 1950. I wonder how it broke."

I didn't want to tell him that I was the one who broke their Picasso plate, years before.

But my father had already moved on. "Now, that's certainly worth something." He was standing below the Karel Appel portrait of my mother done in 1963, not long before their divorce. Keeping it hidden in a closet for years, she had only recently pulled the painting out, and hung it in a position of honor on her dining room wall.

My father smiled at my mother's intense stare. "She was an original. She was interesting. I should never have left."

I looked from the restless man beside me to the image of my mother. The odd thing about the painting was the way Appel had painted my mother's head and neck, like a balloon on the end of a long string. When I was a child, crossing the busy streets of New York, I used to grab *her* hand in an effort to tether us together. Appel had captured that quality of my mother perfectly. My father was right, my mother was interesting; they were both fascinating people. He was the headwater, a source surging in multiple directions. Living beside him, for my mother—and my sister and I—had at turns been exhilarating and overpowering.

Later that night, my father snoring in my mother's bed, I headed up to the attic to find my mother's ancient rotting trunk held together with fraying rope. First I lifted out my mother's old fabric photograph albums, then her scrapbook, all but ending in 1957, the year she gave birth to my sister, and my father's many scrapbooks that she'd continued to diligently compile well into the 1980s—nearly twenty years after their divorce. I set these aside. Farther down, at the very bottom of the trunk, I found what I was searching for: the journals my mother had kept throughout her life, and two shoe boxes full of cassette tapes my parents had made together in the 1990s. She had hoped to write a book about their ringside seat in the art world. Now this trunk of memoirs and stories was part of my legacy.

I had known that my mother kept journals, but I had never been granted full access to them before. I didn't know then what I would do with all this material. My mother was sick and her once-lyrical voice was fading, being replaced by a flat monotone that left me heartbroken. It would take me another year to even listen to the tapes. Just hearing the musical lilt in her voice, my father's rich baritone, my parents' banter as they discussed a world and a life that had vanished and yet still felt present, was like sitting outside a room I couldn't enter, only press my ear against the door. Growing up, too young to be part of the art world, I'd longed to be inside that room to stay up late and go to the party.

When I was little, for a treat, my mother used to read excerpts to Tanya and me. I loved the anecdotes of our babyhood (*At age two, Tanya says she only wants to wear "pity dresses," and Gaby at eighteen months howls with complete abandon*), but my mother's stories and descriptions of the art world were what I truly longed to hear. That night, while my father slept, I flipped open the journal dated 1963:

Karel Appel is painting portraits of people who are part of The Scene— Count Basie, Dizzy Gillespie, Miles Davis—and wants to add me to this jazzy list because he says he loves the color of my eyes. My eyes are not my best feature, but who really knows what appeals to an abstract artist—that green eyeliner I buy at Woolworths? Pete said sure, without even asking me or considering how to find enough babysitters. I put on the yellow jersey and caught the bus down to Walasse Ting's studio. [Ting was a Chinese-American poet and painter of nudes and animals.] *European artists all try to come to New York for a spell if they can borrow a studio. Ting's using Appel's in Holland, I think, while Appel does a series of portraits of folks who are part of The Scene.—I've lost the knack for sitting. I can't stay still anymore. Maybe it's The Scene: what it's done to me. The studio was hot, and I was itchy, and the phone kept ringing. He would answer in Dutch monosyllables and then explain it was his wife, and a few minutes later she'd call again. There was a wonderful painting of her on the wall as a voluptuous reclining Negro nude, with exaggerated features. She is extremely slender: an exquisitely famished looking, very white Balenciaga model with precision-cut features and dark eyes the size of dessert plates. He painted her unseen self. I hate my own portrait! I am furious and pleased. It is a fearsome portrait and Pete says a great painting.*

Though I love art, I am not an artist, a historian or a critic. Yet my mother had bequeathed this story to me. It felt imperative to pick up the threads that she had left behind. This memoir is about my relationship with my mother and father, their passion for each other and their love affair with the art and artists of the twentieth century. To borrow a phrase from my father, it is a pictorial history of the moments we lived through, when art and life came together and defined one another.

Portrait of a Woman (Thalia Selz)
Karel Appel, 1963

PART ONE

New Images

ART IS A FORM OF MANIFEST REVOLT, TOTAL AND COMPLETE.

—*Jean Tinguely*

THE OBJECT OF ART IS NOT TO REPRODUCE REALITY, BUT TO CREATE A REALITY OF THE SAME INTENSITY.

—*Alberto Giacometti*

Chapter 1

Germany, 1919

M y father was born just after the end of the First World
War, into the tiny sliver of hope that followed the turmoil and horror of the trenches. A few months later
the map of Europe was redrawn and the Treaty of Versailles
was signed. That same year, 1919, the United States adopted the
Eighteenth Amendment to the Constitution, prohibiting the
sale of alcohol, and proposed the Nineteenth Amendment—not
to be ratified until the following year—giving women the right
to vote. In Africa, an astronomer tested and confirmed Albert
Einstein's theory of relativity. Mass did indeed cause space to
bend, the shortest distance between two points was not a straight
line because straight lines couldn't exist in a curved universe. In
Paris, Pablo Picasso and Georges Braque had taken their invention of Cubism to its most mathematical conclusion: perspective
in art, like relativity in space-time, was a matter of viewpoint.
Ideas were everywhere, and so was the desire for change. In

Weimar, Germany, the new republic was formed, a democracy to replace the imperial government, and a sergeant major and architect named Walter Gropius came back from the Western Front with a dream. He opened a school that would combine all the arts—painting, sculpture and architecture, as well as the crafts of design and furniture making, under one roof—creating "a total art." The Bauhaus was based on the utopian philosophy that art did not only reflect society, but could actually change it. Bauhaus members believed that art could lead mankind into a better, fairer, more equal world. A world where good design shaped the way human beings led their lives.

The old world, a world of emperors and kings, absolute time and realistic representation, was dying, and history's clock, Newton's clock of an ordered universe, was resetting itself.

Some two hundred miles southeast of Weimar, my father grew up in the crumbling remnants of this old world, in the fairy-tale landscape of the Black Forest. In the predominately Catholic city of Munich, his Jewish family was wealthy and educated. As a child, he was accustomed to affluence and prestige—noblesse, he joked. The family home in the center of Munich took up a city block and resembled a small Baroque palace with turrets, domes and a crown on the roof.

Divorce ran back through my family line like a genetic muta-tion. My father's mother, Edith, was married and the mother of a son, when on a ski vacation in the Alps she met Eugen Selz, an eye surgeon considerably older than her. Eugen was so smit-ten by Edith's beauty that the next day he placed a peach in the snow for her to discover as she swooped down the slopes on her wooden skis. A peach in the snow, a girl in furs, a man in spec-tacles, soon they fell in love and she divorced her husband and

Family home in Munich on Maximilliansplatz.

married Eugen, having two more sons with him. My father was the youngest, and her least favorite child.

Edith had wanted a peaceful girl and my father was an active boy, not good at either tranquillity or silence. He told me he was sent away as a child because he was too energetic—*wildfang*. In an effort to quiet him down he was sent to a Kinderheim, a children's home where rambunctious eight- and nine-year-old boys were forced to hike in the mornings and were restrained to their beds in the afternoons. Though he spent two summers being confined while the sun shone, the experience didn't curb his need for movement. He did not do well in school or his studies, preferring to entertain himself with silly pranks. He liked to dangle a long purse attached to a string over the balcony of the family apartment. Whenever a passerby tried to grab the purse, Dad would gleefully yank the string out of reach of the grasping hands. My father, the mischievous troublemaker, was labeled the child who would never amount to anything.

But his maternal grandfather saw something in his curious, impish grandson. Julius Drey was an antique dealer who specialized in objets d'art and Renaissance paintings, with the occasional modern piece. For a while, a Rodin sculpture sat in his courtyard. In an effort to calm his grandson down, Drey began to take my father under his wing. Just as my father would later introduce me to art, his grandfather brought him along to the museums and galleries where he made his acquisitions. He showed him Titians, El Grecos and Rembrandts. Almost immediately art both calmed and engaged my father.

Through art, the new ideas of modernist thought trickled into my great-grandfather's home and into my father's mind and heart. There, Dad was exposed to the decadence migrating down from the wild cabaret life of Berlin, the freewheeling theatrics of Bertholt Brecht, the films of Fritz Lang as well as the ideas of the Bauhaus, and a circle of intellectuals that included the art dealer Heinrich Thannhauser, whose son would later bequest his magnificent collection of Impressionist, Cubist, Futurist and German Expressionist paintings that now make up a large portion of the Guggenheim Museum's permanent collection.

It was a predictable life. The household ran like an elegant timepiece. Each Sunday morning the family went to hear the army band play Brahms or Beethoven in the old city's central square, then, at one minute to one p.m., they were called to the family dinner table by the gong of a bell rung by one of the servants. But in 1934 when my father was fifteen years old, his grandfather Drey died just as Hitler was gaining power. His grandmother, not knowing the value of the estate, let alone the art business, hastily sold off the mansion and art collection. Years later, when my father occasionally saw pieces on a museum's or collector's wall that had once hung in his grandfather's house, his face would elongate, his eyes droop like a gaunt El Greco figure. "Now, this is very sad," he'd say, nodding his head hello and then goodbye to the Toulouse-Lautrec or the Dürer on the wall.

For the next three years my father watched the world around him change as the Nazi Party established its regime. His father's practice was restricted to only Jewish clients and the family was forced to move into the ophthalmology office, only a block from the Gestapo headquarters. Out on the streets of Munich my father saw the great pageantry of the Third Reich, red banners emblazoned with swastikas, parades of soldiers in perfect goose step. The Bauhaus, with its utopian vision of an art that would lift up the masses, closed its doors. The masses were now dressed in brown shirts and marching with synchronized locked knees and rifles held high. An army of blue-eyed, clean-shaven boys too young to remember the stink of the trenches, only the decadence and poverty that followed. The first wave of intellectuals fled. Finally, when Jews were banned from employment and education and lost their rights as citizens, papers were secured for my father to go to America to complete school. Hoping that the conflict would blow over soon, not envisioning the slaughter that would follow, his parents decided to remain behind.

Now, truly, my father did not want to come to America. He was eager to strike out on his own and go to Palestine to fight with the Zionists instead. Though his family was secular, he was a hotheaded seventeen-year-old boy, angry at being forced to wear the Star of David and denied an education. He argued with his father for months, finally relenting and agreeing on the destination. Once in America, my father reasoned, he would find his way to Palestine.

Before he left, my father remembers seeing his first glimpse of contemporary German art put on view at the Munich police station for the purpose of ridicule for its loose moral values. The Degenerate Art Exhibition would eventually travel to a number of museums in Germany and Austria and be seen by almost three million people. Years later my father would write, *Ironically, the original Degenerate Art Exhibition turned out to be the forerunner of the big museum blockbusters, and its attendance record has still not been equaled.* Crowded on the walls, the first paintings my father saw were by Max Beckmann, followed by Wassily Kandinsky and Paul Klee. Kandinsky, the pure inventor of abstraction, and Beckmann, the great figurative painter, represented the two poles of expression my father would vibrate between for the rest of his life.

But it was Beckmann my father first fell in love with. The most esteemed painter in Germany, Beckmann had developed a style radically altered after his experience as a medic on the front lines during the First World War. *Yesterday we came across a cemetery that had been completely destroyed by shellfire . . . The shells had unceremoniously exposed their distinguished occupants to the light of day, and bones, hair, and bits of clothing could be seen through cracks in the burst-open coffins.* Beckmann didn't turn away. He sketched what he saw and again and again drew his own reaction. Over his lifetime, the number and intensity of his self-portraits matched only Picasso's and Rembrandt's. After suffering a nervous breakdown at the front, Beckmann was discharged. When he again picked up his paintbrush, his once-elegant academic figures had become distorted grotesques crammed on the canvas, moving in foreshortened space, like the soldiers compressed in trenches. His narrow canvases sucked the viewer into the dramas he portrayed. Often he placed an image of himself in these scenes, the artist as chronicler and depicter, the artist as witness and stage manager of history. At the time of my father's birth in 1919, Beckmann was renowned and lauded. But in 1933 the Nazis marked Beckmann a "cultural Bolshevik" and dismissed him from his teaching position at the Städelschule Academy of Fine Art in Frankfurt. Beckmann fled to Amsterdam, where he lived in poverty, using his bedsheets for canvas, eventually making his way to America after the war. More than five hundred of his works were confiscated from German museums, some displayed in the Degenerate Art Exhibition.

To a young man who had been labeled a Jew, the Degenerative Art Exhibition at the police station was a powerful moment of identification. Here on the walls were artists who, in affirming the self, had been branded for their personal expression. My father vowed he would never allow himself to be confined or pigeonholed again.

In 1937, when my father boarded the ship *Europa* bound for America, he wasn't sure he'd ever see his parents again. He had few possessions: a hard suitcase, a little book of Rainer Maria Rilke poetry, an overcoat, a Homburg hat and a pair of plain blue ceramic candlesticks. Standing on the ship's deck a week later, glimpsing the skyline of Manhattan for the first time, so modern and strong, its architecture so sharp and defined compared to the ornate Bavarian buildings of his homeland, my father instantly fell in love with the city. Forget Palestine, New York was where he wanted to be. This, of course, was my restless father in a nutshell: a man who, in fleeing one world for another, learned early to embrace the exhilaration of constant change.

In America he was sponsored by the Liebmanns, a branch of my father's family that owned the Rheingold Beer Company. Though they sent him to Fieldston Academy, a fancy prep school in Riverdale, to learn English and finish high school, he had to live on a tiny stipend, alone in near-poverty. My father was not the only person they sponsored. At least forty Jews owed their lives to the Liebmanns.

Still, my father painted a positive picture of this period of his life, saying jovially, "All the other boys at school arrived in limousines, but I took the subway and had an hour each way to study." On weekends he explored the city, wandering down to the docks and climbing aboard the great ocean liners, wondering if his parents would ever arrive.

A year passed. My father graduated from Fieldston and was called to meet with his wealthy relatives in their large Park Avenue apartment. "What do you intend to do with your life?" they wanted to know.

Reaching back into his memory, he recollected the times when he had been most happy, viewing art with his grandfather Drey. "Perhaps something in the art business?" my father suggested.

His relatives shook their heads. "No, no, we already have a cousin in the art world. But nothing's ever become of Cousin Alfred."

This was how my father learned that he was distantly related to Alfred Stieglitz, the famous photographer and gallery owner. How this notorious cousin had slipped under my father's family radar was a mystery. But Stieglitz, with his multiple liaisons and his habit of borrowing and losing money, was not well thought of by the upstanding branch of the family. In 1907 Stieglitz had scandalized American audiences—and the family—by showing nude photographs. It was one thing to show paintings of nudes, but a photograph was almost real. Then, in 1917, Stieglitz had photographed Marcel Duchamp's *Fountain*, an actual urinal that Duchamp had placed on a pedestal and called art! This was not art, his relatives said, but a bathroom appliance! Like a dog getting the whiff of a scent, my father's nostrils must have flared. Off he immediately went to the American Place Gallery to meet the notorious Mr. Stieglitz, who by then was quite ancient and, when not doing business, napped, regal as a statue and dressed severely all in black, under a white sheet in the back of the gallery. As soon as a possible patron entered his gallery, Stieglitz would throw off his sheet and sweep into the room in a long flowing black cape—he was famous for parading around in a cape, even inside. When asked the price of a painting, Stieglitz would slyly eye the buyer up and down, sizing up the potential of his wallet before inquiring, "What is it worth to you?"

Stieglitz took my father under his cape and introduced him to Dorothy Norman, his paramour, who published his translations of a few Rilke poems in her journal, *Twice a Year*. My father was elated to be in the company of Henry Miller and André Malraux, even if only in translation. He wanted American readers to experience the haunting lyricism of the poet who had sustained him across the sea. *Who now dies anywhere in the world, / without cause dies in the world, / looks at me.*

Word finally came from Europe. His mother and father had barely escaped Kristallnacht, the Night of Broken Glass. It had been the habit of my ophthalmologist grandfather to regularly examine the nuns' eyes at the local convent for free. Early on the day of November 9, before the riots, deportation and deaths began, two nuns, hearing what was planned for the city's Jews, visited my grandfather Selz's office on the pretext of an eye complaint. Disguising my grandfather in a nun's habit, they spirited him out of danger and into hiding in the convent until my grandmother Edith could be fetched. Passage was booked, first on the train to England, then on the voyage over submarine-infested waters to join my father in America. Eventually my grandfather Selz was able to find work for an optometrist making eyeglasses.

By now my father was enrolled in college at Columbia, but he was forced to quit to help support his parents. Employed in a lowly job at the Rheingold brewery, he scrubbed out beer vats in Brooklyn. He hated the hard labor and the fact that, although the business was owned by Jews, all the brewers employed there, except for him, belonged to the German American Bund— brown-shirted members of the American Nazi Party who celebrated each German war victory with beer fests. Even if he was lucky enough to be promoted to beer salesman or manager, he knew he didn't want to stay at the brewery. But as an immigrant with little means and a family to help care for, his future looked bleak.

Again he found his salvation in art. Up until 1942, when he was drafted into the army, my father continued toiling at the brewery on weekdays, but come the weekends he'd immediately go down to Stieglitz's gallery to sit at his feet and meet modern artists like Georgia O'Keeffe. When I was older and heard the story of my father's introduction to the New York art world, I tried to picture him as the gaunt young immigrant who smelled of stale beer and sat at the feet of the white-haired old man in a cape. In my imagination old Mr. Stieglitz looked like a cross between Santa

Claus and the Wizard of Oz. It made me laugh: I couldn't imagine my father at anybody's feet.

Chicago, Illinois, 1939

On my father's side I am descended from a pure Greek line. But on my mother's, the royal blood of the Hamlins goes all the way back to Edward III of England. My mother wrote this in her first diary when she was fourteen. True, my grandmother's family could trace its lineage back past the founding of our republic, all the way to an English king, but they were impoverished New Englanders who had ridden in a covered wagon all the way from the dunes of Cape Cod to a one-room farmhouse in the flat Midwest. My grandmother's parents had been divorced, uncommon in nineteenth century America, and for a long time my grandmother was certain she'd never marry. Men drank and fornicated, and she wanted to be a scholar. She had been the first woman in her family to go to college, on a scholarship, no less, where she'd studied Old English. (Later we grandchildren dubbed her Grammar instead of Grandma.) While at Oberlin, she'd been so poor she lived on lard spread over bread crusts. Then she met my grandfather. In a few short minutes he swept her off her high laced-up boots. Standing across the room at a party, he threw an entire bag of cherries into the white lap of her long skirt, one by one.

He was a Greek peasant, on his way to becoming a chemist, and everyone called him Doc. Boisterous and brilliant, with a square chin and a waxed mustache, he was known for his charm as well as his temper. (He threw more than cherries.) It took Doc three years to convince Grammar to marry him. He plainly stated that he didn't want children. Having survived poverty and famine in the mountains of Sparta when he was growing up, during a time that included the early death by starvation of two of his siblings, he was terrified of losing a child. Grammar gave up her pursuit of Old English verse (although she never stopped quoting Beowulf: *Fate goes ever as fate must*) and settled in Chicago, where she became Doc's helpmate, boxing up his chemicals and editing his lectures and books, and eventually sneaking my mother and then her baby brother into this world by waiting too long to confide her pregnancies.

They named their baby girl Thalia, after the Greek muse for music and dance, but everyone called her Lala. Even though her father hadn't wanted children, she never felt unloved. Years later, she would repeat to me the same words he'd said to her. "I may not have wanted you. But I loved you once you got here." So I knew how those words made her feel. They made her feel special, as if her very appearance on this earth had changed his mind.

While she was growing up, her father's laboratory was housed in a shack in the backyard out of which colored smoke billowed. As a little girl, my mother thought he was a wizard. He'd write her name in fire on the Fourth of July and sprinkle her Halloween costumes in chemical compounds so that when she walked down the street she glowed and sparkled like a real fairy princess.

By the time she was fourteen and began her first journal, she was already five-foot-eight—the tallest girl in her grade. *I am not pretty. Standing before the mirror I have once or twice thought myself so, but in comparison with average girls, I am not pretty. However, I have long, what some people call artistic hands, and I am slender. I have a quick temper, a dreamy and somewhat escapist disposition, and an honest enough heart.*

Her favorite book was *Jane Eyre*, her favorite painting was

Titian's *Portrait of a Man in a Red Cap*, her favorite star was Bette
Davis and her most prominent virtue: honest thinking.

The war raged in Europe. In New York my father worked at
the brewery and escaped to art galleries whenever he had time
off. He had a German girlfriend by then, but she soon fell in love
with an art dealer and broke my father's young heart. Still, he had
paintings to distract him. The first museum devoted entirely to
modern art had opened in New York and those of the European
avant-garde who could escape Hitler flocked to America. In the
Midwest my mother's parents hung over the radio. *They turn the
dial, stop it: across the waters come the words, "Hello! Hello! Berlin!
Britain is at war with you!"*

Strays started to show up regularly at my mother's kitchen door
on Ardmore Avenue, boys from Greece or Italy or even young
Negro men who had been told in the streets of Chicago, "Go find
the Greek Doc, he will help you." There had always been strays
since the Depression, anyone with a real or manufactured need
for charity was welcome, and now they even included refugees.
If they were injured or sick, out came the iodine and alcohol.
Doc would dress their wounds and tend to them, while Grammar
fed them and made up the cot in the basement. The kitchen, my
mother said, often smelled of sick. Sometimes these strays would
stay on for weeks or even months, helping in the laboratory until
they were back on their feet. Working for Doc, they packed up the
indicator dyes that were needed for the war, dyes that could register the presence of poisonous gas and save lives. But no matter
how they covered their hands with gloves, their faces with gauze
masks, in the evenings, over the bowls of Grammar's egg lemon
soup, my mother watched the strays bleed color—red and green
dyes seeped out of their pores, even their eyes oozed wet purple

tears. Like the images in the Expressionist paintings she would later come to love, the war bled down these boys' faces in bright pigments and into the family's yellow-yolked soup.

When she was not in school, my mother would sneak into the lab. Young and curious, she was practicing her skills at flirtation, and would sit and talk to the boys while she did her Latin homework. She had a series of crushes, and to each her father reacted the same way, piping home a female—a secretary or Greek waitress—to distract these stray boys from his daughter.

Did she know that some of these procured women had been her father's lovers? Late at night, through the heating vents, she heard her parents arguing the same way she heard them making love—passionately. When Grammar threatened to walk out, Doc barked, "Man is born free, woman enslaves him." Soon enough the stray would begin dating the girl Doc had found for him, and the danger for adolescent Lala was averted.

Half of Chicago was parked on their front porch anyway, eating, drinking and engaging in fervent disputes. Tempestuous Greeks who, given the choice between talking and yelling, always chose the latter. From the laboratory, along with his rare chemical practice, Doc concocted his *special* brandy even long after Prohibition was repealed and the ban on alcohol was lifted. (Forty years later there was still a store of that potent brandy that I discovered in an old closet and, trying to get drunk at age fifteen, I made myself violently sick instead.) Back then Doc was the noisy beating heart of a population that, outside of Athens, was then the largest enclave of Greeks in the world. My mother said she knew from an early age that if she wanted to see the world, all she had to do was hang around her own house and watch.

On December 7, 1941, my mother was sixteen and she still

favored Titian and Bette Davis, though *Pride and Prejudice* was running a close second to *Jane Eyre*, and her declared virtue had modified slightly: *It is my great effort to be honest with myself,* she wrote from her living room. *Wonderful things have happened to me. I've been to Europe, survived pneumonia and diphtheria, I have two brilliant and fascinating people for parents, many interesting personalities come through my home, I've seen two operas, I wear clothes well.* She was feeling lucky that night in her safe house with the noise of her family all around her. *Japan has declared war on the United States. The President and his cabinet are in a conference. Pearl Harbor in the Hawaiian Islands was bombed early this morning. Everyone seems to agree we will be at war. It changes one's whole perspective. But I am fortunate because I have a chance to make something fine of myself.*

Two years later, my mother did set off to make something of herself. Following in Grammar's footsteps, she went to Oberlin College, where there were almost no male civilians on campus, only the 4-F boys. There, she blossomed from the gawky, too-tall girl into an elegant woman with a swan's neck. She cut her long hair so that it framed her face in thick dark waves. She began to apply lipstick and mascara. After she nearly failed chemistry, she wrote home, *Unlike Daddy I am not the least bit scientific.* She wanted to study art history instead. *I am much more prone to fantasy than fact gathering.* Art history was the study of the most beautiful things on earth: Renaissance paintings, Greek and Roman sculptures of winged Nikes and Adonises.

MY MOTHER ALMOST didn't attend the Art Department faculty tea that afternoon in 1947. For one thing, she didn't drink tea, associating it with childhood warnings to stay away from the TNT (tea-and-tea) explosives in Doc's lab. For another, she was at the University of Chicago, but no longer studying art. Instead, she was enrolled in the English Department, on her way to getting a master's degree. Doc had insisted that she get a degree that was useful, so she would always have a job to fall back on, like teaching English. He didn't trust this newfangled field of art history. Still, she liked to sneak into the art history lectures to look at the slides, which was how she'd been invited to the party. Too shy to mingle, she leaned languidly against the wall, nibbling a crustless cucumber sandwich and mentally taking notes for her journal.

A dark-eyed, handsome man strode across the room toward her with a loose smile on his face, interrupting her reverie with the words, "You are a Modigliani in repose."

"Aren't they all," my mother quipped. But she was immediately drawn in by his deep baritone voice and foreign accent. He sounded like those strays who'd shown up at the kitchen door, only he was far more sophisticated. His voice rumbled with excitement, like a brook tumbling down a mountain. He gestured with his hands, full of the same vitality, but not quite the same decibel level, as her father. He wanted to go places. He talked of art and beauty and philosophy.

By now my father had left the brewery behind, become an American citizen and joined the Office of Strategic Services, the predecessor of the CIA. They'd trained him in Morse code, hoping to drop him behind enemy lines as a spy, though by his own admission my father wasn't good at covert activity. He was always getting caught trying to sneak out of the barracks to find a bar full of pretty girls, a difficult chore since all the recruits had arrived in tarpaulin-covered trucks and had no idea where they were. Luckily for my father, the war ended before he was shipped overseas. Now, in 1947, he'd been discharged, then accepted at Chicago, where on the GI Bill he was fast-tracked to getting his master's degree in art history.

That night, after the tea, as my father walked my mother home, he was charmed when she confided her own passion for art, though now she confessed she wanted to become a novelist—*to write endlessly and with great joy.* He found her a smart and intuitive judge of character, different but not dissimilar, an ideal complement to his enthusiastic nature. The next night he took her out for ice cream, and she laughed when he said that the bright chrome fixtures in the parlor made him feel almost chromium himself. He'd named a chemical element, my god, she was smitten.

Within a few weeks she was sneaking over to his basement apartment for some *sin and sarsaparilla.* They fed on sex, food and ideas. They disagreed, they squabbled: My father believed man's purpose was to express his individuality, while my mother was more inclined to accept that our lives were in the hands of more powerful forces than our own—the fates. He analyzed and dissected, while she conjured and elaborated. "You are just dramatic," she declared. "But I am truly tragic." A few months later he said by way of proposal, "Let's make it legal."

She loved the strong force of his personality and his clear-cut certainty. In her presence my father felt whole, no longer the displaced immigrant boy wandering among the docked ships waiting for his family to arrive. Most importantly, my father respected my mother's knowledge and passion for art history. Always good at recognizing talent, he responded to her ability to understand art as well as grammar, particularly English grammar, which, even if he had translated a few Rilke poems, was not his native language.

They plummeted toward each other. Drawn by a combination of desire, lust and the belief that they could stimulate each other's work. They called themselves *babyandbaby*, a double-headed coin. She was mysterious and thoughtful, he quick and passionate. Together they would achieve great things.

While she was away on a visit back home to the house on Ardmore Avenue, my father wrote to her, *You will write, Lala, and I will study and we will grow together and still stay young.*

Thalia Cheronis and Peter Selz.

First, though, they had to convince Doc.

Though Doc was an immigrant who had made his way from poverty to becoming a professor, a businessman, a writer and the head of the community; though he was raised in the Greek Orthodox Church but called himself an atheist; and though he had taken in Jewish strays during the war, Doc didn't want his daughter to marry a Jewish man.

What he had, my mother later told me, "was a case of the village mores. He was a Greek peasant in his soul and xenophobic, in spite of his marriage to Grammar. Mostly, I think, he just didn't want to let anything go of its own volition."

She accused Doc of being anti-Semitic.

Heaven have mercy, Doc's eyes bulged. "In my house always there are liberals, radicals!" he yelled. Then, addressing the ceiling, Doc shouted, "Who taught her to think of art and poetry, that these are identical with the soul of mankind? How shall I answer her?" His gaze leaving the ceiling, he glared at my mother. "Listen, if you still have the ears on your head you were born with, why don't you have the decency to fall in love with someone I can approve of?"

Ah, my mother realized. More than anything else, Doc wanted her to marry a scientist, preferably Greek.

My father was hardly dissuaded. These were the very things he loved about Doc and about my mother's family. They were passionate people who had brought home the poor and the disenfranchised and believed that creating something sublime was akin to touching the divine. My father set out to win Doc over. He wrote him a letter promising that Lala would finish her degree. He told Doc exactly how much he received from his GI bill and how much he earned tutoring German, and to the penny what his bills were, how much he spent. He bought a life insurance policy on himself—for Lala. More, he told Doc how his own father had just died, Eugen Selz, the famous eye surgeon who had treated the nuns in Munich for free and once left a peach in the snow for his beloved. After Eugen had immigrated to America he could only get a job working in an optometrist's office grinding eyeglasses. In his mid-sixties by then, he spoke little English and had lost, my father wrote, not only his country but his whole identity. After the GIs returned home he was let go from even this menial job and, too shamed to tell his wife, his peach in the snow, he'd continued to leave each morning as if for work, and would sit on a park bench until evening. That's where he'd died, of a stroke in the middle of a heat wave. My father expressed to Doc how much Lala's family meant to him. He called his feelings *a spontaneous liking for you all and your way of living.* In the end he told Doc that with Lala his life made sense.

She had brought home her own stray. What could Doc do but finally accept him?

And my father had found a family. Not just my mother, but her whole extended bohemian tribe.

THEY WERE MARRIED in her parents' backyard on Ardmore Avenue, under a large crabapple tree, surrounded by throngs of Greeks and Doc's pack of barking collies. My mother wore a pale gray dress and my father a dark gray suit, my parents leaning against one another, for once the only still creatures in the flurry of motion surrounding them. Doc toasted them with wine and later some of his—chemically aged with a full dropper of god knows what—Prohibition brew. My father had given my mother a simple, elegant pearl engagement ring, and she'd transferred it to her left hand. There it sat beside her wedding band—except when she took it off to wash the dishes—until one day seventeen years later when she would throw her wedding band out a taxi-cab window into the dark undergrowth of Central Park West, and place the pearl in the cavern of her pocketbook. She kept the pearl and gave it to me on my fourteenth birthday. A ring with a solitary setting, so perfect for my aloof mother. At first the gift of the elegant pearl excited me; slipping it on my finger made me feel like a bride. But I hadn't inherited my mother's slim fingers and the single delicate pearl looked out of place on my thick adolescent hand.

If there were any shadows on her wedding day, they were from the leaves of the crabapple tree. Maybe my mother had a tiny, niggling fear. She admitted to her best friend Joan that she loved my father *too* possessively. But certainly, married, she reasoned, she would grow out of her insecurities. She was the daughter of a scientist and had a college education. This was the twentieth century.

In Chicago they moved into an inexpensive apartment on Maryland Avenue, put their mattress on the floor, made a book-case from wooden boards set on cream-colored ceramic tiles. Around the dining room table my father built from a door, they placed eight molded Eames chairs they'd registered for when they'd married instead of the usual china and linen—back then Eames chairs were not considered works of art, but just cheap plywood chairs. Above their shared desk they hung the first piece of art my father owned, a Max Beckmann drypoint that a girl he'd dated briefly before he'd met Lala had given him. Beckmann had done the large self-portrait in 1919, the year my father was born. "I just said I liked it and she gave it to me," my father told my

Large Self-Portrait
Max Beckmann, 1919

mother. "She must not have known its value." Never shy about his requests, my father had felt an instant affinity for this forceful self-portrait that took up the whole canvas. Later, my father's head came to resemble the one in Beckmann's powerful portrait, just as my mother would come to resemble the image Karel Appel created for her.

Late one night, struggling to come up with a theme for his dissertation, my father looked up into the serious, square face of Max Beckmann and it hit him. He would write about the art from his youth. Those expressionistic, degenerate artists who, like him, had been expunged from Germany. As it turned out, Beckmann and his wife Quappi were living in nearby St. Louis, and my father wrote them. The next time they came through Chicago they invited him for tea at a hotel. In his sixties, Beckmann was a large man, with a glowering expression and piercing eyes. He refused to be seated in the restaurant, but insisted that a table be placed by the front doors of the lobby. He wanted to watch the people come and go through the doorway as if they were stepping onto a canvas, and he wanted to be seen. Even more than that, my father told my mother later that night, "He's consumed with self-scrutiny. Like his self-portraits, Beckmann wants to be seen in the act of looking."

A voyeur? My mother asked.

An artist, my father answered.

Both my parents were completing their degrees and both were working part-time: my mother edited a journal for the Office of Naval Research, while my father taught his first art history class at the Institute of Design. The ID was the new Bauhaus, which, like the old Bauhaus, was founded on the belief that the marriage between art and technology would not only create beautiful, useful items, but these aesthetically perfect and functional creations would revolutionize people's lives and thus change the whole world. Grand ambitions, but America had just helped the Allies win the war due in large part to technology; it was a heady time. My father later said that the Bauhaus was a potent idea, never fully realized in Germany or in America, but what was more important than the aspiration of an art for the masses that could alter human existence? He, the industrious one, was forever chasing a distant but perfect future, while my mother, the true Hellenist, was tied hook, line and sinker to the dreamy past.

Baby Dormouse, he called her. *My sleepy dormouse.*

When either of them worked late and they missed seeing each other in the apartment, they left love notes.

She: *I thought of your hair and eyes and mouth. I could cry or shout. Please come soon. I live in your house.*

He: *Dear Baby, where is your little head with lots of hair on my shoulder? Love Baby.*

She: *I love you piece of mankind, three times today as much as yesterday. Baby, please come home so I can fight with you.*

He: *I have left a cream puff treat to fatten up my dormouse.*

Then one night he asked, *Baby, how about some babies?*

Not yet, she said. *I'm too unsure of myself, maybe I always will be. Besides, you don't know what you want from me.*

Of course I do, I want a wife. I want you.

You only know what you don't want. You don't want your mother. He didn't. He was contemptuous of his own mother, a woman who had spent most of her time while he was growing up visiting her parents or having tea with her friends engaged in "*silly talk.*"

I want someone with a brain, someone with interests, someone willing to make a go of it. That's you!

She didn't see how she could do it, not all of it, the writing, working on his book as well as her own stories, the part-time editing she took in, and then there was how much my father loved to entertain and go out. Already they hardly ever stayed home. *Besides*, she told him, *I want to have fun first.*

In early 1950, they sailed to Europe for a year, my father on a Fulbright scholarship, my mother spending her days in their Paris pension writing chapters for a novel she would never finish and love poems to him: *You will remember, my love, plunging with a great cry, tearing flank from thigh* . . . He was working on his dissertation on German Expressionism but at that time there was no course of study for him to follow. *Pete asked the top man in his field at the Sorbonne if he could work under him; the fellow said no, not unless he picked something where everyone was dead!* But Dad didn't want to study dead artists; he was interested in living ones, in what was happening now, rising out of the crumbling rubble all around them. So he invented his own program. Abandoning the library (those tombs) and the lecture hall, my father did his research in the galleries, cafés and studios, discussing the influence of existentialism on postwar art with artists like Alberto Giacometti, whose emaciated figures looked as thin as knife blades and who liked to take my dad up to see the girls in Pigalle; and Jean Dubuffet, who, though he preferred a simpler married life, made collages that often resembled the drawings of an insane child.

Splintered postwar Europe, ravaged cities swarming with refugees, engulfed in a housing shortage, a food shortage and, save for Paris, which was awash with women clad in full skirts and cinched waists courtesy of Christian Dior's new look, a clothing shortage. Still, everywhere people crammed together in movie theaters, where, thankfully, there was heat, and lovers stood locked together in arched doorways. *We are so wealthy by comparison*, my mother wrote. *We live in luxury, in a room overlooking a garden with a marble fireplace, 3 lamps, and a bathtub large enough for both of us to drown in.*

On their first full day in Paris they raced through the Louvre, so fast they felt like they were roller-skating along the polished marble floors, then came back to take it a section at a time. Seeing the *Victory of Samothrace*, the great winged Nike flying off the top of the grand staircase, so alive and airborne my mother put out her hand on impulse as if to stop Victory's impetuous flight.

On extended forays they traveled by train, by borrowed car, even by hitchhiking across the continent. Everywhere they went

they drowned themselves in paintings, their fingers becoming
stiff from taking notes. *Two vagabonds*, my father dubbed them,
on our own pilgrimage. To Basel to see a German Expressionist
show, to Brussels to learn what little there was to learn about
early twentieth century Flemish painting (only James Ensor and
René Magritte), then on down to Venice to stand on the stone
floor of the Basilica di San Marco, which looked under their feet
as if the ground were still heaving and buckling from the waves
of the Adriatic. They took arty photographs of city squares, pretended to know more than the other tourists (they did), visited
churches where they took turns swearing over the holy water,
then listened to desultory services for penance. Riding through
the Soviet-occupied sections of Austria in a "sealed" train they
listened to people speaking in low voices about the *next* war, the
one with Russia. Disembarking in Munich, the city of my father's
birth, they stepped onto the platform. The place looked all right
to my mother, a large paved open space with funny pillars scattered here and there, until she saw my father's face. He was gazing around with a baffled half smile. "But there was a roof?" he
said quietly.

That baffled looked remained on his face for the four days
they were in Munich, walking through the scorched shell of the
city. Bomb-gutted buildings that hurt their eyes, steeples gone,
roofs gone, walls all gone. Finding their way to my father's family house, they discovered a few shattered windows and the dome
still in place, then to his former school, which was nothing but a
blown-out building. *I spoke their dialect*, my father wrote, *but no
longer their language. Where I thought I would see familiar places, I
found holes.*

Finally, in the small town of Colmar, seemingly untouched

by war, they stood in front of the *Isenheim Altarpiece* for two solid hours. Just about the most beautiful thing either of them had ever laid their eyes on. A multipaneled masterpiece by the late-medieval German painter Mathias Grünewald, it unfolded around them like a symphony. One section depicting the Annunciation in rich gold and warm red; another, the Crucifixion's barren landscape all in stark gray; and the final set of panels, made of gilded gold, showed Christ transformed, rising into heaven. My parents saw this creation as the embodiment of the extremes of the human condition: all they had witnessed, all they'd experienced in Europe, journeying from the exultation of their arrival in Paris, through the catastrophic darkness of Germany and to the rapture of Resurrection through art.

In his dissertation, my father wrote of the influence of Grünewald's altarpiece on the German Expressionists: *His form was the vessel of his emotion, the mastery of light, color and line was used only for the expression of inner feeling.*

And my mother wrote her parents, *We feel we would know nothing, we would understand nothing, if we hadn't come here and seen this for ourselves.*

Only art could accomplish such a great feat, fathom the depths of the human soul and its heights. Art was their tea leaves, their road map and their destination. For my parents, art explained the world.

Chapter 2

My father was a man of enthusiasms. What truly lit him up, other than discovering a great painting or holding forth at the head of his dinner table surrounded by art luminaries or perhaps pursuing a beautiful woman across the room, was discussing the history of the Museum of Modern Art. Then his eyes would blaze, his finger point heavenward and he'd pronounce, "Not only was it the only modern art museum in America, it was the only one in the world!" As if the museum were at that very moment springing fully formed from his brain. Of course, Dad wasn't just thrilled that it was the original, the very first of its kind; what excited him and what he identified with was the audacity of MoMA. It was a bold, unconventional idea. It sought to exhibit art created by living artists as opposed to warehousing the art of dead ones. However, the part of the birth story of MoMA that my father never revealed was that in the male-dominated art world, the Museum of Modern Art was conceived by a woman.

In April 1929, the intrepid collector Abby Aldrich Rockefeller wrote her son Nelson, then only twenty-one and studying
at Dartmouth College, that she was going to have a luncheon. *My
mind is full of ideas for a new Museum of Modern Art for New York, I
have great hopes for it.* Only six months later, along with her two
girlfriends, also art patrons, Lillie P. Bliss and Mary Quinn Sul-
livan, Abby opened the doors to MoMA. It was November 7, 1929,
just nine days after the great stock market crash. The museum
was affectionately known in our household as MAMA and not
MoMA—in honor of Abby and her daring assemblage of female
chums, according to my mother.

The public's response was better than Abby had hoped. The
first exhibition lasted only a month and attracted over forty-
seven thousand viewers. Abby quickly formed a board of directors, and Alfred H. Barr, Jr., a young graduate student studying
Cubism, was hired as the museum's founding director. Barr drew
up plans for a multidepartmental museum that was based on—of
course—the Bauhaus. Every art form, including furniture design
and film, would have representation. Ten years later, when my
father first wandered the streets of New York City as a young
immigrant boy looking at art, the Museum of Modern Art had
just found its permanent home on West Fifty-third Street.

My father was not the only nomad on New York's streets interested in art at that time. Back in the thirties, art programs didn't
exist in most high schools in the United States and, though one
heard a few stories of Americans fleeing the country for expat
life in Paris, in reality not many could afford trips to Europe to
study art, let alone attend college. If you wanted to be an artist
and live the bohemian life, there was really only one place to go:
Greenwich Village and its environs. In 1924, Willem de Kooning,

a strapping twenty-year-old with swept-back blond hair, managed to stow away on a ship sailing from his home in Rotterdam and by the mid-1930s he was working as a house painter, living in New York and had seen the first Cubist and Surrealist shows at MoMA. In 1930, after being expelled from high school, Jackson Pollock was lured east from his family farm in Wyoming by two older brothers, also artists, and began studying at the Art Students League. By the early 1920s, Mark Rothko had dropped out of Yale to study theater in Portland, Oregon. His favorite actor was Clark Gable, and for years portly Rothko, with his doleful gaze, sported the same tidy mustache as the suave and dashing Gable. By 1925, Rothko had finally settled in New York and on painting as his true medium. When Rothko later met my father, he informed him that when he'd first walked into the Art Students League and seen the naked models he'd thought, "Now, this is the work for me." Ad Reinhardt was born in Buffalo, but grew up in New York and was studying art history in the thirties at Columbia University. Philip Guston, from Canada, moved to New York in 1935 by way of Los Angeles. And, in the late thirties, about the same time my father fled Germany for New York, Franz Kline escaped the coal mining town of Wilkes-Barre, Pennsylvania, and Robert Motherwell, the son of the president of Wells Fargo Bank—the wealthy one, Dad called him—arrived from California.

All born within a twelve-year span, by the time these men sat around our dining room table in the late 1950s drinking their various muddy-colored drinks and flirting with each other's wives (how well my mother remembered Rothko's long pianist's fingers—his translucent skin—on her knee) they were not only established, they were famous. And no longer young men.

Rothko, born in 1903, was the oldest; Motherwell, born in 1915, the youngest.

Before they became the first and maybe the greatest American art movement thus far, they had to persevere. The Depression brought jobs in the form of the WPA—President Roosevelt's Works Project Administration, which in turn created the Federal Art Project. Asking my father about the WPA usually caused his face to flush with the passion of the true socialist he believed himself to be and pronounce, "Look what can happen when the government comes to the rescue of the artist." Lee Krasner, Philip Guston, Ad Reinhardt and Jackson Pollock all worked for the WPA. For a short time, Mark Rothko, who didn't become a U.S. citizen until 1938, hid the fact that he was Latvian in order to work for the WPA; and Willem de Kooning, a Dutchman, painted

A young Philip Guston working on a mural for the WPA.

for the project until he dropped out. They might not have liked the government telling them what to paint, but for their work at the WPA they were paid a stipend of $24 a week. The WPA was their club, their school, their common ground and their bread and butter. They painted not just easel paintings, but billboards, murals and signs, learning to work on a massive scale, with huge brushes and rollers. If it weren't for the WPA, Pollock, Rothko and de Kooning might not have survived long enough to become the holy trinity of Abstract Expressionist art.

As the Depression ended and the WPA was dialed down, World War II tossed not only my father across the ocean and eventually into my mother's arms, but it also flung onto the shores of New York a cavalcade of European artists. Surrealists like Max Ernst and Salvador Dalí arrived with their ideas of the unexpected juxtaposition of objects—pictures of melting timepieces and ships bedecked with the masts of butterfly wings—the natural realm clashing with the mechanical, the brave new world roaring out of the mouth of the old regime. The German modernist Hans Hofmann landed and eventually opened his own art school, teaching the likes of Lee Krasner and Helen Frankenthaler his ideas of the flat canvas and geometric forms of colors. (Learned, my father informed me, from looking at Rembrandt's use of light and shadow. Five years old in the Metropolitan Museum, all I wanted to see was the canopied bed in the French eighteenth century room, but Daddy was adamant. Lifting me from under my armpits, he held me in front of Rembrandt's self-portrait so I could examine his dour and magnificent face. "Squint," he said, "and you can see how Hofmann later replaced the lights and shadows with blocks of colors.")

From Holland via Paris and London, Piet Mondrian arrived in New York with his pure paintings, with their thin black and blue lines, and his belief, paramount to these young men, that art was a spiritual endeavor. And Marcel Duchamp, who with his ironic readymade *objets*—a urinal, a bottle rack, a mounted bicycle wheel, all carefully smuggled out of France—suggested that art could be anything.

Now these young men who longed to bring the art within them to life had work, they had change in their pockets, and, most important to an artist, they had time on their hands. Time to paint and time to talk, time to meet and, like their European counterparts, time to sit in cafés. They frequented the same cheap establishments: the Waldorf Cafeteria, open twenty-four hours a day, or the automat, where macaroni and cheese could be had from a coin-operated vending machine. Later, they gathered in the same bars, drinking beer, smoking cigarettes and arguing about art. Not many had telephones back then. When they needed company they went to each other's studios or met for coffee.

My father said, "For an artist to be around people who cared about what he did meant almost as much as the ability to do his work."

Having survived a depression and a world war, my father told me these artists shared a reservoir of emotional content. Later, he would write about Abstract Expressionism, *Rarely in the history of art has there been a group of artists so engaged in an ambitious commitment to a personal authentic style, no matter what the results might be.* All these young artists needed now was sponsorship. That came in 1941 when Peggy Guggenheim fled Nazi-occupied France for New York. Peggy Guggenheim was a promiscuous, eccentric millionaire collector, married to the Surrealist painter Max Ernst, when she opened Art of This Century on West Fifty-seventh Street in 1942. By this time Pollock and de Kooning had been introduced to each other by Lee Krasner when all three were included in a group show. And Rothko and Pollock would both have their first one-man exhibitions at Guggenheim's gallery. Already Jackson Pollock had begun to envision a style of painting that would revolutionize the process of making art. Abandoning the easel, he spun the act of painting from the wall onto the floor. In a recognition that painting was a kind of performance that involved the body, Pollock's poured, dripped and splattered surfaces became repositories of energy in motion, of a dance-like encounter with the canvas. After Pollock's radical motion, an easel painting looked precious, old-fashioned and artificial by comparison. Painting was no longer about an image, even an abstract image, but a record of an actual event. In the words of the art critic Harold Rosenberg, it had become "an arena in which to act." In Pollock's 1943 application for a Guggenheim fellowship—started eighteen years earlier in 1925 by Peggy's uncle Simon and which Pollock didn't receive—he wrote, *I intend to paint large movable pictures which will function between the easel and mural.* In fact, Pollock had just begun the first of these paintings, his revolutionary *Mural*, a commission from Peggy Guggenheim for the entryway of her New York brownstone. In creating this breakthrough painting, Pollock was forced to take the canvas off the stretcher simply because he needed to make the painting portable in order to deliver it to Guggenheim's home when it was completed. The story Pollock put forth was that he stared at the blank canvas for months without inspiration. Finally, shortly before it was due, he had a vision. In one night he attacked the canvas and created *Mural*: *It was a stampede . . . [of] every animal in the American West, cows and horses and antelopes and buffaloes. Everything is charging across the goddam surface.* A twenty-foot-long rush of gesture, color and action that, rumor had it, was originally eight inches longer, but had to be cut down in order to fit onto Guggenheim's vestibule wall. Influenced by Picasso's *Guernica*, which had been on view nine years earlier when Picasso had sent it to New York to help raise money for the Spanish Republic, *Mural* combined the idea of painting on a heroic scale with the use of industrial materials learned from working at the WPA. Critics immediately recognized *Mural* as apocalyptic, a new form of American art, more emotional act than picture. As de Kooning later said, "Pollock broke the ice for the rest of us."

When Dad met Pollock in 1951 he had just returned from Europe. Both my parents were now teaching at the Institute of Design, and my father had become the only nonartist member of Exhibition Momentum. This was a group of local artists

Mural

Jackson Pollock, 1943. © 2013 The Pollock-Krasner Foundation/ Artists Rights Society (ARS), New York. Image courtesy of: The University of Iowa Museum of Art, Gift of Peggy Guggenheim, 1959.6

endeavoring to get their work hung in places of distinction, and my father was their honorary academic. Once a year they held juried exhibitions and invited renowned artists or curators to come and evaluate their work. In 1951 Jackson Pollock took his first plane ride across the country to jury the exhibition along with the older American Cubist painter Max Weber. Though he liked the plane ride, Pollock claimed to have hated the work of juror. Each painting Weber lauded, Pollock shot down. "He was already liquored up when he arrived," my father told my mother. Dad was disappointed by Pollock's lackadaisical performance. While the

Jackson Pollock, Max Weber (seated) and
Peter Selz (standing).

aging Weber advised the kids to stay away from booze, Pollock sat on the couch drinking straight from the bottle. Apparently someone in the crowd around Weber had called him "Jack the Dripper." At one point Pollock burst out, "You think it's so easy to splash out a Pollock." Turning to Dad, Pollock growled at him, "Where are all the girls? I was promised girls!"

With my mother's editing assistance, my father finished his dissertation. In 1954 it was one of only two dissertations ever done on twentieth century art. Together, my parents decided that they would also seek a commercial publisher for what is now titled *German Expressionist Painting*. Back then, my father's approach of placing art within a political and social context was novel. Up until that time art history had been primarily concerned with stylistic method and provenance, but my father chose to investigate the theories, philosophies and ideas in vogue at the time the works were created. He wanted to know what the artists read, whom they socialized with and, most importantly, their own writing about their work. *The book (Peter's) has gone off— we kissed it and breathed a prayer*, my mother wrote her parents. The book articulated my father's belief that the Expressionist art of the twentieth century—in prewar Germany and happening in the forties and fifties in New York—was characterized by an emphasis that shifted from the *outer world of empirical experience to the inner world* and required the active participation of the viewer. Quoting Oskar Kokoschka's eulogy to fellow painter Edvard Munch—*As in love, two individuals are necessary*—my father wrote that personal involvement between artist and viewer *is perhaps the most important single factor in the development of the expressionist movement*. The viewer was no longer gazing at a pictorial

landscape or a portrait, but being allowed entry into the soul of
the artist. This type of art required emotional connection and
commitment.

That book and that statement, positioning the observer in a
place of importance next to the work of art itself, was the beginning of my father's identification with the artist. He couldn't
draw, he couldn't paint. He once made a ceramic bunny in a studio art class he'd been required to take at Columbia, and, except
for the strange mustard-yellow glaze, his rabbit was clumsy and
ordinary. He knew he did not possess an artistic talent. What
he had was a sweeping sense of history and a deep affinity for a
created object.

By the mid-1950s my father was often traveling to the East
Coast, staying with friends and looking for entry into the New
York art world. It was on one of these trips that he met Ad Reinhardt and began to frequent the galleries that were showing
abstract art. Like my father, Reinhardt was politically active
and wrote about art. A fastidious man, Reinhardt was part of
what was called the New York School, but as an oppositional figure. Instead of Expressionistic brushstrokes or drips of color, he
favored geometric patterns and a limited palette. The first time
my father came to Reinhardt's studio, Ad told him he wanted to
abandon color, shape, space and form. "Then what are you interested in painting?" My father asked.

"The ineffable," Ad replied simply. A few years later he started
work on his black-on-black canvases. Seeking to paint works that
transcended easy definition, Reinhardt, like many of the New
York painters, agreed with my father's proposition that the art
they were creating couldn't be understood with a mere glance.
They believed their work, like human relationships, needed the

presence, the deep personal involvement, of another being. My father wanted to be that audience. More importantly, he wanted to help this work gain the attention he thought it deserved.

In 1955 he was offered a good job, not on the East Coast, but out in California. At Pomona College he would chair the Art Department and direct the gallery. It was not New York. Still, my father knew if he was ever going to convince my mother to have a baby, he needed a well-paying job. He saw the position, running his own department and gallery, as an opportunity. His life had never followed a straight course, and it was in his nature to embrace opportunity whenever it came along.

Chapter 3

My parents had only been in California three years when, in early 1958, my father announced his big news. He had been offered the position of chief curator of painting and sculpture at the Museum of Modern Art. "Can you imagine?" He leaned toward my mother, his eyes shining with excitement. "When I fled Germany I never dreamed I'd have such an opportunity."

Sitting beside him in their blue Studebaker, her hands folded on top of her round pregnant belly, my mother was silent. It was twilight, her favorite time of day, and as they often did at the end of a long, hot Southern California afternoon, they'd driven to the outskirts of Claremont to relax and talk. My one-year-old sister Tanya lay sleeping in the car bed in the backseat. My mother gazed out the window. To the north sprawled Los Angeles, to the south the desert, west was the Pacific Ocean and to the east rose the San Gabriel Mountains. She liked the safe feeling of being held between the mountains and the sea.

"But we have a good life here," she protested. "Good friends."

"It's all I've struggled for," my father said.

My mother, pregnant with me, felt uneasy. To her, Pomona felt like home. For one thing, at Pomona they both had positions on the faculty. Not only did my father chair the Art Department and run the college gallery, he had just published his book on German Expressionism, and he was becoming well known for introducing cutting-edge shows on the Stieglitz Circle (the group of painters championed by distant cousin Alfred Stieglitz included Georgia O'Keeffe, Arthur Dove and John Marin) and hard-edge painting. Even though he hated labels, Dad, along with Los Angles Times art critic Jules Langsner, had coined the term "hard-edge" to describe the work being done in Los Angeles—flat fields of color separated by clean, sharp lines. My mother taught film studies and wrote. They lived on a tree-lined block in a nice house with a cat named Sybil and one-year-old Tanya.

They had been married ten years. If my mother had hoped on her wedding day that she would mature, in many ways she had. She knew how to throw an impromptu cocktail party for sixty, a spring fling for twenty-five and a sit-down dinner for ten (borrow a few chairs); she'd finished her master's with honors before they'd left Chicago; she'd published a short story, and a joint article for *Art Digest* on Flemish art with my father; she enjoyed teaching, especially the theatrical aspect of standing in front of the class with a profound or witty comment on her tongue. She was still shy in an unfamiliar crowd, and, as she freely admitted to my father, peculiar. A daydreamer who liked to withdraw into her own writing world, she'd been content in their universe of two, and any intruder—my father had already had a few affairs, which he'd felt compelled to confess—set off her alarm bells.

She'd worried a baby might come between them. But after my father enlisted Doc to help convince Lala that she would indeed love us once we got here she'd relented and become a mother. The kind of mother who never felt comfortable holding a baby in her arms, though she was quite fine when that baby lay on the pale yellow "blankie" spread on the lawn beside her while she wrote. In response to my father's affairs, my mother had wept, felt stone-cold disgust with both his appetite and her own possessive nature, then rationalized a fling of her own.

Now he wanted to uproot them. She sensed that a move to New York into the fast-track art world would prove too enticing a contender for my father's affections, and she tried to dissuade him.

"I don't know if I can see myself in New York," she told him. "What is there for me?"

"Oh, my god, Lala," he said, his finger pointing east, toward their future. "Let me tell you how it was." And he relayed again the story of how, on his recent visit to New York, he'd brazenly walked into MoMA and asked to borrow a Georgia O'Keeffe painting for his small provincial college gallery show on the Stieglitz Circle. That's when Alfred Barr, the legendary director of MoMA, had said to my father, "We should have someone like you here."

"You should," my father had replied.

In the car my unconvinced mother said, "I don't know, Pete."

But he continued, telling her that along with René d'Harnoncourt, the museum's sophisticated European director, who stood over six and a half feet tall and was a former diplomat and a count, the venerable Alfred Barr and William A. M. Burden II, an heir to the Vanderbilt fortune and the president of the board—he, her Pete, would represent MoMA to the world. To be part of such a circle of luminaries was both my father's dream and his ambition. "I can't go without you," he said.

How could my mother deny him? Even though she had her reservations, she adored him and what she referred to as his big, noble forehead.

Within a month, right after she had given birth to me and before the Stieglitz show opened at Pomona with the Georgia O'Keeffe painting on display, my father's new job was official. He was returning to the city he had first fallen in love with from the deck of *Europa*, the ship that had brought him to America. Barr and d'Harnoncourt had liked the fact that my father had a solid background in art history as well as a passion for new ideas. My father became the youngest curator hired by MoMA. To hear him tell it, he was also the first one who was ever paid a full salary.

As for my mother, she made her peace with the decision, packed up their life and gave Sybil, their tree-climbing cat, to a friend. She still had her doubts. Fidelity was not my father's strongest suit, but he'd promised to be "trustworthy." The next time my father traveled east, my mother wrote him about the

Press release from the Museum of Modern Art.

reason she had agreed to the move to New York: *It is an act of faith. And I realize that an act of faith is simply an act of love.*

It's you I love, you know, he replied. *All I ask is that you believe in me. We have both come so far.*

On a hot September day in 1958, holding the hands of my sister Tanya, my parents boarded an airplane for New York City and my father's new job. However, in their rush to depart, they neglected to remember their one-month-old baby—*me*—wrapped in a traveling blanket and left behind on a chair in the terminal. The plane was called back to the gate. They found me where they had left me, still asleep in my white traveling blanket.

"Weren't we silly, not remembering our baby, but you were so very brave," they would recount laughingly and repeat for years. I loved this tale of their brief, accidental abandonment. It made me feel strong and resilient, and I liked the image of my parents as brainless characters in a 1930s screwball comedy, leaving their baby at the gate. In fact, my parents were anything but silly. They were just very inattentive, and New York, with its continuous swirl of activity, would only increase their distraction.

It took my mother less than twenty-four hours to be seduced by East Coast glamour and sophistication. In her journal the day after her arrival she wrote:

I am drunk, drunk, drunk on New York and all my worst characteristics are showing. I enter the bathroom across a marble threshold, and in the bedroom we sleep in a king-size bed. First time either one of us has ever slept in one. Or even seen one. Though we have seen the beds of kings. This bed is a savannah. Where are you, Pete? Hold my hand. Thrown over us an exquisite muslin spread on which has been stitched

"D S duP." For three stories this monogram on sheets (such percale! I could lick it!), bath towels, bath mat, kitchen towels, glassware in the high-ceilinged dining room (I gaze in awe at 12 champagne glasses at a time), the wide silver frame of a wedding picture in the parlor. D S duP, my unknown benefactress, I stand on the lavender urns in your oriental rug and in my hand I hold a family History. Published, yet. Even with a hard cover . . . There she stands in her wedding gown— yards of snowy taffeta—a plain, undistinguished looking girl with her hair parted in the middle and rolled harshly to either side. Oh, Doris duPont Stilliman Stockly, I could do it so much better. Well, maybe not, but I would sure love to try.

She was ensconced in the mansion of a wealthy benefactress of the museum while she and my father looked for an apartment. Across the river in Brooklyn, my sister and I were placed in the care of Doc and Grammar. Doc had recently been hired by Brooklyn College to run the Chemistry Department, though he still maintained a laboratory and a farm in Illinois where he grew engineered crops because, as soon as he retired, Doc and Grammar intended to feed the hungry of the world just as he had once quenched the thirsty of Chicago.

On her side of the river, surrounded by urbanity and elegance, my mother was as giddy as a teenage girl. She was beside my father on this new adventure, two vagabonds again as they had been in Europe:

Pete and I walked on the Esplanade in Brooklyn Heights and stood and gazed at lower Manhattan glittering in the cold dark and huddled before the sea wind and the challenge facing us, two babes from the

boonies. Turning, I saw a woman—smooth, civilized shape standing
in a lighted window—juxtaposed to the long winds off the night water
and the humor and desolation in the warnings of the foghorns.

Because my father's job required a fair bit of entertaining,
my parents were advised on the importance of an uptown, Central Park West location. An address deemed slightly more formal
than downtown, while suggesting a more congenial attitude than
the staid East Side. Within days my parents found an apartment
in the same building as René d'Harnoncourt, my father's boss at
MoMA. The Turin was dark and cavernous, with a caged elevator
that ran up through the center like an artery. The elevator, with
its brass gate and giant shiny crank, was our thoroughfare and
nexus. When I was seven and Tanya nine, the elevator men went
on strike and we and some of the other children of the building
were charged with running this majestic machine. For nearly
a week, paired with a buddy each, we ferried our parents out of
their apartments, down to the lobby and off to work. With its
beaux-arts façade, the Turin was in the ballpark of elegance, but
turn the corner and walk down Ninety-third or Ninety-fourth
Street and rows of brownstone tenements were vacant, gutted
and boarded up. Yet the Building, as it came to be called, turned
out to be an intellectual and psychological gold mine.

In the late afternoons, Pauline Kael, the opinionated film
critic who reigned at *The New Yorker*, glowered from behind a
cloud of cigarette smoke as she ascended to her apartment—a
few floors above ours. "Careful, girls," she'd growl as we jerked
the elevator to her stop. Her often-whimsical decrees ruled the
cultural and Hollywood filmscape. Once, right after the movie
Cleopatra premiered, even Elizabeth Taylor and Richard Burton

came to pay their respects to Pauline Kael at the Building. Kael, in her inimitable way, had blessed their film in her review with the words, "Oh, go see it anyway!"

Upstairs also lived the frail poet Adrienne Rich with her husband and three sons. This was before Rich became the voice of lesbian, feminist poetry. I can barely remember her three sons, who must have been on elevator duty the week of the strike, only fierce-looking Rich, her round face rimmed with short hair, propped between two crutches. She suffered from acute rheumatoid arthritis and her hunched body reminded me of Tiny Tim in *A Christmas Carol*.

The social heart of the building lived up on the ninth floor. A wild-haired Russian Marxist named Roz Roose, who hosted salons each Sunday afternoon and invited everyone—kids and all—over for lox and bagels and smoked fish. An irresistible, nonstop talker, Roz immediately embraced my parents. Norman Mailer came to Roz's parties along with whomever he was married to at the time. So did the film director Arthur Penn and the comedy team of Mike Nichols and Elaine May.

With Sunday salons, museum events, and the Artists' Club down on Eighth Street where the New York School of painters and sculptors gathered to exchange opinions—and where one night my father nearly got into a fistfight with the Beat poet Allen Ginsberg after Ginsberg called him bourgeois for working for MoMA and my father called Ginsberg even more bourgeois for publishing in *Time* magazine—fairly quickly my parents were in the thick of it all.

These were the years my parents referred to as "the red carpet years" and my mother called "that life." Describing a party she attended soon after they arrived, she wrote:

The movie actress Hedy Lamarr came through town and wanted to buy a painting from one of The Boys (Rothko, Guston, Motherwell et al) and so there was a party and she arrived—beautiful, with an enveloping magnetism—carrying a pad and a pencil under one arm with the blithe insistence that each of the artists draw her a birthday greeting (for free of course) right on the spot. This wife drunk, that wife jealous, Hedy offering Franz Kline's girl a screen test. Franz Kline yelling, "We'll draw her a picture, boys, and then do you know what we'll do??? We'll FUCK her!" Well of course they did all draw her a picture—except Cavallon. And Cavallon's wife found him later in the kitchen with Hedy—a hand on each of her breasts.

Called the Irascibles, the New York School, or the Abstract Expressionists, my parents referred to the guys who smoked, drank and argued about painting whenever they got together simply as the Boys. Even though they were older than my father, they were still boys. There were women artists, Helen Frankenthaler, Hedda Sterne and the grand dame Louise Nevelson, but these were ladies—especially Helen, who had a manicure every day after she finished painting. When my mother was introduced to Helen Frankenthaler, at one of my father's first formal events, Helen snubbed my mother, saying her evening dress looked like a wrinkled nightgown, and poor mortified Mom's face crumpled like the flimsy garment she had on. This was before Mom began dressing up, and maybe Helen had something to do with the metamorphosis of my mother's wardrobe, because the very next day Helen sent her a beautiful black dress with satin piping at the hem, and they remained friends even *after* my parents' divorce.

These women painters were good artists, but they certainly didn't hang out drinking at night as a group. When I was older, my father admonished me never to refer to this coterie of famous artists as Abstract Expressionists. "Some are abstract painters, denying anything but color and form on the canvas, while others are Expressionists. Meaning, Gaby, they allow their feelings to enter their paintings."

Upon their landing in New York, my father immediately took my mother to visit Mark Rothko and his wife Mell at Rothko's studio because Dad wanted to put together a Rothko retrospective at MoMA. Mark rushed forward and clasped, not my father's hand, but my mother's. It turned out that a few years earlier in 1954, Doc had tried to save Rothko's teaching job at Brooklyn College. Doc might have been born a peasant who didn't know much about modern art—though he had a strong affinity for the art of ancient Greece—but after he'd seen one of those exuberantly colored Rothko paintings he'd burst into tears, not an uncommon reaction to Rothko's work. When Rothko told this story to my mother, he related how Doc had stood up at the faculty meeting and thrown behind Rothko all the weight of his chaired position, which meant in true Doc style he'd screamed and yelled and flung an eraser at Ad Reinhardt, who was voting to keep on the lesser painter Jimmy Ernst, the son of the surrealist painter Max Ernst. Though Rothko's contract wasn't renewed, he'd remembered the name of the crazy Greek with the waxed mustache twitching in agitation. My mother couldn't have been more pleased. In this unfamiliar landscape someone important, someone my father respected, knew her, or at least her father.

And, then there was Willem de Kooning. Literally translated, his Dutch surname meant "the King," and he was. After years of poverty, de Kooning was finally becoming commercially successful. He had gained renown in the late forties when he'd covered his canvases with swaths of black-and-white enamel paint, because he could get it by the gallon, cheap. He was still one of the Boys but also, due to his fame, slightly beyond them. But Dad always said that even though de Kooning was credited with inventing Abstract Expressionism, he was never purely an Abstract artist; you could always spot a subject in his paintings, somewhere. When my parents met de Kooning he was already in his fifties, though he still had a boyish face, and a stocky build. They carted him home for dinner and fed him at the dining room table my father had constructed from a simple plywood door using steel piping for the legs. It was a very Bauhaus-looking table, both elegant and utilitarian, and the only thing Dad had ever made with his own hands except that mustard-colored ceramic bunny that he'd sculpted in college. All the artists loved the door-table, especially de Kooning. He would later create a whole "door series" of garish female figures six feet tall painted not on canvas, but on simple wood-paneled doors. These were not based on my father's table, but done because de Kooning had ordered the wrong size of doors for his house in the Springs. Still, making his table, seeing those door paintings, made my father feel like he, too, was an artist at heart.

It was a small circle, more of a cluster, really, who met for cocktails, openings, the theater or dinner a few nights a week. My parents had been used to busy lives, but nothing had prepared them for the whirlwind and the saber-toothed competition of life in New York. Dad was the new guy, the young guy, the guy the *New York Times* had dubbed Mr. Modern Art, and he was on everyone's invitation list.

My mother, who hadn't expected to enjoy this life so much, was now smack-dab in the middle of what she called *life finally happening. No more waiting around. Though our babysitting fees are exorbitant.* She wrote friends back in Claremont of swirling from party to party, then tumbling exhausted into bed. *I rise each morning with barely three hours of sleep to care for the children. Standing in front of the 5th floor apartment window I still get a jolt. There instead of the mountains of Southern California are the green trees of the park and the Guggenheim Museum, hovering like a large snail over Fifth Avenue.* She hadn't made the psychological move across the country yet, and for a few short minutes she'd wonder if she'd ever find a way of binding herself to this world as more than just a decorative element on my father's arm.

Then the day would begin and my father would hurry off to his office downtown. God, he loved walking in the front door of MoMA. "My shows are decided by me and me alone," he told my mother. In fact, he did have to get the okay from d'Harnoncourt in curatorial meetings, but they were his ideas. His research was extensive. Where were the paintings to be found? What could they borrow? Back then insurance wasn't the huge factor it is now, but there were no computers to help locate the art. However, my father had traveled extensively and would continue to do so for the museum. From back when he was a young boy he had visited museums frequently. He knew where many of the paintings might be located. And yet art, particularly modern art, was always moving. Constantly in search of new art, Dad had meetings and lunches with artists and dealers. He wrote his own catalogue essays and oversaw the production and installation of his exhibitions. When he first arrived at MoMA he barely knew how to hang a show, and René had to demonstrate how it was done. The most important work was hung at the entryway of the show. The middle of the painting should be right below eye level and all the works in the room should "speak" to one another. Before each show was hung, Dad played with a little model on his desk of the gallery spaces. It looked like my dollhouse (my sister and I shared a Bauhaus dollhouse of Modernist design), and he'd spend hours happily rearranging the tiny pictures on the tiny walls before the show opened. "It takes a lot of finesse," he told my mother.

At home, after my dad had left for work, my mother set off for the playground across the street with my sister and me. By all accounts, I was a contented though rambunctious child, dark, sturdy and Herculean, while Tanya was what my mother called *fey*, cautious, delicate and as pale blond as corn silk. Already, in my toddlerhood, I was aware of the frantic quality of my parents' lives and of how quickly my mother disappeared into her own liminal space, conscious of our need perhaps for a coat, but not fully present. Whenever my sister and I slipped our small hands coyly into hers, she'd squeeze our fingers gently, then shake them free. She didn't like to be held on to, not by us. While we played in the sandbox at her feet, she read or scribbled in her journal.

Gradually she was drawn into conversation with the other mothers around her. Women who were married to television producers, psychotherapists or UN delegates. They sat in a semicircle above their children, shrouded in cigarette smoke. Periodically one of these mothers would stop chatting, and like a puff of a smoke signal a warning would drift down to us children to watch out for broken glass and dog poop. Like the derelict buildings on the side streets, Central Park had yet to be refurbished; it was a minefield of dog droppings, needles, rusty nails—you name it, and you could find it under your bottom on the playground. But the women who sat above us were glamorous, regal as statues in their stockinged legs, high heels and sprayed bouffant hairdos protected under bright Pucci or gauze scarves they tied under their chins. They swung their pocketbooks, lit each other's cigarettes and talked gaily about lives prior to their marriages and babies, when they had pursued careers in publishing or advertising.

My mother, with her subtle eye for drama and fondness for intrigue, loved the gossip of the playground. By now, she joked, "I have a closet full of evening dresses and nothing to wear to the playground." And it was true. Even at the park she wouldn't be seen without a pair of large, decorative earrings dangling almost to her shoulders. There, sitting in the cluster of moms, she told stories about her Pete, who was at that very moment being lionized somewhere, lunching with the Surrealist painter Joan Miró. *Miró has such hypnotic eyes*; or perhaps Jean Arp, *whose aging girlfriend is the former mistress of D. H. Lawrence.* If he was traveling then, Pete was in London accompanying the Queen Mother through the Tate Gallery, or in Paris carousing with Alberto Giacometti, who sculpted in daylight, painted at night, and drank between shifts. In Germany he was awarded the Order of Merit by the federal republic for his work on German Expressionism. "Everything that happens," my mother said, "happens to Pete."

Roz Roose, our upstairs neighbor and a rabble-rouser extraordinaire, inspired my mother and her friends to join a protest against the atom bomb down at City Hall. After dropping their children off with the babysitter, they dressed up in their heels and white gloves, and trooped down to join the demonstration. *I expected ten to thirty people, but this is New York, and there were about five hundred. The Beats were out—the girls had brushed their long hair and made up nicely and put on their prettiest pants and earrings, the* guys trimmed their beards for the occasion. The only other men in the crowd were a few Ivy League types and Norman Mailer who was talking to Dorothy Day, the old pacifist from Catholic Worker. It was like a cocktail party at lunchtime until the paddy wagon showed up. Mom and her friends, with our instinct for self-preservation, put on dark glasses, just in case a photographer tried to snap their picture. After all, they had husbands with prestigious jobs and children waiting at home for dinner. Right before she was almost carted off in the paddy wagon, my mother sweet-talked the cop into letting her go.

Still, she wanted to do . . . something! In particular, she wanted to be known for her writing. As she explained to my father later that night when he found her standing by the sink, hands in soapy dishwater, "I couldn't even let myself get arrested!" Pausing over the suds. "I want to step into the sphere of my own importance."

"But you are so wonderful." My father stroked her back. "Everybody seems to know it. There is no one quite like you."

She was unique like a painting. Each afternoon at four o'clock when my father wasn't off traveling, my mother began her transformation. She'd found an inexpensive seamstress in the neighborhood, bought her fabric cheap down in the Garment District, and had the outfits she saw in paintings copied. With a little magic of white silk she soon resembled a Singer Sargent or, in oriental-patterned sarong and red sash, suddenly she was as decorative as a Matisse. If she was worried about other women stealing my father's attention, she also sensed that art was his truest love and the real contender for his affections; she would not be outdone by a painting. With a tease to her hair, a brush of scarlet to her lips, a dab of gardenia-scented perfume at the nape of her neck, she'd slip her feet into gold-scalloped high heels and turn us over to the babysitter. Then, shawl thrown over her shoulders, she'd blow us a good-night kiss as she sailed with my father out the door.

They were off to the races: flying into the elevator, then into a taxi and into another elevator and then—whoosh!— arriving in someone's apartment already full of people drinking expensive liquor. *It is hi to Mark and Mell Rothko, to Philip and Musa Guston who hovers like a bird over her drink. Mark is now the self-declared Prince of Painting, telling Pete that he's dubbed himself with this name after being introduced to David Rockefeller, the Prince of Finance!* My mother identified with Mark's sense of irony and drama, as well as Mell's lack of illusions about the art world. Besides, she was their third wheel, accompanying the Rothkos to openings when Dad traveled. *And how do you do Sir John Rothenstein* [for this particular reception was honoring the esteemed director of the Tate Gallery in London]. *Mark beaming upon this little grinning bullfrog of a man and swelling out his chest and in his precise way saying,* "Sir Rothenstein, Sir Rothenstein, I am an ambitious man, I wish to be buried in Westminster Abbey. How am I to accomplish this?" *Who even remembers Sir Rothenstein's reply.*

At some point my father would call my mother over to look at a painting on the wall or to hear what he was proclaiming about the painting on the wall. *Pete always repeats his words to make sure I've heard him—ha-ha—at the same time someone yells in my ear, "And I just want to tell you, before you disappear. I love your black stockings and pink satin ballet shoes, like a Degas dancer!"* Then, invariably, because one party a night wasn't enough, my father beckoned and my mother slipped into her wrap, snaked her delicate hands into their long white gloves, kissed her hostess goodbye and dashed

Thalia Selz

with my father into the foyer, where for one still, quiet moment they took it all in—*that life! Then, back onto the elevator and into another taxi, zipping off for supper among the New York psychiatrists, whom one should never take seriously, or with the wealthy, whom one should always take seriously because they love being thought important so much, or the artists and that is enough like breathing so one doesn't have to be careful at all.*

The artists, because that's why they had come to New York, for the art and the artists.

In the late fifties, when the art world was still in the grip of abstraction, my father wanted to show art that hadn't abandoned the figure entirely. Not exactly figurative art, but art that showed man in the tumult of the second half of the century. My father had come up with the idea for this show even before he left Pomona. And both Alfred Barr and René d'Harnoncourt were behind him. But critics like Clement Greenberg believed that after the war, "High art must be abstract." Liberated from the confines of the image, purged to its essentials, abstract painting was free. It was pure art. To paint any other way, to include subject matter or illusion, was a violation of the progress of modern art. Greenberg had even sidled up to Willem de Kooning at a Jackson Pollock opening and intoned, "Now it's impossible to paint a face," and de Kooning, the great reinventor of the face, not to be displaced, replied, "Yes, and also impossible not to."

My father, a man full of the power, vigor and emotional passion that had generated Expressionism, found Greenberg's approach too narrow and formulaic. Besides, my father liked going against the grain and believed great art, whether abstract or not, was the expression of deep human experience. Like de Kooning, he wanted to wrestle with the question of what had happened to the image of man in the ascendance of abstract art. Where had the figure gone and what did it look like now? My father saw the figure as not just physical, but spiritual in nature. He was not the kind of man to be swayed by the prevailing wind. Already he thought of himself as a maverick, like his charismatic and uncompromising cousin Stieglitz. In the age of abstraction, rediscovering the figure was a radical act. His show *New Images of Man* debuted at MoMA in the fall of 1959. Though he had chosen the young artists (Robert Rauschenberg and Helen Frankenthaler) to represent America at the small Paris Biennale for MoMA the year before, *New Images* was my father's first major show for the Modern. It included the attenuated spindlelike sculptures of Alberto Giacometti, the early graf-fiti scratches of Jean Dubuffet, Francis Bacon's macabre paint-ings of the Pope (nobody understood Bacon, my father said; his paintings could be picked up for $1,000) alongside Rich-ard Diebenkorn's bright forms residing in fields of color, Karel Appel's gaudy heads and Willem de Kooning's famous series of women. It even included some of Jackson Pollock's late black-and-white tormented shapes that hovered between figurative and abstraction. Like my father, the show was a mix of Euro-pean and American influences. While the reviews were mixed (*Art News* called my father's inclusions of artists outside of New York, such as Diebenkorn and Leon Golub, a sign of his "talent-scout-mentality," but the *New York Times* wrote that "the exhibi-tion is disquieting and unsettling precisely because it ruthlessly invades our inner privacy"), the exhibition was a whopping suc-cess and broke museum attendance records. But many of the artists of the Abstract school felt threatened by Dad's desire to feature the reemergence of the figure, let alone sculpture. The well-known painter Barnett Newman, an Abstract Expression-ist (*sorry!*) who divided fields of color on his large canvases with vertical zips of pigment, was upset because the show included sculptors. "Sculpture," Newman told my father, "is what you back into when you look at a painting."

It was not a show that returned to the figure in the traditional sense. A lot of the images were twisted, contorted and barely recognizable as forms at all. But Willem de Kooning's women epitomized the ideas my father was trying to put forth. De Koon-ing's women were wrestling with life. They were opulent, flesh-colored, aggressive, creamy-smeared and had humorous or scary faces that glared out of the canvas, they were engaged in a full-on

Woman and Bicycle 1952-53
Willem de Kooning

battle between image and background. My father said that de Kooning was merging the symbolic representations of women through the ages with the present, modern generation he saw all around him.

De Kooning had told my father that his women did not emerge out of the act of painting, but were received rapidly when he saw a woman walk into a room, a bar or at a party. It was essential to him to catch these glimpses and tie the images quickly down on canvas. He would affix the head and the legs first, then often cut-and-paste the mouths from toothy smiles of models in fashion magazines. "Flesh," de Kooning said, "was the reason why oil painting was invented." Dad called them "the earth goddesses of the advertising age." They were funny, luridly gorgeous and sharp-tongued-looking women. The sort of women who talked openly about the Oedipal complexes they had transferred to their psychiatrists. They were like the playground moms who wore high heels and red lipstick even in the morning and who, when they weren't watching their children, knocked back cocktails and flirted with—sometimes slept with—each other's husbands. They marched in protests, baited police, grinned behind dark glasses at photographers and sometimes got hauled off in paddy wagons. They were like my mother, quintessentially 1950s, struggling to be seen and heard as more than just ornamentation.

My mother, who had helped with the research and editing for the catalogue, was proud of my father's first New York show and of how far he had risen so fast. Only a year earlier he'd been a university professor, and now he was Mr. Modern Art. She referred to him jokingly as the small monument in the center of her life. But she, too, wanted to come out of abstraction and into definition. On a special tour right before the opening of the *New Images* show, they rode an elevator up to the penthouse of the museum and stepped out onto the balcony. All of New York was spread out below them like a glittering sea. My father had made the leap across the ocean and the dream he had pursued for so long was real. They had scaled the shining cliffs of the city. Throwing his arms up in the air, he cried out, "It's ours, baby, all ours."

And for that brief moment it was.

Chapter 4

Six months after *New Images of Man* opened, my father was sitting in his office at MoMA when the Swiss kinetic artist Jean Tinguely came to see him with a proposal. En route to New York on the ocean liner *Queen Elizabeth*, Tinguely had conceived of a plan, a sculpture whose sole purpose would be to self-destruct. He wanted to call this suicidal machine *Homage to New York*, after the vital city which was constantly in a state of decay and renewal and whose giant skyscrapers looked to Tinguely like shiny, magnificent precipices. Most of all, Tinguely wanted *Homage* to go off "like a burst of Chinese firecrackers" in the Museum of Modern Art! However, not everyone at the museum felt the same imperative. Dorothy Miller, another curator complained, "We are in the business of preserving art, not destroying it."

"Let us change with, not against movement," Tinguely declared. He insisted that his piece was not so much about destruction as about "freedom." Everything was doomed to obliteration eventually, even art. Never one to resist the words freedom and art in the same sentence—especially when there was a hint of chaos in the mix—my father pushed forward with the idea. He'd seen one of Tinguely's beautiful apparatuses a year earlier and was delighted by its humor. Undeterred by MoMA's resistance, Dad said, "Art hasn't been fun in a long time." He believed that as an institution that supported Modernism, MoMA should be involved. After a good deal of pressure and persistence, Dad's bosses finally agreed. Tinguely was given a section of the sculpture garden in which to build his machine.

With the help of friends like Robert Rauschenberg, Tinguely scoured the city and New Jersey, collecting junk—bicycles, a baby carriage, hammers, saws, pulleys, banners, a bathtub, even an antique piano—and carted it all back to the museum. Soon Tinguely was secretly constructing his "machine" inside Buckminster Fuller's geodesic dome, which was sitting in the garden from a previous exhibition. Not even my father knew what Tinguely was up to inside that dome. All Tinguely would say was that there was much better junk in America than in Paris.

Finally, on the evening of March 17, 1960, a crowd of 250 selected guests—among them Governor and Mrs. Rockefeller, the other trustees, an NBC film crew, and artists like Jasper Johns, Marcel Duchamp and Robert Rauschenberg, who had contributed a toaster to the master machine—gathered in the garden. The dome was dismantled and there before them rose a whitewashed gleaming tower, an engine of debris that glowed against the dark night sky. To Tinguely's dismay, it had snowed that morning, and try as he might, he couldn't convince the museum workmen to spray-paint the snow black so it wouldn't distract from his pristine machine. Luckily the snow had mostly melted to slush by the time of the performance. The critic Calvin Tomkins quoted my father as saying, "I had no idea how beautiful it was going to be. One had a real feeling of tragedy that the great white machine couldn't be preserved somehow."

There stood Tinguely looking clean-cut in his V-neck sweater and collared shirt. With a few twists, turns and flicks of switches, he set the sculpture in motion. It sputtered and spurted, shuddered and shook. White balloons inflated and collapsed. One mechanical arm beat out a rhythm on a washing-machine drum; another painted black paintings on a roll of white paper that immediately rolled itself back up again. A radio turned itself on and off, the piano played a sad tune and gradually pieces of junk clanked and clattered to the ground. Guests surged forward, snatching up little bits of debris and stuffing them into pockets and purses. Then, suddenly, to everyone's shock, including Dad's and Tinguely's, the white piano in the middle of the pile burst into flames.

People applauded, retreated, but wouldn't leave the spectacle. The fire department was eventually called and, to great boos from the crowd, extinguished *Homage* and the performance ended abruptly. Apparently the machine was in danger of destroying not just itself, but the museum as well.

Dad was surprised. "Tinguely never mentioned a fiery piano," he said with his winter fedora cocked at an angle. "But Tinguely is showing us how the artist must destroy what he sees in order to see differently." My father had wanted the fire department to allow the suicide to continue. But at the reception following the dousing, both my father and mother were shunned. Not even

René d'Harnoncourt or Alfred Barr would speak to them. A little over a year earlier, three months before my father came to work at MoMA, a huge fire at the museum had destroyed one of Claude Monet's eighteen-foot-long *Water Lily* paintings. Barr had thrown a chair through a window to rescue women and children from the fire and d'Harnoncourt had burst into tears. The night of the Tinguely fiasco, my mother wondered if this was the end of my father's honeymoon at MoMA. They rode home in miserable silence in the cab, hands clasped in the space between them, both of them staring dejectedly out their respective windows at the inky darkness of the park. The very next day, however, the reviews in the *Times* praised the event. *Homage* instantly became art world history and my father's reputation as a daring innovator at the museum was cemented. Even though his freewheeling

Homage to New York
Jean Tinguely, 1960

attitude wasn't to everyone's taste, there was little question that he had a gift for walking the fine line between belonging to the establishment and acting like a provocateur.

My father, busy on his mission to introduce the world to art, spent limited time with us when we were small. At the time of the Tinguely *Homage*, I was a baby at home with my sister and babysitter. On the evenings Dad was in town, while my mother got dressed or fed my sister her supper, he would come to my crib, flip me onto my belly and stroke my back as I drifted off to sleep. My mother told me that I became so used to this ritual that when I heard his shout of hello at the front door, I would begin to cry until his large face with his spreading smile appeared up above me.

More and more frequently he was called away. Not only across the continent and to Europe, he was also now flying up to Maine and the summer estate of William A. M. Burden II for top-level museum meetings. The purpose of these retreats was to talk about "our museum" with the Rockefellers and the Fords. Back in 1952, Nelson Rockefeller—the son of the indomitable Abby—had set up the International Council at the Museum of Modern Art with the purpose of selling Abstract Expressionism to the world as a symbol of American political freedom. This was supposedly a hush-hush response to the Cold War and the fight against communism. None of the artists were privy to this agenda—a few even had leanings toward Trotskyism. In the early 1960s my father was not involved in this strategy, but nevertheless the feeling persisted that the museum had an important role on the world stage, as a harbinger of modernist beliefs and freedom of expression. From these meetings, Dad returned not with stories of vanguard thinking and political intrigue, but with descriptions of

how the rich lived. My mother wrote her brother about one such
occasion:

*Pete was chock full of bits of casual gossip (Nelson Rockefeller particu-
larly requested his son via long distance telephone to announce his
engagement two days earlier than planned so as to share the headlines
with Nixon the day Nixon arrives in Warsaw), extraordinary food and
wine (the wine course at one meal—not an elaborate one—consisted
of a peach floating in champagne), and a conviction that the rich are
protected from the elements not only by their money but by National
Selection (he was surprised, for instance, that the Rockefeller ladies
actually ran for shelter during a thunderstorm. I suppose he expected
the rain drops to part, rather like those curtains of water in medieval
renditions of the baptism of Christ!).*

She resented his disappearances, pouting until his return, at
which point she would cheer up and cook an elaborate dinner:

*I served him swordfish steak (poached the night before in milk with dill
and oregano) with homemade mayonnaise, he took up his fork, jabbed
at it two or three times, and announced querulously that he had supped
the preceding night on roasted quail and for that day's lunch (at a picnic on somebody's goddam island, by Christ) had eaten lobster freshly-
caught (presumably by a special lobster-trolling-butler Burden keeps
for the purpose) served with "just the best white wine I have ever had
in my life." Served in cut crystal by liveried servants to picnickers who
sat on rocks. "Rocks?" I queried, unbelieving. "Big rocks," said Pete.*

For my father, that world of privilege and power was more
engaging than our domestic life. From his own childhood, he

had retained a patrician sense of belonging to wealth, culture and prestige. A lifestyle my mother had not been born into and did not aspire to join. Given her parents' predilection for taking in every panhandler in Chicago, she was deeply skeptical of the wealthy and their privileges. Soon, more than physical distance began to separate my parents. After the Tinguely event and his trips to "Burden Island," my father began to complain that my mother didn't fit in the world that he wanted to be part of. He accused her of being too shy and frivolous, too eccentric for a serious intellectual man. When she arrived at the Guggenheim ahead of the throngs of partygoers, the guards would allow her up to the top of the long, curving spiral before the opening started. There, in the dome of Frank Lloyd Wright's Cathedral, she'd take off her pretty shoes, clasp them in her hands and skip through the museum all the way down the ramp in her stocking feet. At first Dad had been charmed by her playful display, but people began to whisper. This behavior was forgivable in an artist, but not for the wife of a man who wanted to direct his own museum. Increasingly he looked at my mother with a critical eye.

Now, when they went to parties, he pressured her to circulate. "Don't sit off in a corner, engrossed in a conversation with just one person," he said.

"I am too sensitive to others and too unsure of myself. I always will be."

He objected to her solitary ways and complained when she was too possessive. "You must stop sulking every time I talk to a pretty woman," he told her.

"But I'm not good at masking my vulnerabilities," she said, and wrote in her journal that *around every corner I fear a horror is taking place.*

As for my father, he believed that his minor encounters with other women were no more important than a tennis match (though he'd never played tennis). Her constant harping on the subject was wrecking what they had between them.

Her own father had been a lothario and she'd watched Grammar's tight-lipped embarrassment for years. My mother didn't want to be long-suffering like Grammar, yet she found herself in the same predicament. She believed she had profoundly failed my father, not only sexually—he claimed to have the bigger appetite—but in her role as art world wife. And so they went back and forth and the fact that he was rarely home and indiscreet in his womanizing sent her spinning into fits of jealousy. When he left town she wrote him daily of her depression and the parties she attended to "circumvent" her loneliness:

Mark and Mell [Rothko] *just called and invited me to see* Così fan tutte *the Mozart Opera. That should be fun. People are very kind, but I hate my widow's weeds. I miss you more and more and find it difficult to parry thrusts about beautiful women. Theodore Roszak told me he had an elaborate fantasy about how you were at that moment seated in a Paris nightclub with some glamorous brunette—fantasy, that is, emanating no doubt from his own desires. It's probably not a fantasy where you're concerned. Any normal human being would be jealous in my place. I know you are having a much better time.*

Perhaps their time apart was not as perfect as my mother imagined. In his letters to her he wrote of jet lag and miserable nights sleeping in unfamiliar hotels—*I took a pill last night and managed to sleep a few hours*—of racing through museums and visiting artists who were often in despair about their work and in need of reassurance. *Giacometti has a tiny studio in a poor section at the end of Montparnasse. He seemed delighted to see me. It was an experience to see him among his tall figures, but he says the work is all no good.* For the most part my father ignored my mother's distress. He wanted to hear about her nights out, who was there and whether his name was mentioned. *You have such a witty way with anecdotes,* he wrote her. *I miss you. Kiss the girls for me.*

And my mother replied, *Don't pretend the children make up for it, they don't.*

Deeply angry and desperately unsure of herself—at once frightened of people and exhilarated by them—my mother had always been prone to exaggeration and mythmaking. At heart she was a storyteller and so she created monsters where there were only ghosts. Yes, she loved us, but she loved our father more. She wanted to be in Paris gallivanting by his side, as she had when they were first married. Later when we were older she said, "Thank god I can talk to you like adults." My mother had never wanted to be stuck at home with kids in the first place. She complained that she hadn't slept through the night in three and a half years, which was normal for a parent of two young children, but untenable for someone with a desire to write and who indulged in a rigorous party schedule.

Raised in a time and place where fathers didn't participate in the "domicile," rejected first by his frivolous mother, then nearly expunged by his "Fatherland," my father still wanted to belong, to my mother, to our home, but without its cramping his style. A marriage shouldn't limit a person's freedom, he said, and why couldn't my mother just adopt a more sophisticated attitude to his dalliances? More than anything else, the force of my father's enthusiasms drove him. That those enthusiasms were for both art and women took its toll on my mother.

He was unfaithful, that much they both agreed on, though he had promised that he would never let a third party come between them. But in the spring of 1960, right as he was leaving for a trip to France, she suspected that he was having an affair with someone in their circle. She began keeping track of when he showered. She noticed how he looked at himself in the mirror. Was he checking for lipstick on his cheeks? She examined his shirt collars and even his undershorts. *I am either paranoid and should be put away,* she wrote him of her suspicions as soon as he left, *or I am right in my convictions or at least correct about the fact.* She had gone to a party and confronted the woman. *I do like her: she lies so convincingly. I have great respect for that girl; I wish I were that smart.*

He replied from Paris categorically denying her accusations. *Blaming me across the ocean. If there was any lipstick on my washcloth, it could only have derived from two very hearty kisses, one on each cheek to be exact, that Alicia* [Alicia Legg was my father's assistant at MoMA] *gave me before I left. Nobody else kissed me—you didn't.* He went on to relay his news about the trip: *Marc Chagall is making trouble about lending some windows to MoMA. Now I must go and see a difficult and cross Dubuffet and have lunch with Tinguely and be picked up by Copley's* [William Copley was a collector of Surrealist art] *chauffeur to spend this evening at their castle.*

Later that same day he sent my mother another message by telegram. *Love you and miss you more than ever Paris sad without you.*

Your cable came this morning, she answered. *I sympathize greatly with your plight (namely, me!)* She wanted to go away for a while to think.

He cut his trip short and returned to New York within two days, claiming that this time he had done nothing wrong and her fears were unfounded. He promised that on the next trip abroad he would take all of us with him. Even though my mother never fully believed my father about this affair, she loved him and was obsessed with him. She had begun to doubt her own judgment. She believed that only her writing could save her.

For the nearly two years they'd been in New York, except for her letters and journals, my mother had barely scribbled a word. She noted this sad irony in her journal:

A flash of insight comes and with it the urge to give back to life what it has given me—and then the compulsive daydreaming, the terrible desire to have all desires fulfilled takes over. I am filled with wretched yearning and a secret knowledge that whatever I desire at such a time will surely be denied me because I am so unreasonable and insistent in my demands.

My mother's anxiety and distraction, her need to either be beside my father or disappear, frightened my sister Tanya. Just as my mother hovered over my father, Tanya was reluctant to leave our mother's side. A pattern developed. Back from a night of parties, my mother would fall exhausted into bed, only to wake at four or five a.m. to find Tanya silently standing inches from her head, in her long white nightgown, her small hand stroking the coverlet, a little ghost with a reproachful frown on her face.

In the early summer of 1960, four months after the Tinguely performance, my entire family, Doc and Grammar included, set sail for Italy. Dad needed to research an upcoming show on Futurist art, the twentieth century movement that emphasized speed and the energy of restless modern life with images in furious motion, sculptures and paintings that looked like they were in the processes of splintering apart from too much dynamism. My mother, not to be left behind this time, was excited to be again traveling with her husband. We sailed on the *Queen Elizabeth*. Disembarking in Genoa, we continued to Pompeii, Merano and then up to Tyrol. The plan was simple: After a week together in Italy my parents were to travel on alone while my father worked. My sister and I were to stay in Italy with our grandparents. Our parents had left us with them before when they first moved to New York. This time, however, uprooted and disturbed by the overseas voyage, Tanya became inconsolable. Doc refused to be burdened with her. He wouldn't agree to take us and not even Grammar could convince him otherwise. My mother worried. If she stayed with us, or returned to America, what would her husband do and whom would he seek for company in her absence? In Tyrol, in an act of desperation, clouded judgment and fatigue, she made the decision to leave my sister and me behind in a Kinderheim—a children's school in the Alps.

Twenty-two years later, on my birthday, my mother sent me a letter about that trip:

Of course I should have packed up the three of us and gone down to Genoa and caught the Elizabeth I *back to the U.S. Had I had the understanding and foresight to surmise what the consequences of our act would be, I would have done so. But I was immature, ill-advised, and uneducated in child-rearing.*

Located in a meadow, the setting of the Kinderheim resembled the opening shot of *The Sound of Music*, complete with brilliant green fields, towering snowcapped mountains and an alpine village in the distance. My mother told me later that she remembered thinking, *My baby is just beginning to speak*, when she kissed me goodbye.

Tanya and I were in a foreign country, surrounded by people we had never met. We did not understand a word of German and our caretakers knew little English. Trying to make the separation as easy as possible, the nurses advised our parents to tell us they would only be gone for lunch. They took our clothes and dressed us in the red-and-blue-striped outfits of the camp. Our mother reassured my sister that in her new German play clothes she wouldn't get her pretty dress dirty. Our parents kissed us goodbye and drove out the gate. Two months would pass before they reappeared. I was about to turn two years old, I only retain a memory of playing in a damp sandbox and trotting across that green alpine meadow on my chubby legs; but Tanya, a year and a half older, had a sense of time, she could question why our parents didn't return.

I was so tired, my mother wrote. *Even now writing to you I feel that sense of exhaustion return.*

But on that long drive over the Alps, she went on to explain, *I remember just sitting there looking down at you, stroking your hair from time to time and readjusting you in my lap, and then suddenly awfully realizing that I was about to lose you for two whole months and that you would turn 2 years old without me there. I thought, "I love this child; I LOVE her; I never knew how much I loved her before. She's been around all this time, and I was so blind I didn't know how much I loved her."*

The trip did not turn out as my mother had hoped. My parents were no longer the same adventurous young couple who had once set off across a ruined continent in search of art together. She sent no chatty letters back to friends and wrote nothing in her journal. After a month of traveling together, while my father continued to pursue his research and an affair, my mother returned to the foot of the mountain below where my sister and I waited. She took a room at a hotel on the banks of the Inn River, and though she could have come up to visit us, she did not. Instead, she finally began to write a novella that would be published the following year in *Partisan Review*. In the opening scene she describes a woman remembering her past in a Tyrolean hotel surrounded by folktale woods. At the end of that month when my father rejoined her, my mother had finished the rough draft of her novella. Together they journeyed back up the mountain, where my sister and I awaited in our pretty dresses for their coming.

Chapter 5

Ever since my father had come to the Modern, he'd wanted to do a Rothko exhibit. Back then it was rare for a living artist to have a one-man show at MoMA. Jackson Pollock was given a memorial retrospective after his death. But if Pollock had been thought of as the crude barbarian cowboy from the West, hurling paint at the floor, Rothko was considered erudite. An educated connoisseur of poetry and opera, a lover of Mozart, Rothko was an artist whose meditative work sought to contain emotion rather than explode it. Even though Rothko's paintings were often on a large scale measuring eight, nine or ten feet long by six or seven feet high, they still created a shocking state of intimacy. He wanted his work not to overwhelm the viewers, but to be large enough to take them in. My father told me that Rothko had gotten to the essence of what he was about, capturing the cadence of both ecstasy and tragedy on the surface of the canvas.

I was three; most of my father's words flew far over my head, but the reverent tone of his voice, the look of wide-eyed wonder on his face when he talked of Mark Rothko, lit me up inside. Later I learned that in preparation for the show my father and Mark spent long afternoons discussing the frescoes from the walls of Pompeii and the idea that painting could not just represent, but *become*, symbolic space.

To stand in front of a Rothko painting was to enter a space of contemplation. His floating rectangles of radiant color—oxblood-red, charcoal-black and washes of pink over maroon—glowed with transcendence. They were portals through which the viewer could dream. Even as far back as 1945 when he was still painting surrealist figures, Rothko wrote in a personal statement, "Art for me is an anecdote of the spirit, and the only means of making concrete the purpose of its varied quickness and stillness."

Red on Maroon
Mark Rothko, 1959

My father came away from his meetings with Rothko saying that Rothko approached art like an old master, on a majestic scale, but the core of his paintings—those portals—were compressed to embody the drama of being human. "He has succeeded in reconciling the ideas in his head with the physical objects he creates. There's no illusion to be found when gazing at a Rothko painting, it just exists, like a man."

When Dad explained that viewers responded to Rothko's work as if it had a human presence, "the paint breathes and expands," he said, I understood. My picture books came to life with talking bears and cats that wore hats. At night, when my mother turned off the lights and the shadows from the street danced across my bedroom floor, my bright orange Eames rocking chair transformed into the bow of a ship that sailed me off to sleep. Of course a painting was mutable and alive. Especially these paintings that my father said absorb "every ounce of emotion Rothko gives them—can't you feel it?" There was never any doubt in my mind that art could step off the walls and walk among us.

Not my mother. My mother took a long time to warm up to Rothko's paintings. "They're just big splotches," she said. "As if he can't see."

"He can't, really," my father agreed. He had run into Mark at the Department of Motor Vehicles, both of them renewing their driver's licenses. Even with his glasses on Mark had asked Dad to help him fill out the form. "I can't read this," Mark confided. My father refused. "You shouldn't be driving, then," he told Mark. But when my mother said Rothko couldn't see to paint, Dad said, "He sees exactly what he needs to."

For the MoMA show, which opened in the winter of 1961, the paintings were hung to Mark's specifications, in groups like siblings, the walls repainted off-white, the large paintings only inches from the floor so that they confronted the viewer on his own terms, like doorways. Rothko wanted the lighting in the galleries dimmed. "The pictures have their own light," he said. He wanted his paintings touching the floor, but Dad said the cleaning lady wouldn't be able to see and would swish water on them. As it was, the museum was already upset that Rothko was getting special treatment. MoMA had a practice of getting a 10 percent commission on work that was sold from its exhibits, and Sidney Janis, Mark's dealer at the time, made a stink, sending a letter to the museum stating that Mark's work already had a waiting list. Everybody wanted a piece of Rothko by then. Rothko paintings were selling for the same price as Picasso's, and both were selling for more than Courbets or the Impressionists. When my parents went to parties, people said, "I collect Rothko." As if it were possible to own the man along with the art.

Mark Rothko had just backed out of his commission to paint a series of mural-sized paintings for the Seagram Building—claiming the Four Seasons Restaurant was too pretentious to display his work—and this act made him all the more famous as an artist protective of his creations. Rothko was willing to sacrifice commerce for the integrity of his paintings. He had always felt deeply ambivalent about showing, and was depressed and sick during the time of the exhibition at MoMA. This retrospective was a moment of reckoning, my father said, not just for the critics but also for Mark himself, who was never quite satisfied, but always looking for something more. Still, Rothko came nearly every day to sit in the museum and visit with his paintings. He told my father that he'd had to quit painting the beautiful orange and pink canvases because people weren't paying attention to the subject. They were simply seduced by the color!

By this time, when my father was home, I was spending my Saturday afternoons alone with him. Ever since we had returned from the Kinderheim, Tanya had become irritable, angry and anxious. She didn't want to leave our mother's side and threw temper tantrums at the slightest provocation. Mom brought Tanya to the Child Development Center. While they were gone, my father took me to look at art. With me riding atop his shoulders, we visited the galleries on Madison Avenue and Fifty-seventh Street. From my position, my little hands clasping his forehead, my legs wrapped around his neck, I felt like we were one giant fused creature and I ruled the world—or at least my father's domain.

"What's that?" My father would ask whenever we entered a gallery, proudly demonstrating my expertise to his friends. "Gaby, tell us who painted that picture."

"Manet!" "Monet!" "Renoir!"

I wasn't exactly a child to him. I was a captive audience. I was greedy for attention and I took every word he uttered as pure fact. "Artists are the guardians of individualism," he told me thumping his chest and my little leg at the same time. "Be yourself and nobody else."

Six months after Mark's show opened, my father was away in Europe meeting with Jean Dubuffet whose textured, angst-riddled figures would be my father's next retrospective. Dad was excited. He wrote my mother that Americans had never seen Dubuffets before, and this show would be another first. What my father loved, almost as much as the art, was being the first on the scene. While he was away in Europe, back in New York, Franz Kline died. The first of the Boys to go, Franz Kline was considered the quintessential action painter for his surging black gestures on white grounds. Although often worked out as sketches first, his paintings expressed an explosive immediacy. With huge brushes and common commercial paint, Kline sought to focus the artistic act to sheer energy in motion. Warned by his doctor to quit drinking and smoking, he'd ignored the advice and died of heart failure. My mother attended the funeral service alone. Bernard Reis, the accountant to the art world (Reis did our taxes for free and Bernie and his wife Becky were collectors, host and hostess to the art scene), who at that time represented Rothko, Kline, Guston, Motherwell and de Kooning in their dealings with their galleries, came over to her and exclaimed, "What a fine turnout we have, just like at an opening." My mother, aghast, wrote in her letter to Dad that night, *It's all status-seeking. These guys are all suicidal. All but Rothko. He'll outlive them all, I bet.*

Even after Kline's death, the cocktail party that had started in the fifties was far from over. Elaine de Kooning called that era "a decade-long bender." Hard alcohol was served at all the openings and the Boys still drank competitively, flirted competitively, painted, sold and showed competitively. After Dad returned, he traveled down on the train with Mark to see the Franz Kline memorial exhibit in Washington, D.C., and told Mark that he wanted to mount a de Kooning retrospective. As soon as Mark next saw Bill, he said, "I hear the next show at MoMA will be *your memorial*." A Freudian slip, perhaps, because Rothko wanted to be the only living artist shown at MoMA. Was he suggesting that de Kooning, like Jackson Pollock, only warranted a show after his death? Dad said that de Kooning looked terrified and later wondered if this might have been one of the reasons he backed out of his MoMA show. More likely, Bill Seitz, the curator Dad had put in charge of the retrospective, had annoyed de Kooning with his constant mention of the work of Marcel Duchamp. "I'm not interested in Marcel Duchamp," de Kooning snapped at Seitz. Or perhaps de Kooning had recognized that he wasn't ready to have his moment of reckoning. His work was still mutating between figuration and abstraction, and would for many years to come. He would not have a MoMA retrospective until 2011, fourteen years after his death.

A month after Klein's memorial show, the Sidney Janis Gallery—which represented the work of most of the Boys— decided to mount an exhibition of Pop art, and all the Boys except de Kooning resigned in protest, convinced that Janis had lost faith in their work. Pop art was the antithesis of the soul. Pop artists like Warhol painted soup cans, they said, an item to be found in the supermarket. They did not want to be associated with a gallery that displayed such slick commercialism. That was when Bernard Reis, their solicitous accountant, stepped in and introduced Philip Guston, Robert Motherwell and Mark Rothko to a new dealer and gallery: Frank Lloyd of Marlborough Fine Art. A self-inventor like many of these artists, Lloyd was born an Austrian Jew named Franz Kurt Levai. He'd fled the Holocaust and eventually emerged in England, where he renamed himself Lloyd after Lloyd's Bank of London and named the gallery he founded after the Duke of Marlborough.

My mother wrote: *I know what people sell their souls for, to live here against this shining cliff and think it is for them, their poor cockroach selves, scuttling around at its base. For which delusions I have great sympathy, being myself so deluded.*

Finally, though, she was finding her footing. Her novella, the one she'd written in the valley below the Kinderheim and which she referred to as "the long thing," but was actually titled *The Education of a Queen*, had just come out in *Partisan Review* and would appear in the *Best American Short Stories* and *O'Henry* collections the following year. After the opening scene in the Tyrolean hotel, she'd spun the rest of the tale from an anecdote she'd heard about Joseph Cornell. Cornell had fallen in love, and silently stalked, but never approached, a woman selling tickets in a glass booth in front of the movie theater. Mom had set her version of the story in Chicago, where a fragile naïf artist appears one evening at Doc's laboratory, and later is introduced by the magnetic Doc to a haughty young ticket-seller because Doc thinks all hot-blooded men need women. But the naïf artist's desire for the girl is not for who she is—crass and small-minded—but for how she appears, as if conjured from his own imagination, a trinket behind a wall of glass, a readymade Cornell box.

The particular Joseph Cornell box that had inspired my mother when she was writing her novella was an untitled piece referred to as *Penny Arcade Portrait of Lauren Bacall* (circa 1945–46). After Cornell saw Lauren Bacall in her first movie, *To Have and Have Not*, he went back to watch it four more times. His box displays a central framed image of elegant young Bacall trapped in a deep blue penny arcade as if she is a prize to be won with the roll of a marble. Cornell has surrounded his Bacall in a shrine of tiny photographic peep-show-like windows: a childhood photo, the skyline of Manhattan where she grew up, a dog that might have once been hers. Cornell pinned down and preserved his prize, the bewitching young nineteen-year-old Bacall, like a butterfly behind a cage of glass.

Now, when my mother went to parties, the artists in her circle took her aside and whispered, "We knew you were one of us":

Mark [Rothko] *greets me at a gathering at his place with his wide embrace, "I believe that in your novella I detected your parents."*

"Oh, no," I say.

"Never mind, I know how an artist lies."

She was happy; better than happy, she was content:

Though Pete doesn't like the title, says it reminds him of a story about homosexuals, he is proud. We make love while dancing. This is always good for the sake of admiration. Well, it is genuine, too. I am very tolerant of him tonight. He is as gay as a child and so handsome in his tux. Earlier this evening we had been "shot" at a pretend happening for a French movie: Only One New York. *When we start drunkenly for home it is snowing. A soft wet whiteness drifting down through the black air, the early AM. I lift my satin evening skirt and tiptoe through the whiteness in my black satin shoes. When I remove them before going to bed my toes are encased in shells of black dye. My feet look like two small black rowboats. The party has bored me ineffably but I love him.*

She had made her peace with my father's affairs and had given up begging him to stop or threatening to leave. She would never leave him, and he in turn would always plead with her to stay. *Pete can be so unexpectedly sweet.* She flew to meet him in Europe, where he was overseeing the U.S. Pavilion for the 1962 Venice Biennale, an extravagant contemporary art exhibition that since 1895 had taken over the Renaissance city every two years. When she stepped off the train that carried her into Venice, my father greeted her with violets and brought her to their hotel. Their room had a tiny balcony and a view of the scrolled buttresses of Santa Maria della Salute because he'd remembered how she loved that crazy church. When he nuzzled into her big wild mass of hair, he said, "My place."

Later that evening they celebrated with their crowd, sailing off across the brackish lagoon to a baroque palace on the island of Torcello in a fleet of gondolas for a candlelit supper given by a wealthy collector. *The high-rolling art collector Peggy Guggenheim shoots past in her own private gondola with her own private young Italian. As she disappears up ahead a voice in another boat calls out, "He's yummy, darling! How much will you take for him?"*

Sitting beside my father, who glowed with confidence—even his white hair radiated self-assurance—my mother felt thrilled, finally an acknowledged member of that life. It was decadent,

Mom and Dad in the gondola with Friedensreich Hundertwasser, his wife, the Japanese artist Yuko Ikewada, and Giuseppe Santomaso.

absurd and glamorous, and it was now fully hers, for she, too, was producing art. She had a right to be there. She knew she was neither on firm land nor completely at sea, but she was on the boat, beside my father, her small monument. *We joke that we are aboard the great deck of the ocean liner and it is called Modern Art.*

Chapter 6

In 1962 Dad opened his newest retrospective, on the work of Jean Dubuffet. Dad had met Dubuffet, a bald-headed French-man with big ears like Popeye, in Paris with Mom in 1950 and become impressed with his work. He had shown him as one of the artists in *New Images of Man* in 1959 and then gone back to Paris to select the work for this exhibition from Dubuffet's warehouse. Dad thought that the work of this artist who shunned the intellectual and cultural in favor of a naïve style would appeal not only to a large New York audience, but also to children. To my sister and me. *Dubuffet wants to enchant and amuse rather than elevate . . . His subjects are common people and most ordinary occurrences,* he wrote in the catalogue.

Tanya and I were indeed transfixed. They were paintings of children with buttons as big as their heads, and naked ladies riding bicycles, and cows and goats with silly smiles. Pictures of flowers made entirely of collaged butterfly wings. Sculptures made of tree bark and sponges. Drawings done in chalk and crayon like our drawings. At home our mother had given us a wall in our playroom to scribble on and it was covered not only with our pictures but with our dirty thumbprints. Dubuffet's paintings and drawings were like our wall, scratchy and marked up, infused with dreamlike faces that looked as if Dubuffet had painted them with his toes. He was fascinated with what Dad called "graffiti," which he explained was sort of like modern cave painting. There were images of distorted funny-looking men, one of which Dubuffet gave to my father, a biomorphic figure with a large face and a bug-eyed stare that now hung in our living room and could look alternately goofy or frightening. Dubuffet

à Peter Selz
Jean Dubuffet, 1962.

collected the art of the insane and the untutored. He would come to influence a whole movement in art (Art Brut—now called Outsider Art), which focused on art created outside the boundaries of the professional arena. Dubuffet believed that this type of work had a more pure impulse and was therefore more powerful. In the 1970s, artists like Jean-Michael Basquiat would be inspired by Dubuffet's primitive style.

Although my father was playful in his choice of shows from Tinguely to Dubuffet, he never got down on his hands and knees and played with us. Mark Rothko, not my father, sank to his haunches at his own Christmas party in 1963 and played a game of pick-up sticks with me. He let me hold his new baby Christopher, called Topher, in my big-girl lap while he thoughtfully untangled a stick. Topher gurgled while Mr. Rothko took his time. He brought his face down close to the pile of sticks and peered through his thick eyeglasses. His pupils swam behind them like pebbles in pools of water. My mother was right: Mr. Rothko was blind as a bat, constantly adjusting his glasses until finally he delicately leveraged a stick free.

Up above, in the realm of the grown-ups, my lordly father held forth. He had authority and power and a way of deciding, just by the cast of his gaze, what was important, even precious. The closest he ever got to actual play was taking me to look at art or pointing out design features in the man-made world. Museums were my playgrounds. "Let me tell you what I saw today," my father would say, and I would follow his lead into the realm of art, of design, of the constantly re-created world. "Look at the mark of man's hand on the landscape!" he told me. "It is the mark of man that matters." Once my father told me the world was designed for a five-foot-ten man, and I believed him. Architects and furniture designers, he said, particularly modern ones like Le Corbusier, used set specifications when they created buildings, doorways, tables and chairs that were "based on the ideal-sized man." At five-ten himself, he was an elegant man, and, I saw that, in a doorway surrounded by the wooden molding, he was indeed perfectly framed, like a portrait.

That was the year my mother had her portrait painted by Karel Appel. Of her life with my father my mother wrote, *It's like being in a montage.* My father continued to put on his exhibitions, one on the work of Emil Nolde, the German Expressionist painter whose brushstroke and colors, he said, were "visual equivalents to physical dynamism," and another on the sculptures of Auguste Rodin. "Can you believe this is the first ever Rodin show in America?" Dad said with dismay. "In the age of abstract steel shapes of David Smith, Rodin's tortured emotional forms may have fallen out of favor, but he was the progenitor of modern sculpture." Then Dad went off to Germany to research his next retrospective on Max Beckmann.

While he was away, my mother went to sit for Appel, one of the artists included in my father's *New Images of Man* at MoMA. Karel Appel was a CoBrA artist— a group of Dutch and Danish painters who shared an interest in surrealism and complete freedom with color and form. Some of Appel's paintings looked like a wild mixture of the colors of Matisse and Joan Miró with a little of the chopped-up, reassembled facial features of Picasso. At first Appel painted my mother to look as elegant and refined as a Modigliani. But at the last moment he said, "It's not right, come back tomorrow." When my mother next saw the painting, he'd replaced the graceful woman in the picture with a wild, windblown and uncontained figure. She looked like a goose whose head was about to be chopped off. Appel had caught the darting gaze, the fretful pouting lips and the tousled unkempt black and blue zigzag mass of her hair, the look of a woman struggling to maintain an unraveling marriage. She was so heartbroken with his changes that even though my father admired the image and asked her to display the painting, she buried her crazy likeness in her large walk-in closet. There it remained, a secret visage behind her fancy dresses, until one day years later she realized, like Dorian Gray in reverse, she'd aged into her own portrait. That's when she pulled it out and proudly hung it on the wall.

When my father was at home, my mother was charged with purpose. She threw parties. Big ones. She prided herself on making her own dishes and for two days she cooked until the shelves of the refrigerator sagged with platters: poached salmon mouse, stuffed mushrooms, deviled eggs, chicken liver pâté and little meatballs on the ends of toothpicks dripping with a lemon sauce that were called Königsberger klopse and that she learned to make in honor of my father's heritage. Sometimes she even stuffed grape leaves with nuts and rice in honor of her own Greek background. Whatever was their newest gift—the little red Rothko, a somber Leon Golub head, the squiggly Dubuffet figure, or a pivoting George Rickey sculpture—would be put on proud display. The women—nearly, but never quite as beautiful as our mother—chatted, calling each other "darling!" calling us "little darlings." Staining the edges of their glasses with crimson or scarlet lipstick, they sipped their cocktails as they eyed their famous artist husbands. At least once during the night my sister and I would stumble on a guest in the pantry off our kitchen pressing his large, paint-stained paws up against the wrong wife's décolletage.

The Boys! Klein was dead and de Kooning had moved to Long Island, but otherwise they still included Mark Rothko, Philip Guston, and Ad Reinhardt, and the Expressionist painters Adolph Gottlieb and Theodoros Stamos. Huddled near the bar, they philosophized about the meaning of color, form, shape, gesture, myth, music, God, man and the current sales of their work—a topic that always made some of them yell and some of them sulk. Philip Guston would argue with Ad Reinhardt as to whether abstraction really existed once you put a mark on paper. Reinhardt was in favor of a purer, emptier canvas, while Guston would soon abandon abstraction entirely for his own vocabulary of cartoon-style figures—faces covered in stubbly whiskers, eyes the size of grapefruits.

Slinking through the crowd, as elegant as a tulip, our mother helped pass the food, *"Did you make this all yourself? Imagine!"* Amused, Mom nodded, one ear cocked to the gossip that perfumed the air. Occasionally she'd rush off to the kitchen where she kept her grocery list, a long scroll of paper hanging on the wall. Underneath tomatoes and lemons she wrote the cocktail chatter down. *Philip Johnson, the architect, hired a Japanese houseboy because, said Philip, "At least I've found someone the right scale for my house!"* and *Robert Scull is a big, nouveau riche collector who recently bought a new piece of Pop Art by Tom Wesselmann: a nude sitting next to a real telephone. Bob was speculating about what would happen if the phone actually rang; what would the voice on the other end of the line say? Adolph Gottlieb shot back, "Hello, Schmuck!"* Gottlieb was one of the painters who had resigned from the Janis Gallery in protest of the Pop show.

Larry Rivers, who painted what my father called "semi-realistic paintings," but who my mother said was not "semi about anything," invariably arrived late, his hair frantic, ringing the doorbell repeatedly and rushing inside without so much as a hello before demanding a pill from my father. "What kind of pill do you want, Larry?" my father asked, eyebrows arched, as he guided Larry toward our medicine cabinet.

"Any pill, just give me a pill!"

And then there was Ruth Kligman. When Ruth arrived she enthusiastically clutched all the men—especially Dad—to her bosom. Ruth had been Jackson Pollock's girlfriend, the sole survivor of the car accident that had killed Pollock and her friend Edith Metzger. After Pollock died, she'd hooked up with de Kooning. My mother called Ruth "a tragedy in the making" because she so badly wanted to attach herself to a famous artist. Poor Ruth hoped de Kooning would divorce his wife Elaine, marry Joan Ward, the mother of his daughter Lisa, then divorce Joan to marry her. This woman and her saga of lovers fascinated Tanya and me. When we weren't jumping on the bed or rubbing our faces against the fur coats, we trailed Ruth through our apartment, only to have her bolt the bathroom door when we tried to follow her inside.

At bedtime my mother would usher my sister and me into the living room. Dressed up in matching red-and-white-striped nightgowns and nightcaps—my mother's sense of fun and fashion—we were paraded in to say good night to our parents' guests, then quickly forgotten. But we crept back and stood at the edge of the party, giant girl-sized candy canes.

Watching my father in the center of that room, dressed in his tuxedo, I thought he looked like a prince. So handsome and merry, his face bright and laughing with enthusiasm, his arms spread along the back of the couch as if he could embrace the whole room. When he spoke, his lilting Bavarian accent and deep baritone voice commanded attention. My mother leaned toward him. Outside the apartment windows, across the park, the city lights hung like a great, glittering backdrop. For years I held on to this image of my father and our home—investing the memory with every drop of enchantment my six-year-old heart could conjure. Everything I loved was inside this lit-up container of space.

We spent the summer of 1964 in a house named Loveridge on the outskirts of Sag Harbor. A run-down, shingled cottage with white shutters, a bright red front door and a long path meandering through woods of pitch pine and scrub oak, then among tall marsh grasses where egrets nested, over dunes, down to our own private beach on the lapping bay shore. It was a brief idle, as summers are. Mom wrote in the mornings, then took her walk along Ferry Road to an old family graveyard around the bend. My sister and I spent the day with our father at Georgica Beach in East Hampton, where Dad lounged on his beach towel, the art world gathered under big sun umbrellas and everyone gossiped about whether de Kooning was working, on a binge or drying out.

On our way home, we'd stop to visit Alfonso Ossorio at his Italianate mansion, the Creeks. Ossorio was an affluent artist from Manila, a stocky man with a sweet smile, who lived on a sixty-acre wonderland of driftwood sculptures and evergreen trees. He whizzed around his property on a golf cart and was given to throwing extravagant parties. Pollock had been en route to one of those parties in the summer of 1956 when he'd crashed his car and died, taking Edith Metzger with him and sparing Ruth Kligman. Ossorio had befriended Dubuffet in Paris and now collected his work, which was how Dad first got to know him. Now, à la Dubuffet, Ossorio was covering everything in sight: walls, floor, rocks in the garden and his art, with a thick encrustation that he called "congregations." In his studio, rows of tables held trays containing shells, bones, dolls' eyes, agate marbles, plastic pearls and costume jewelry that he used in his heavily caked artworks. While he discussed his work with our father, my sister and I pretended we were princesses and his trays of fake gems were our jewelry boxes. We sprinkled jet beads and blue-green abalone shells in our hair. When we left the studio, Ossorio allowed us each a handful of his trinkets to stuff into our pockets and take home. Artists, I thought, had the best toys.

In the evenings, when they weren't attending a shindig, my parents threw dinner picnics on our slice of bay. Blankets were spread on the ground, Larry Rivers rattled over on his motorcycle, the cartoonist Saul Steinberg came with his wife, Hedda Sterne, the only female painter among the original Irascibles, Mark Rothko sat with one-year-old Topher in his lap, drinks were poured, and my sister and I wore matching dresses that looked like Mondrian paintings with huge color blocks outlined in black ribbing. We all watched the fireflies darting and disappearing into the night sky. Once, a few of the Boys piled into the bay and tried to swim to the lighthouse but it was dark and the lighthouse was on the other side of the island and far away.

Besides baby Topher, I knew very few children in the art world back then, just these mischievous adults who played with shells, built sand castles, painted and ran drunk into the sea. We, their children, were loved, surely, but always after the main course: art. Who could compete with a masterpiece, with the time and energy, the lifeblood it took to create the work or to tend to the egos, as the wives did, of those who toiled at this? We didn't even

Mark and Topher Rothko,
Loveridge House.

Tanya and Gaby,
Loveridge House

try. There was Kate Rothko, Topher's older sister, whom we still
called Katie then, but she was a big girl, already fourteen. In a few
short years, angry with her father for her parents' separation, she
would scream at him that she hated his paintings, and after he
died she would spend years trying to get them back. There was
Lisa de Kooning, but she lived with her mother. I only remember seeing Lisa once, waiting for her father to show up at a party.
She'd stood vigilantly by the door all night but he never arrived.

Waiting for a man to return had not worked for my mother.
She'd ceased her attentive guard over my father. Fretting and

watching over him had caused her to leave her children behind in a foreign country. Now, after a day of writing, a quiet pleasure enveloped her.

This was the summer "I Want to Hold Your Hand" was playing all day long on every radio. It was the Freedom Summer of protests in Mississippi when over a thousand students attempted to register African-Americans to vote, thirty-seven churches were bombed or burned and three civil rights workers were murdered; it was the summer Lyndon Johnson finally signed the Civil Rights Act into law; out on the West Coast, it was the summer the Free Speech Movement was born on the Berkeley campus. But in the idyllic Hamptons we hardly noticed. We cranked up the radio, boogied around the Loveridge cottage in our cotton underpants, rode bicycles into town and tried to see *A Hard Day's Night* at the local theater, only to stare at the backs of throngs of teenage girls who stood screaming for the entire show. Out on the street, our mother sang the Beatles lyrics, her summer skirt blowing in the wind. When we reached for her, instead of dropping our hands like she used to, she kissed our fingers and promised we'd all be back next summer.

As if heralding the end of our holiday, one rainy night in late August a car careened around a hairpin turn off the dark road, crashed through the split-rail fence of Loveridge House, skidded over the wet grass and slammed through the bedroom wall where my parents slept, stopping inches from my father's head. We all awoke to headlights streaming in the room and a drunken man stumbling from the car. Tanya and I, rushing in from our adjacent room, found our father calling out, "Lala," our mother cradling him in her arms, examining his head for glass wounds, saying, "I know this head like it's one of my own bones." Luckily,

Dad had escaped without a scratch. The man was brought into the kitchen for a cup of coffee while the police were called, and my father sat at the table, repeating, "He lost control of the car. Happens out here all the time. Remember how Pollock died on Fireplace Road, in a car crash on the way to Ossorio's. That could have been me!"

After the debris was cleaned up and the hole patched temporarily with plywood, my parents told the story again and again at the beach, naming the event "the rude awakening," making light of how close Daddy had come to departing this world. "Joking about things," my mother explained, "is as necessary as licking honey off a thorn."

"Who licks honey off a thorn except a deer?" Tanya asked.

"All of us do," our mother said.

But in her own journal she wrote:

Every letter I write is a lie. It's been this way for a long time. The details are all true, but the vision is warped because of what is left out. I leave out the thorns, or joke about them. But this obsessive need to get the details down before it's too late. Too late for what?

Chapter 7

For a few years now my father had been longing to direct his own museum. In the summer of 1964 he began to sense that this was not going to happen at MoMA. For one thing, no Jew, not even a secular Jew like my father, had ever been asked by the trustees to direct a major American museum. Dad had reached the Jewish "glass ceiling," at least on the more conservative East Coast. When he spoke to both René d'Harnoncourt and Alfred Barr, neither encouraged him to hang around for an eventual position of director at MoMA. Though they did not say why, my father was viewed as too ambitious, not possessing the finesse of a diplomat. He was accurately regarded as a man more capable of goading the establishment than coaxing donations out of their bank accounts.

In his six years at MoMA he'd done shows on Mark Rothko, Jean Dubuffet, Emil Nolde, Auguste Rodin, Futurism, *New Images of Man* and Art Nouveau. In 1964 he was working on two big retrospectives: Max Beckmann, the major German Expressionist, and Alberto Giacometti, the French existentialist, both of whom were great figurative, *humanistic* artists. But his taste was in conflict with the prevailing New York wind, which had moved on to Pop and Minimal art. Never one to shy away from expressing himself, my father (like the Boys) spoke out against the art market's growing love affair with Pop art. As far as my father was concerned, Pop pandered to the market. It was bright but limp, a regurgitation of consumerist desires onto slick surfaces. There was no humanity to be found below this surface. Pop art lacked imagination. Andy Warhol himself had admitted as much: "If you want to know all about Andy Warhol, just look at the surface of my paintings and films and me, and there I am. There's nothing behind it."

My father was not a fan of Warhol, though years later he did admit that Warhol was the one Pop artist he'd been wrong in denouncing. Dad enjoyed his Factory parties: the walls covered in silver tinfoil, Andy's white moon face trailed by boys and girls in translucent clothes. Even an existentialist sculptor like Giacometti wanted to make "Andy's scene" and insisted when he visited New York that Dad bring him to the Factory to meet the strange, enigmatic artist who went by his first name.

Minimalist art, too, was breathing down the heels of Expressionism. My father admired Ad Reinhardt's flat dark canvases and the "zip" paintings of Barnett Newman, both of which predated and influenced minimalism, but he had little patience for the rest of that crowd. He believed in art that had a human touch and displayed profound emotions. Art should have depth. Minimal art and Pop art, in reaction to Expressionism, endeavored to remove the hand of man from the surface of the work. "This type of art," Dad said, "doesn't point inward or even beyond itself.

Good art is a visual metaphor for significant human experience."
Of the artists he did like, the critics complained that Dad had
"too much enthusiasm for art."

Perhaps critics thought that my father's impassioned connection to art didn't give him the appropriate intellectual distance
to be a discerning curator. My father could be a polarizing personality, very didactic and full of the certainty that the shows he
curated, even when they were historical in nature, were canon-
challenging exhibitions.

The old guard was being pressured to make way for the next
wave. One day, having forgotten his watch and rushing through
the museum, my father stopped the young artist Frank Stella.
whom he'd spotted standing in the entrance hall, to ask for the
time. Stella was a Minimal artist whose paintings lacked any
illusion, space, depth or spontaneity. Stella wanted to strip a
painting down to being an object. In the 1960s he'd famously
called a painting "a flat surface with paint on it—nothing more."
Now Stella rocked back on his heels, looked at my father and
clipped, "Time to leave, Selz!"

The paint, if not the writing, was on the wall. And my father
was an adventurer at heart. He needed a new enterprise. The
University of Berkeley came calling with the offer to found a new
museum, to be the director, to gather a significant collection of
art together and to teach. For this as-yet-to-be-built museum,
Dad would have a million-dollar annual acquisition budget.
No small change in the days before the rocketing prices of art.
Peggy Guggenheim pledged her personal collection of Surrealist art and Mark Rothko promised to give this new museum,
should my father choose to direct it, a suite of paintings from

his retrospective at MoMA. With the light, the water and the art, my father proclaimed, "It will be like Venice on the West Coast."

When my father came to my mother with his proposition to move to Berkeley (home of the burgeoning Free Speech Movement!), she was not excited about the news. She hadn't wanted to be uprooted from their previous life in California. Now she didn't want to follow him off on yet another adventure. With the success of her novella, she felt like she was just getting traction in New York. Would my father have her become just a spectator again? "I feel like I will be losing rather than gaining." She told him. "*IT'S JUST NOT FAIR!*"

"I can't just stay put, Lala."

She didn't believe him. She thought he was simply restless and his infatuation with California, like his infatuation with other women, would pass. It was inconceivable to her that he might leave MAMA *and* his family. Her own father had had many affairs, but the old Greek patriarch had never abandoned the family. He had died recently in a car crash. For the first time in her life, my mother was left without the indomitable, lovable, magical tyrant and protector. She was bereft. In her grief, she withdrew from my father, who liked constant attention when he was home—wanting the *intensity of being together*—but she didn't fight with him.

When my parents were around, there was a constant sound in our apartment—the rapid-fire tapping of the Olivetti typewriter that sat on the big black desk in their bedroom—because one or the other of them was always working on a piece of writing when guests weren't filling the house. I loved the busy, industrious, reassuring sound of the typewriter keys, the inky smell of carbon paper, the burnt odor of my father's pipe tobacco, the waxy feel of my mother's lipstick kisses on my cheeks. "Kiss both cheeks," I said. "Make them even." When Dad traveled I looked up in the sky whenever an airplane passed over the playground, and waited with Mom for his postcards and letters that arrived daily. I drew funny pictures on cut-up pieces of construction paper to stuff in her envelopes, to make him think of us in Zurich or Venice, or Paris or London or Basel. When Dad came home, the first thing he'd do was drop to one knee so we could rush into his arms.

He was home now, putting together a show and the accompanying book on Max Beckmann, the German Expressionist artist who had inspired him in his youth. Quappi, Beckmann's widow, often came to our apartment for drinks and dinner. One evening she pointed to the wall over our couch. "I'm going away to India, why don't I loan you *The Argonauts* to hang there until the opening?" The spot was already occupied by a large painting by Reva Urban, but hardly as grand (or as famous) as this last triptych by the great German Expressionist. The Urban was quickly removed and up went *The Argonauts*, three panels crowded with Greek gods and goddesses in luminescent stained-glass colors which for some reason reminded me of the noisy crowds at my parents' cocktail parties. "The painting tells a story," my father explained. "About art and inspiration."

I stared at the panels. I couldn't recognize any of the Boys. "Where's the artist?" I demanded.

"That one." With the end of his pipe my father indicated a tortured, unshaven figure with a brush. "Beckmann painted himself in the image of Vincent van Gogh." Then Dad added soberly, "This was the last painting Beckmann created. He died a few days after completing it."

The Argonauts
Max Beckmann, 1950

With the painting up on our wall for the five months before the exhibition, my father was able to study it in detail. He paced up and down before it, sucking on his pipe. He had recently taken up smoking a pipe, and fussing over the pipe, lighting it, puffing it, knocking the tobacco ash into the glass ashtray, gave him a contemplative, professorial air.

Though my parents had stalemated about their future, they were united in their fascination with *The Argonauts*. Pulling up chairs as if they were on the deck of an ocean liner, they sat for hours—drinks in hand, the sound of Charles Mingus's deep bass strumming over the record player—in the rapt grip of the painting up on the wall before them. To them this depiction of the myth of Jason and the Argonauts was an altarpiece to the glory of creation. The left panel showed the artist guarded by a sexy naked sword-wielding muse. "I doubt any of the artists' wives we know would appreciate that," my mother mused. In the middle Beckmann depicted Jason's quest for the Golden Fleece. "Art is about a search," my father observed. In the last panel the Greek chorus strummed lutes and recounted the tale of art. This was my favorite section of the painting—no one was naked in it, and all the figures looked happy, as if they were at a cocktail party. The chorus, Dad wrote, *is the intermediary between action and audience*, the filter through which the creation was seen. Quappi shared with Dad Beckmann's feelings about *The Argonauts* and in the catalogue for the show, Dad wrote about what she'd confided: *If the left panel symbolizes the commitment to art, the center, the adventure and fulfillment, the right is reserved for comment and interpretation by the chorus.* Mom called this *the three-pronged process of creation*.

Paintings are meant to seduce; they can't speak (usually), and so they hold us enthralled by their visual grandeur, their poetry, their magnificence or their repose. The spell this triptych cast over our house, the spell my parents' tranquillity under its power cast over our home, seeped down to my sister and me playing at their feet. Whatever was so important about that painting, we wanted to be a part of it. We drew paper dolls dressed in togas and cut them matching paper wreaths to wear on their heads while they danced to lute-playing paper muses.

Five months after the painting went up, it came down. My parents' chairs sat empty and eventually were moved back into the dining room. The magic spell was broken. *The Argonauts* was shipped off to the Boston Museum of Fine Arts, where the Beckmann show was opening before it came to New York, and my father again pressured my mother to leave for the West Coast, where *so much experimentation is going on.*

"We can't really afford to experiment any longer. Not in terms of living, that is; only in terms of art," she said.

"Why can't we?" My father wondered. "There are so many possibilities and I feel ready for a new challenge."

"Because I am always going to be too much of a lone and oddball wolf to make myself over into a useful, nice, chatty, charming museum-director wife. Would you really want me to be an organization woman? Stop and think."

But he was too busy barreling forward, onward, to stop and think. Up to Boston for the big opening, she forgot to bring the studs and white bow tie for his tuxedo. *Somehow I remembered his cufflinks. Pete is furious. I've always been our ace packer. The Maître d' comes to our rescue and swiftly fashions a tie out of a paper napkin, looking almost like the real thing. Fastens it in place. His efficiency and tact calm us but can not salve our humiliation.*

During the opening of the show of my father's resurrected hero, my mother was filled with *shame and dread.* Standing glumly in the receiving line next to Ralph and Charlotte Loring Lowell of the Massachusetts Lowells (uncle and aunt to the poet Robert), she listened to a lady swathed in veils of pink chiffon tell her how she'd just redecorated her "hall." "I wanted to test the acoustics without having anyone see the place, so I arranged a fine concert performance to which I invited the entire population of the Perkins School for the Blind. Because, you know, I'm that Mrs. Perkins!"

I can't understand what is happening to me. My life is closing around me like a fist. I feel utterly locked out of Pete's world. In part by my own contempt for it.

Back at the hotel room, my parents undressed for bed. Outside the window a car horn traveled swiftly past, keening as it receded down the avenue. My mother turned to my father.

ME: *We must talk. Say what you think.*

PETER: *Well, I was thinking two things about you all evening long. First, that you looked marvelous. You were beautiful! You were without doubt the most beautiful woman there . . .*

ME: *Yes, you were?*

PETER: *Um-hm. And the second thing I was thinking was, why isn't there somebody who appreciates it more than I do?*

ME: *(staggered) WHAT?—What do you mean?*

PETER: *You should be married to somebody who's* mad *about you!*

ME: *And you aren't?*

PETER: *No.*

After he had gone to sleep, or perhaps two days later when they returned to New York, she typed up their dialogue on a separate piece of paper and pasted it into her journal. It must have shocked her to her core, for she wrote it out like a script. She had always been adored, just for being herself. *I loved you once you got here, just for being you.* But now my father was telling her that he no longer did. Maybe he was mad *at* her, but he was not mad *about* her anymore.

We have become a cliché, one child in therapy, living on more than we earn, both of us seeking other people. Yet despite the pain and disenchantment they were still very much a couple, *babyandbaby* wrapped up in each other's lives, reading each other's work. If not mad about each other, if not mad at each other, still deeply intertwined and connected.

Dad imitating Beckmann's dark expression in front of Max Beckmann's *Departures* at MoMA opening.

By the beginning of 1965 my father was hard at work preparing for what would be his last show at MoMA, an Alberto Giacometti retrospective due to open in the spring. But he had also made his decision to leave for Berkeley and his own museum. My mother flew out to California, far too overdressed for all the sunshine, in her leopard-print swing coat and black high heels, to look at houses. She was trying to acquiesce.

In mid-January my parents attended Marcel Duchamp's opening at the Cordier & Ekstrom Gallery, not knowing that, save the Giacometti exhibit, this would be the last big event they would ever attend as husband and wife. The gallery had sent out an invitation that was in fact a real readymade Duchamp. A postcard reproduction mounted on a playing card of Leonardo da Vinci's *Mona Lisa*, with the inscribed letters below *L.H.O.O.Q.* (a pun, since the French pronunciation of the letters produces the sentence *Elle a chaud au cul,* or She has a hot ass). Years ago, Duchamp had playfully defaced a repro of *Mona* with his own mustache. This time he'd defaced his own defacement by shaving off the mustache and writing the word *rasée* (shaved) below. My father was charmed by the invitation and later had it framed, but *the endless circle of Duchamp's irony* irritated Mom.

That night, my parents rode up in the elevator with Salvador Dalí and his wife Gala. The young receptionist recognized my parents but asked Dalí to identify himself before she would let him pass. "But I am Dalí!" Dalí kept sputtering and pointing his finger in the air. "I am Dalí! Dalí!" Watching Dalí's waxed mustache grow at least three inches in agitation amused Mom more than the *graceless objects* on display. Across the room, Marcel Duchamp sat puffing his cigar as quiet as one of his favored chess pieces. Andy Warhol was there, too, in his James Dean sunglasses and mop of blond wig over his forehead, documenting the whole extravaganza. *All of them acting like caricatures of their own art works.*

Four large rooms and the hallway were packed with Duchamp's old readymades. Through the crowds, caterers bore trays of beautiful food, salmon that were two feet long and magnificent pheasants with large maraschino cherries clasped in their beaks. That night, the collectors Mary and William Sisler bought the entire show so that they could send it on a tour of all the major museums.

There was no hint that Duchamp was even still making art. It

had been years since he'd done anything more than play chess
and show up at events. When pressed for answers about his work,
all he'd say from behind the smokescreen of his cigar smoke was
that he liked chess.

It was a ruse, of course, a façade. Three years later when
Duchamp died, the art world discovered that he'd secretly been
working away for twenty-five years on a piece called *Étant Donnés*.
It was not a readymade object. *Étant Donnés* was carefully crafted
and representational, a door with two holes cut in it, through
which the viewer was forced to peep and spy on a naked girl lying
in a wooded landscape. It was beautifully constructed. But by
casting the viewer into the voyeuristic act of looking, the piece
alluded to what Duchamp had been thinking about for years. The
idea that the creation of art was a threesome: an unconsummated
love affair between the creator, the piece of art which was the

object of desire, and the viewer. Like Beckmann, Duchamp had found a way to express the three-pronged process of creation. But in his work, the audience had supplanted the chorus, and the spectator now deciphered and interpreted the work of art.

Way before Warhol and Pop art, when Duchamp had created his first readymade in 1913, he'd suggested that art could be anything. He opened the door to an avalanche of new ideas about what could constitute art: Pop, Conceptual, Happenings, Performance and Assemblage art all flowed through Duchamp's door. In 1921, photographed by Man Ray, Duchamp had dressed as his alter ego, the vixen Rrose Sélavy, and arguably crafted the first piece of performance art. Duchamp used chance as an element in his work—later a device employed by the artists who created Happenings—when he'd fired paint from a toy cannon to resolve parts of his monumental work *The Large Glass*. Happenings, open-ended, organic events, were the rage in the sixties art world. At Black Mountain College in North Carolina, John Cage read poetry on a ladder while Merce Cunningham danced; in France, Yves Klein threw gold coins into the Seine; in Tokyo, Yoko Ono draped herself in fabric and presented the audience with a pair of scissors and the instructions to cut the cloth from her body until she deemed the artwork complete. These artists believed, as Duchamp did, in the fun and importance of breaking down the limitations and boundaries of art. Duchamp's visual puns paved the way for Andy Warhol, who hung with bated breath at Duchamp's knee that night of the opening at the Cordier & Ekstrom Gallery. Warhol had already popularized the idea of art as a series of factory-made replicas when in 1962 he'd silkscreened his favorite thing, the dollar bill. In creating *200 One Dollar Bills* Warhol parlayed Duchamp's idea of the readymade art object one step further: a multiple silkscreen of an object was as close to forgery as you could get without quite slipping over the line. But by 1968, two years after Marcel Duchamp's final exhibition, when Andy Warhol displayed five hundred Brillo boxes, it became virtually impossible to distinguish an object that was art from an object that wasn't. Without Marcel Duchamp, that door might still be closed.

In one form or another, all great artists tackle the rich tradition of the past. Some by superseding previous constructs, some by merely engaging in a dialogue. By the mid-sixties the Boys had reached the apex of their careers. A few critics thought they were receding, though not my father, who turned out to be right. Mark Rothko would still produce his great dark masterpieces for the Rothko Chapel in Houston, and Willem de Kooning would return to a looser form abstraction. Robert Rauschenberg had even paid great homage to de Kooning, the father of Abstract Expressionism, by trying (with de Kooning's permission) to erase one of his drawings. Visiting de Kooning with a bottle of Jack Daniel's, Rauschenberg had explained his strange request. Could he have a de Kooning to obliterate? De Kooning was not thrilled with the idea of being erased, but at least he understood the importance of this action. "I'll give you something I'll miss," he said, and found a very difficult drawing for Rauschenberg, telling him, "This will take you a while." Indeed Rauschenberg spent a long time working over that de Kooning, but never quite eliminated the older artist, whose ghost lines still appear like scaffolding underneath the smudged eraser marks.

It is in the nature of creation to re-create. De Kooning took on Picasso, Duchamp defaced da Vinci, Philip Guston's later figurative works would never have existed without Max Beckmann, who in turn owed Rembrandt. Rothko was beholden to the American painter Milton Avery. Their muses were many. Now a new army had stormed the castle gates. Not just Pop and Minimal art, but a form that engaged with the land, with the world. It was indebted to Expressionism without being contained by it. This art was flying off the canvases, off the walls, out of the museums, and spreading across the country. Or at least that's what my father hoped.

Years later my mother said of the Duchamp show, thinking of her ride up the elevator, "I remember being so startled when Dalí, such a strange-looking man, so famous, was not even recognized. There was a new group taking over, a new era, and it was not us."

Chapter 8

I n the early spring of 1965 my mother went into the hospital
to have a hysterectomy because a tumor had grown on her
uterus. Her tumor turned out to be benign but the hospital stay was longer than expected. The doctor had left a sponge
inside Mom and had to go back in and fetch it.

While she was convalescing in the hospital, brewing over her
collapsing marriage, she befriended a lapsed Catholic, lesbian
alcoholic named Barbara who was dying of a brain tumor in the
next bed. Each night, these two very different women coaxed
each other out of their misery by talking until sleep overcame
them. Mom was there for two weeks. While her new friend
slipped in and out of consciousness my mother tried to face what
was happening in her life, mulling over a question that Barbara
had raised regarding the end of her own: "What will follow now?"

At home, Dad was in charge of us. On the Saturday midway
during our mother's absence, he took Tanya and me, not to visit

the galleries, but to the carousel in Central Park. We twirled on painted steeds to sweet calliope music and were introduced to his new friend, Norma. Norma had wispy blond hair, a sharp chin and long slim legs draped sidesaddle over her wooden horse. After a few turns around the carousel—because one time was never enough—we all went to Schrafft's, sat in a booth and, while Norma and my father sipped cocktails, Tanya and I were allowed a scoop of ice cream served in a silver dish, *and* a ginger ale. Since our mother had never allowed us to drink soda before, this was a great treat. The next morning, when Dad brought us to the hospital—the staff agreeing to a quick visit in an effort to placate Mom, who they feared might sue over the sponge incident—we immediately reported the event to her. "Daddy took us to meet Norma and let us have soda!"

My mother glared at him and he hung his head.

It turned out Mom knew Norma, everyone in their art world circle knew her. In fact, Norma and her husband had come to parties at our house. Like our mother, Norma had a degree in art history; she was younger and from a wealthy family. She possessed a cold, edgy beauty and, most importantly, Norma knew how to circulate in a crowd.

Still, even though this affair was out in the open, my mother decided to wait it out. Maybe Mom believed that because Norma was married and had two sons, it would blow over. Dad flew to Paris to meet with Giacometti and rendezvous with Norma. Back at home, Mom secretly took her own lover and flew to Puerto Rico with him. My mother's affair hit the rocks over the Atlantic, but my father's survived the crossing. In Paris, Norma and Dad decided they were in love. As soon as Norma agreed to leave her husband and run off with him to California, my father dubbed her Nora. "Norma," he said, "sounds like the name of a cleaning lady."

Early that June, my mother and father attended his last show at MoMA, the retrospective of paintings and sculptures by Alberto Giacometti. After the show closed at MoMA it would travel across the country and, like my father, end up on the West Coast. Norma was at the MoMA opening with her husband that night. My father wanted "everyone to get along." But my mother, in her long white satin dress, sailed off in a huff. She wandered through the rooms of MoMA whose walls were covered with Giacometti's paintings, their solitary figures trapped in the middle of soft gray voids. Everyone was still downstairs at the bar, so, save for the guards, my mother was alone with the elegant, elongated sculptures with their enormous feet.

Born in Borgonovo, a narrow village on the Swiss-Italian border that is now part of Stampa, Giacometti was as gaunt and elongated as his existential figures. He was in his mid-sixties dying of heart disease by the time of the MoMA exhibition. Dad said Giacometti was never satisfied with his work, forever complaining that it was no good. "But you're better than the rest," my father reassured him. "Well, yes," Giacometti agreed. "But even Cézanne failed. We all fail." My father wrote, *His work, neither imitated nor slandered, is out of competition. Like a saint, he is placed in a niche by himself.* Dad called Giacometti "a spectator as painter." Once, seated at dinner in Stampa, Switzerland, Giacometti told my father that he couldn't really see him. *I was a conglomeration of vague and disconnected details. But each member of the family sitting across the room was clearly visible, though diminutive, thin,*

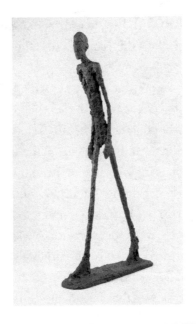

Walking Man I
Alberto Giacometti, 1960.
Art © Alberto Giacometti Estate/
Licensed by VAGA and ARS,
New York, NY

surrounded by enormous slices of space. Giacometti, my father said, was grappling with *the relationship of the figure to the enveloping space, of man to the void, even of being to nothingness.*

In the museum my mother sat down. She thought about what her husband had written in his book, how the rough-hewn bronzes encircling her *do not allow us to come into intimate contact with them. They remain unreachable and can only be seen at the distance from which they were modeled or painted.* Though Dad had been writing about Giacometti's sculptures, my mother said later that at that moment she wondered if he'd been writing about himself as well. *To be in a room with a figure by Giacometti is not to enjoy an object but to experience a presence.* Did she make up her mind then that this would be her last visit to the museum? She wouldn't have cried. She was too proud to cry in public, and probably too angry. Under her slinky satin skirt, she would have slipped her shoes off one last time. That night she wrote in her journal, *So many hours together. Seventeen years. We all fail.*

Spring was in full bloom in Central Park when my parents sat my sister and me down and told us they were getting divorced, a word I had only heard once before, in reference to Willem de Kooning.

"What does that mean?" I asked. Was our father leaving us for Ruth Kligman, too?

"It means that Daddy will be staying across the park," Mom explained. She sat between us, her hands in her lap, long fingers folded together.

I giggled until I saw that my mother's hands were white little knots in her lap.

Across from us, Dad sat in one of the eighteenth century brocade chairs with the gilded arms that had once belonged to his beloved grandfather Drey. He twisted on the seat of little golden bees buzzing on a green background and pointed out the window. "We can wave to each other."

Wave? Dad explained that he would be staying in an apartment across the park before he moved to California. The only thing I knew about California, other than that Tanya and I were born there, was Disneyland.

Tanya and I got up and went to the window together. Looking out, we saw the park, where the apple and magnolia trees flowered. Curled up in the distance was the Guggenheim—the mark of man's hand.

A week later our mother drove us out for a visit to the Loveridge House in Sag Harbor. There we splashed in the ocean and ran along the shore linking hands like a line of untethered rope. Our mother kept her sunglasses on and pointed out to sea where a lone ship struggled across the horizon line. On the way home she pulled the car to the side of the road below the old family graveyard and told us to wait. In a flash she darted across the road, her wide flowered skirt billowing out like a sail, and then climbed up the hill disappearing into the small graveyard. A few minutes later she returned carrying a stone. It was a tombstone, or part of a tombstone, a broken fragment of Mrs. Jemima Payne's stone whose curved top showed part of an angel's wing and her name.

Why did she take Jemima's stone? As I grew older my mother explained that Jemima Payne was Mr. Payne's second wife. His first had died in childbirth, though how my mother knew this I never learned. She insisted she stole the fragment of her gravestone—which was about the size of a toaster—because my father was leaving her to remarry and take on a second wife. Because Mom couldn't steal Norma away, she wanted to steal, metaphorically at least, this particular second wife away. "I wanted to leave Mr. Payne with his first wife, alone and intact, the better to work out their marriage problems in eternity."

By the time we arrived home, Dad's suitcases and boxes were stacked by the front door. Pieces of furniture—the gilded armchair!—were being lifted and hauled out and placed in a moving truck parked in front of the building. Just then Dad walked in from the bedroom with a pile of striped ties dangling from his hands.

"Oh, you should have been gone by now," our mother sobbed, clutching her stone against her chest, Tanya and I holding on to her skirt on either side. "You agreed you would be done by now!"

He had tears in his eyes, too. "It took longer than I thought."

I had watched my father pack for trips before, but I had never seen the contents of our life uprooted. The undersides of everything exposed. Against the walls, the backs of the paintings were turned outward, the remaining furniture lined up and tagged. Even his slippers were packed. Paintings off their hooks left empty ghostlike spaces behind. The Beckmann triptych had long since disappeared, and now the little Rothko, the de Kooning, Dubuffet, Feininger.

In the long dark hallway I stood beside his last suitcase. Inside it contained everything that was his—his boxer shorts and socks, his slacks, white shirts and dark suit jackets and now all his ties—a careless jumbled pile like my doll's clothes in the back of my wooden dollhouse.

"Just don't marry her," my mother said.

Without answering, he placed the very last items, two candlesticks, into the big gray suitcase. So last-minute, I thought they were an afterthought—except they were his. They had always been his. These were the blue ceramic candlesticks that he'd traveled on the boat with out of Germany at seventeen, carrying them inside his first suitcase, across an ocean and onto this shore. Having barely escaped the Nazis, he hadn't known if he'd ever see his parents again. But he'd held on to those ceramic candlesticks, and for years kept them side by side in the corner of the bedroom.

When my father laid them down on his pile of rumpled clothing and shut the lid of his suitcase, I began to cry.

My father began to bellow, too, a long, sorrowful, echoing wail. Setting his suitcase down, he opened it, retrieved the candlesticks and came toward me, placing them in my small hands. "Hush," he said. "There, there. It will be all right."

The blue candlesticks, which had once been his talisman of a life left behind, were now mine.

PART TWO

On and Off the Wall

THE KINETIC ARTIST USES MOVEMENT ITSELF...AS THE

PAINTER USES COLOR.

—*George Rickey*

THE THING THAT'S IMPORTANT TO KNOW IS THAT YOU NEVER

KNOW. YOU'RE ALWAYS SORT OF FEELING YOUR WAY.

—*Diane Arbus*

Chapter 9

The first time Tanya and I visited our father and *Nora* across the park, we threw a bunch of toys that we thought were her sons' out the window. Over a lunch of crustless sandwiches—our mother served her sandwiches on crusty baguettes—we were told that Dad, Nora and the boys (who were conveniently off with their father that afternoon) were soon departing for a big house in California, which *we* would get to visit. Up until that moment, I don't think we understood that our father was going to be part of another family. Now he said, "You'll have stepbrothers. They're your age."

"We don't play with boys." Tanya said.

We were only seven and eight. We played paper dolls, Easy-Bake Oven and trolls with our girlfriends.

But our father reassured us we would like *these boys.*

At the end of the lunch Dad and Nora left us alone for a few minutes in the living room, probably for some "smooching," Tanya explained. Immediately, and without any discussion, we gathered a selection of the boys' toys from a basket beside the couch and headed for the window. Climbing up on the sill, we leaned out and one by one tossed the toys eight floors down onto the pavement below. Minutes later the doorbell rang, and when our father opened it, there stood the doorman in his blue uniform brandishing the baseball glove. Our father's face went red with rage. We didn't yet know Nora well enough to understand that narrowing her eyes and raising an aloof shoulder meant that she was angry, too. "Don't you know you could have hurt someone?" the adults asked.

"What am I going to say to the owners?" our father asked. Apparently this apartment wasn't where Nora and her sons lived. They lived in a brownstone next door to Walter Cronkite. This was just a sublet our father had taken until the house in California was renovated. We had tried to destroy the property, not of our future stepbrothers, but of unknown children who were away on vacation. Hanging our heads in shame, we followed our father into the taxi. He sat between us, frowning. "Your mother hasn't raised you two very well. I want you to call me Papa from now on." Nora's children, who did not splatter the sidewalk with paper money and plastic cars, called their daddy "Papa."

"Papa?" we both spat out the word for the first and last time.

Of course, the boys played their own mischievous prank on us later that summer while we were vacationing "*en famille*," as Nora said, on Fire Island. They climbed the scrubby trees outside our bedroom window and spied on us while we changed out of our bathing suits. Hanging from the branches like monkeys, our new brothers laughed and pointed at our naked bodies, our exposed "things." Then they all left for California and Tanya and I had little interaction with the boys. They were put on a similar visiting schedule with their papa. When we flew west, they flew east. We were not going to have boys to play with after all.

In the months following our father's departure, our mother sank into a depression. At thirty-nine, she'd been left with two children three thousand miles from their other parent. An event she'd never anticipated. She had gone from the circle of her family to college to graduate school to my father. Before Dad left she had never balanced a checkbook. She began locking herself in the bathroom, turning on the faucets, both the sink and the bathtub, and crying under the noise of running water, hoping that my sister and I wouldn't hear her. But we did hear her.

Sitting outside on the floor, Tanya would whisper, "Go call Daddy," and so I'd call my father from the kitchen phone all the way in California and if I was lucky enough to reach him, he'd say, "What can I do?" Then my sister and I would start to cry and he'd say how much he wished to help but was far away. I'd hang up the phone and Tanya would take out our crayons and we'd draw pictures, slipping them under the bathroom door. Eventually Mommy would emerge, clean, quiet and powdered, to sit down on the floor between us and say, "Oh, what would I do without you two, you settle me!"

In between her crying jags, she dated. Once a man with thick black hair and the large beaked nose of a bird came to the front door to pick her up. He was introduced as Jerzy Kosinski, the author of a controversial book my mother had on her shelf, *The Painted Bird*, about a boy surviving the Holocaust. They didn't go out for long. Kosinski was an eccentric who liked to disappear. Mom once discovered him curled up and hiding in a large bureau drawer. He was too strange for her tastes.

With my mother out dating, Tanya and I were again left in the care of babysitters, and soon just ourselves. I became afraid of the dark, surrounding myself, in the nearly empty apartment, with my stuffed animals. Though I knew they were just toys, they provided the pretense of guardians. Slowly it dawned on me how different this thing called divorce was from a long business trip. I placed the blue candlesticks on the top of my bureau and sometimes I pretended that my father was gone for good and that these two objects were all I had left. Then the night would come, and my father's face would rise in front of me like a distant light, a star I hung my dreams on. When his calls and letters arrived, they, too, reminded me that he hadn't entirely vanished from our lives, he was just obscured by the brilliant sunlight of his very busy life.

Having come from the Modern, when my father arrived in California he was considered art world royalty. He was at the height of his game, a demigod in the provinces and he was jubilant and electric. Though the museum wasn't built yet, he opened in a temporary space—the Powerhouse Gallery—with a show on Kinetic sculpture. Dad had planned the show for MoMA, but now that he'd left, Kinetics would inaugurate Berkeley, or at least the idea of the future Berkeley museum. "Heavy metal figures," he wrote us, "beautifully pivoting and swirling like ballerinas." My father's shows had always reflected aspects of his personality, and Kinetic art, with its focus on perpetual motion, its nervous intensity, was no exception. *Over 70,000 people so far and damn good publicity*, he wrote, quoting the attendance in his letter to my mother. For even after a quickie Mexican divorce and a rushed marriage to Nora—who had her own quickie divorce—my father still felt the need to report back to Mom about all his various accomplishments. And my mother liked the fact that he needed to confide in her. His dependence on her good opinion gave her

Dad in front of a Kinetic piece, Len Lye's
Fountain.

a measure of power. She replied that even in New York, *everyone
is talking about your show.*

The Kinetic show had sprung out of my father's relationship
with the sculptors George Rickey and Jean Tinguely. Five years
after *Homage* had burst into flames and been unceremoniously
quenched, in what my father referred to as a *Keystone-cops finale*,
he now felt the time *for the high art of motion* had finally come.

Basic to the philosophy of Kinetic sculpture was the idea that
the only stable thing in the universe was movement. If the work
of the Abstract Expressionists had in part been about the depiction of inner turmoil and change, and the belief that the map-
ping of an interior landscape in paint could redeem mankind,
then Kinetics pointed outward. Kinetics was part sculpture, part

performance. These were the early years of the Apollo space program, with the goal of sending a man to the moon. Kinetics was
about the promise of the future.

Kinetics could be dynamic like a Tinguely piece; it could capture the magnetized, quivering energy of a loop of steel, as Len
Lye did in *Flip and Two Twisters*; or feature the slow movement of
a peg sinking into a plywood board, as Paul Bury's *Oak Pegs on a
Background of the Same* painstakingly demonstrated; or Kinetics
could, as my father's friend George Rickey showed in his monumental *Two Lines—Temporal I*, measure time and space. Rickey's
two steel blades, thirty-five feet high, pivoted, oscillated, swept

Two Lines—Temporal I
George Rickey, 1964. Art © Estate of George
Rickey / Licensed by VAGA, New York, NY

and danced above the ground, appearing to intersect, but never quite touching.

Dad had met George Rickey in the 1950s in Chicago and later got to know him in New York when, right about the time we moved to Central Park West, George Rickey and his wife Eddy bought an old farmhouse in East Chatham, New York, in the foothills of the Berkshires. Before my father left for California, we used to visit the Rickeys each summer. George Rickey had come to sculpture late, after journalism. He looked like an intellectual, with Buddy Holly short hair and horn-rimmed glasses. Eddy was a fleshy woman, full of gossip and already chain-smoking at her kitchen table when I would tumble down the back staircase of their home in the morning. My mother would be seated across from her in a backless summer dress, the wings of her shoulder blades exposed, listening to all of Eddy's latest news. Across their green yard, which was peppered with Rickey's gleaming sculptures, I would scamper off to find my father and George huddled in the barn over cigarettes and coffee cups, discussing the perfect balance of a Calder mobile, or the way Rodin trapped motion in marble. Rickey was particularly fascinated by the harmonic motion of the pendulum. His grandfather had been a clockmaker and he was constantly tinkering and tuning the little models for his sculptures in his studio. Showing my father and me how the blade cut both ways, swinging back and forth in a predictable arc unless he altered its length or accelerated the force that moved it.

And then there was chance. Rickey, who wrote the introduction to the Kinetic catalogue, believed chance was nature's contribution. *Chance is an elusive concept. It has other names—luck, hazard, accident, risk, and even fate (which could be thought of as the opposite of chance) . . . Such randomness without interference now serves the artist.* The way fire interacted with a Jean Tinguely performance, or wind came into play with one of his sculptures. Chance was both an unpredictable element and a probable occurrence. My mother understood the precariousness of chance. If the Kinetic artists wanted to inject instability into their work, that was fine in a piece of art, but life was unstable enough without the constant exposure to providence. But my father was willing to gamble. To him chance was a stroke of luck that, if he chose, he could bend to his advantage. What nature did by accident, a man could assist with deliberation. He had done this before when lucky breaks had led him to America, to Steiglitz and to MoMA. He had met Norma by chance when she and her husband bought the property next door to the Rickeys in East Chatham, and he'd parlayed that encounter into an affair and then a marriage, a happy accident for him, an unfortunate one for my mother. I didn't have to be an adult to understand that the thrill of chance came with risks, but that sometimes one had to leap anyway. What if Pollock had never acted in frustration over the canvas for Peggy Guggenheim? What if Beckmann had never seen the corpses tossed out of their coffins in World War I? Or what if de Kooning had refused to give Robert Rauschenberg a drawing to erase? You had to try, didn't you? To move forward you had to tempt fate, and that risk might obliterate you or someone else. Chance was as unforeseeable as it was inevitable, and one never knew how it was going to turn out. The Kinetic sculptors believed that chance was nature's way of effacing the ego of man. Maybe de Kooning, like the Kinetic artists, was willing to let chance efface his ego; he understood the nature of time. But my father's ego was another matter.

Now, even though my father was situated on the West Coast, New York was, as my mother wrote, *abuzz with your activities*. In May 1966 he opened *Seven Decades,1895–1965: Crosscurrents of Modern Art* simultaneously in ten of New York's primary galleries. The show was a benefit for the Public Education Association. My father, the hater of labels and "-isms," arranged the show by decade and subject matter, instead of by movement and school. *Unlike science*, he stated in his catalogue essay, *art does not submit to categorization*. Instead art was displayed by time and theme: a Cubist Picasso mingled with an Expressionist de Kooning and a Fauvist Matisse in a corner of André Emmerich Gallery because they were all painted in the 1950s and depicted naked women. From Rodin to Rauschenberg, every major artist in the last seventy years, excepting the Pop artists—my father was a stubborn man—were represented. In The Talk of the Town, Calvin Trillin wrote:

> As waiters squirmed through the opening night throngs, champagne was spilled on patent-leather pump and desert boot alike, T.V. cameramen ground out impartial footage of Galanos-sheathed heiress and vinyl-skirted Mod, and the critical lion lay down, so to speak, with the creative lamb. Madison Avenue itself seemed transformed by the new spirit. Perfect strangers kept bumping into each other at the various galleries or on one or another of the two special buses (Sardi's red London Transport double-decker and the Lutèce Restaurants green-and-cream Paris autobus marked "Porte de Montmartre-Gare Montparnesse") that had been chartered to ferry opening-nighters between the two main gallery centers at Fifty-seventh and Seventy-ninth Streets.

With exhibitions showing on both coasts, paid by MoMA, as well as Berkeley and Mrs. Victor W. Ganz, who was the vice president of the Public Education Association, which funded *Seven Decades* and had the largest private collection of Picassos at that time, 1966 was my father's big year. He thought he was invincible, a superstar answerable to none. He had begun amassing a collection for the University of California, Berkeley Art Museum: a huge selection of Hans Hofmanns, an exquisite Rubens, a sixteenth century pietà, a Tiepolo and of course his twentieth century favorites: Pollock, de Kooning, Rothko, Tinguely, Frankenthaler, Sam Francis and Max Beckmann.

My mother had just published another novella and finished a draft for a novel. She, too, felt proud of her work that year. Interestingly, both her stories had as their central conflict a woman caught in a triangle: loving an egocentric and unfaithful man; desiring to pursue her own art; struggling with motherhood. In each story the woman is confronted with *the terrible desire to have* all *desires fulfilled.* She is forced to choose. She can have two, but never all three of her wishes. My mother sent both the novel manuscript and the novella to my father to read, as they had always shared their work in the past. "This funny book," my father said when he called her. "It's real good, but (quite seriously) it's too familiar."

Later that summer Dad and Nora stopped off in New York on their way to Italy for a vacation with the Rothkos, and my father invited my mother for drinks with Mark. It was just the three of them, sitting under the Maxfield Parrish mural at the King Cole Bar in the St. Regis Hotel. Where Nora was, I don't know. Rothko was already at work on his murals for a chapel in Houston commissioned by the de Menil family and said, referring to his present enterprise and the trip ahead, "Soon I will have realized which of my conjectures was impossible." Unlike the spontaneous Kinetic sculptors, Rothko was not a man who flirted with chance. His paintings were born from a methodical process, as if he were attempting to crack a code. He wouldn't even let his paintings out of his sight for fear they might be looked at the wrong way. It was like old times, my parents sitting with the artist. They toasted to Mark's commission, my father's museum, my mother's publication. In Italy, my father drove Mark to visit the Piero della Francesca murals, which Rothko thought too crowded, then on to the Fra Angelicos, which Mark loved. They were simpler, more elegant and had a darker palette.

By the end of that summer Dad's correspondence with Mom had taken on a more affectionate tone. He addressed her by her diminutive name, Lala. He wrote that Europe with Nora, even with the Rothkos, wasn't the same as Europe with her. He pined for "my family." He wanted to know, if he would leave Nora, would my mother pack up kit and caboodle and follow him west?

Dearest one, I missed you all over Rome. Surely, I wouldn't choose this erratic course, if I didn't have very deep feelings for you. As for my mother, she'd progressed from being furious after he left, to relishing the need he still had for her. Now she longed for him and the life they had built together. *If it's a choice between peace and Pete, I choose Pete (!),* she wrote in her journal. And to him, *It's fun to be in life again. I love dreams, as you know, and need them and I know you do, too, but good old life is great!* She felt that during their year apart they had both matured. Though how she could interpret her response—Pete rather than peace—as mature is hard to fathom, such was my mother's craving for the force of my father's nature. She hoped that by now *we know a lot of the worst and a lot of the best about each other and maybe we won't expect the impossible anymore.*

It had been only eleven months since he'd walked out our front door. Soon Dad was flying in for frequent visits without Nora, and Nora was none the wiser. On her coffee table our mother placed tempting dishes of appetizers. Tanya and I had seen the movie *The Parent Trap* with Hayley Mills, we understood what was at stake between our parents. We decorated the house with WEL-COME HOME DADDY banners. We dressed up in flounced skirts and curled our hair in ringlets like our *Little Women* dolls, as if by imitating our dolls' appearance we could re-create a more perfect vision of family life to entice our father home.

As she had done throughout their marriage when he traveled, my mother kept him abreast of the goings-on about town. *I went to Ad's opening at the Jewish Museum: mobbed, Ad drunk, Rita* [Rita was Ad Reinhardt's wife] *looking so beautiful and glad to see me as I her but awfully tired. Ran into Ilse and went to her apartment along with Mark and Mell. She is sick, all right, and very manic, but insists that Herbert was not to blame for her incarceration . . . Mark says you spoke to him?*

In a year, Ad would die of heart failure, and in two years, Mark would leave Mell and begin dating Ad's beautiful widow, Rita. *Manic* Ilse and her husband Herbert Ferber were friends of the art crowd: Herbert was a dentist who aspired to be a sculptor, and Ilse had worked with my father at the Modern on the book that accompanied the Art Nouveau show. In Rothko's will, Herbert was named the guardian of Mark's children. But when Herbert institutionalized his wife and then ran off with his dental assistant, Mark removed him, at least as the guardian of Topher.

None of that complicated mess had happened yet. Mark was still alive, still witty, still painting his soft-focused dark master-pieces. *He is*, my father wrote in his reply to my mother's letter, *a wise man. I spoke to him. He knows, but doesn't say much.*

Ad Reinhardt and Mark Rothko had always been competitors, both intellectuals who experimented with color as a composition. For years, Reinhardt had been interested in taking the idea of abstraction to the extreme—down to starkness. His paintings at the Jewish Museum retrospective that night were all grada-tions of black, and now Mark was working with a dark palette as well. But where Ad's squares were flat, hard-edged and reduced, Mark's forms blurred with a powdery surface that made them seem both throbbing with substance and ethereal. He sought to use darkness to unfold a revelation.

Soon my parents' letters turned into hotel room visits. Dad proposed they remarry, even suggesting that they find some-place else to settle, like Princeton or Philadelphia. There was an additional factor contributing to Dad's about-face regard-ing his move west. Just as my father arrived in Berkeley, Ron-ald Reagan was elected governor of California, and one of his first actions was to fire the university president and slash the university budget. This caused Peggy Guggenheim to back out of her promise to bequeath her collection to Berkeley. Instead, she set up a foundation in Venice, stating that her choice was based on her mistrust of Reagan. Dad was in turmoil, rethinking all his choices, both with Berkeley and with Nora. The success of the *Seven Decades* show—Calvin Trillin had called the show "brilliantly unorthodox" and advance sales opening night had exceeded expectations—had rekindled his love affair with the

East Coast. But my mother wasn't quite ready to jump back into the waters with my father until he told Nora, and Dad wouldn't tell Nora until Mom said yes.

I don't remember much about my stepmother Nora. She was a strikingly attractive and thin woman who ate Oreo cookies all day. Aside from a birthday party she gave me in the big house in Berkeley that she'd paid for, I only recall one other nice thing about her—she showed me how to walk like a prancing ballerina, pointing my toes with each step, and I thought that was very elegant. But she also told Tanya and me not to hug her. "I don't like clutchy children," she said.

Down the hill from my father and Nora's house, the Rothkos rented a pink villa for the summer of 1967, my father having arranged for a visiting regent professorship for Mark at Berkeley. Nora's boys were back East at camp, and since I really didn't know any kids out there, even though I was eight and Topher only four *and* a boy, I was excited to have a familiar friend only a few blocks away. I don't remember if Kate was there that summer, but I suspect she was. She was seventeen then, practically a grown-up. Tanya kept her head buried in her book and secretly called Mr. Rothko Mr. Fatso when he was out of earshot. Topher and I played on his wooden rocking horse while the sunlight spilled in through the large windows. Outside, the adults drank cocktails, and whenever we'd run out to join them, Topher would climb up into his father's lap and I would climb into my father's. From our perches, on opposite sides of the patio table, we would settle against our fathers' chests while they talked. Dad loved the pink villa, the cocktails, the sunlight, the view in the distance, but Rothko complained. Leaning back in his chair, he would say how uncomfortable he was with the opulence of the house.

Then, almost as an afterthought, he'd add that he really loved the salmon-pink color of this mansion, it reminded him of the color of the villas in Rome. Eventually Topher and I would scamper off to explore their garden.

Finally, art world gossip in the form of Eddy Rickey reached Nora and she learned the truth. Her new husband was having an affair, and with his ex-wife, no less! A week after the Rothkos departed back for New York, Nora came to say goodbye to Tanya and me in the garden where we were poking with sticks at the lazy carp in the goldfish pond. We knew something was amiss when she told us to make sure to feed the dog. It wasn't even our dog, but her sons'. Then she *kissed* us. As soon as Nora's back was turned, Tanya and I made a beeline for the black rotary phone in the master bedroom. Tanya dialed our father's office number, her little finger spinning the dial as quietly as possible. When we finally heard his voice we both clutched the receiver, sharing the weight, and burst into tears. He came home just as Nora was climbing into her station wagon, heading for the airport. "Couldn't you have waited until the end of their visit as we agreed, Nora?" he wanted to know.

Apparently not. With chin and toe pointed east, Nora said, "It's Norma, Peter, NORMA!" Then she drove off.

Within a few days our mother joined us in California. It happened so quickly, she must have caught Nora's tailwind. Seeing my mother in the California sunshine made my head spin. My parents cuddled and kissed and met with a Modernist architect named Donald Olsen. Dad wanted to design a new house, either Selz 1 or Selz 2, in the open style of his hero Le Corbusier. Selz 1 would be big enough for all four of us, Selz 2 wouldn't. The house, Dad said, "would be a work of art in itself!" Tanya and I circled

Tanya, Mom, me, Dad.

our parents, as excited as pollinating bees, while they looked at floor plans. Dad took us to view the construction on the museum, where we had to wear hard hats. Then, *"en famille"*(!), we drove to a cabin in Desolation Valley, a bowl of glacier lakes in the mountains of the Crystal Range.

Standing outside the cabin on the rock face of the valley, Tanya and I heard Dad ask Mom to "try and understand this new way people are living on the West Coast, free and open."

"Not this again, Pete."

"You can't control me."

"Who's trying to control who?"

"Stop it," Tanya and I yelled in unison, and they did stop quarreling. Dad built a fire in the fireplace without opening the flue and when smoke filled the cabin, our mother calmly suggested we drag the thin mattresses outside and sleep in our sleeping bags. I was thrilled to be surrounded by my family in the dark,

all of us on individual beds, like boats nudging up against one
another in a harbor. Opening my eyes in the middle of the night,
I saw showers of lights, hundreds of shooting stars plummeting
across the dark sky.

But three weeks later we returned to New York, exhausted and
dispirited. "We're just two very different people," my mother
said by way of explanation. "Your father wants to have it all."
She frowned out the airplane window. Still, Dad didn't give up.
In the fall he flew back to New York, unrolled floor plans of Selz
1 for our perusal and talked about what fun we'd all have once
the kinks were worked out. I thought he meant the kinks in the
house, but he meant the kinks between his way of thinking and
our mother's.

He was so determined, more the child among us than either
my sister or me. Both my parents, having once shared a mutual
dream, were reluctant to let go of the possibility that another
dream could encompass them. Dad waged his crusade with phone
calls, letters and more visits back East, giving our mother forlorn
stares and once dangling a jade and pearl earring in front of her.
"The other," he said, "is waiting for you in California." This made
her laugh, and then he'd pulled the earring's mate out of his coat
pocket and we'd all squealed with delight.

In a weak moment, Mom said yes, then perhaps, and finally,
"No, I can't leave my life behind when I don't have a dependable
situation, Pete." Even with Norma gone he was unwilling to agree
to fidelity. And besides, Eddy Rickey in an act of symmetry had
made a phone call to Mom and warned her not to take up with
Dad again, though he was in all other respects a great man. By
this time, their discussions, reunions, breakups and reconcilia-
tions had been going on for three years. All the while they'd been

reconsidering each other, they had both kept their options open. Since the breakup Mom had had relationships with a series of men, mostly in the literati world, quite a few were encounters with married men up at the artist colony, Yaddo, and they had invigorated her. I know this because one morning, in the beginning of 1968 when she had the flu, she listed her lovers in her journal, starting with my father and ending with N.R., the composer she was seeing most recently. He had a dimple in his chin and was ten years younger than Mom. Back in California, Dad had asked his newest girlfriend to move in with him—he hated being alone. As for his museum, even with the reduced budget, Dad's persistence had managed to keep the project on track. He would not be leaving California. He shelved the plans for Selz 1 and began construction on Selz 2.

Maybe the Picasso plate had nothing to do with what was happening between my parents. Maybe it was just a chance mistake of an idle child. My parents had bought the plate together when they were in Paris. A beautiful gray ceramic plate with a white dove painted in the center. My father had told me that not only was the bird a sign of peace, for Picasso it was also a tribute to his father, who had taught him to paint. Picasso's father had specialized in depicting natural bird images. In the 1940s Picasso had begun to create ceramics because they allowed him to be more spontaneous, playful and free than a formal canvas permitted. The Picasso plate sat in the middle of our dining room table in New York and I knew my mother prized this plate far more than any other work of art she'd kept after the divorce, for she forbade me to touch it or pick it up. But she was gone that afternoon, with her young composer boyfriend. I was home alone and bored, entertaining myself by spinning around the table belting along with a 45 of Petula Clark singing about going downtown where troubles were forgotten. When the song ended, our apartment was again filled with the big, heavy silence of an empty house. Downtown was where my mother was. Before I could think through my actions clearly, I lifted up the plate and placed it on top of my head to see if I could... balance it! One step, just one, and the plate slipped and crashed to the floor, breaking into three pieces. Knowing how enraged my mother would be when she found it, I tried to cobble the plate together with Scotch tape. At nine, I repaired everything with Scotch tape. Of course, my mother discovered the broken plate as soon as she came home and cried for hours. She could tell the Scotch tape was my handiwork. "I'm sorry, Mommy," I said, weeping. I felt really awful about that plate. Eventually she carted the plate off to the china repair shop. It came home cemented together, this time with china glue. But it never looked the same again. Two big scars ran up through the center of Picasso's beautiful bird of peace.

Chapter 10

He was my summertime father, my single-month-out-of-the-year father. My father who sparkled like a firecracker, whom I craved, idolized, but didn't really know. When Tanya and I flew in to see him each year to the golden grassland of California, he would greet us at the airport brandishing a bouquet of wildflowers. California poppies, purple lupines and star-shaped asters that were not actually from the wild, but pilfered from a neighbor's yard. Dad had no sense of property lines. He was the father who threw parties full of strange colorful people, girls in tie-dyed skirts and boys in velvet pants and the billowing shirts of pirates. The father who arranged for us to ride a helicopter over San Francisco Bay, to see Joan Baez when she played at the Greek Theater—because who had ever heard of a soprano singing folk songs before? The father whom everyone knew, whose friend, an artist named Harold Paris, told me, "Your father is more like us. Inside he's an artist!" But Dad wasn't an artist. He just wanted to live like one.

Dad playing with Warhol's Mylar *Silver Clouds* at the Air Art Show he brought to Berkeley, 1968.

The Bay Area in 1967 and '68 was the place where policemen were called "pigs" and money "bread" and "flower power" was the metaphor of the moment. It was the place where people came to shed their pasts as easily as their clothes, longing to return to a childhood state, a romantic state, a state of freedom. But the gulf between my father's European intellectual history and his current reinvention as a California hippie appeared even more obvious, at least to his children.

He tried to grow his white hair long, but it stuck out like Albert

Einstein's. He wore open-collared shirts with strings of love beads hanging down his neck, which became tangled among his black and white chest hairs. He smoked pot but couldn't get high, couldn't *tune in*, *turn on* or *drop out*. He dated girls with long hair whose breasts bounced behind loose peasant blouses and who were also "free spirits." He told us our mother was "uptight" and "hung up" and "a square."

He wanted us to have "total freedom" when we were with him. The summer after Nora left we were eleven and ten years old. "Big girls!" he said when we came to visit, and taught us how to hitchhike home from day camp. Well, he taught Tanya, because she was the older one. "You just stick out your thumb like this." He demonstrated, a hook in his hand, an angular thrust to his hip. After that, each day when the other mothers came to pick their kids up at camp, Tanya and I walked down from Strawberry Canyon, where we learned archery and water ballet, bought pink peppermint ice-cream cones at the bottom of Euclid Street and then, while I stood beside her licking my ice cream, she stuck out her thumb. Dad was too busy with his museum, and his shows, to stop midday and pick us up. I don't remember feeling scared when I followed my sister into the backseats of unfamiliar cars. By then Tanya and I were used to being on our own. We didn't think that something bad might happen to us, lost and kidnapped children had yet to make their appearance on milk cartons. Yet Tanya and I knew enough, without a word ever passing between us, not to mention our mode of transportation to our mother.

Dad was gone during the day and he was gone at night, to openings, events, parties, dates. He must have felt uncomfortable around us.

He explained that in California we were expected to cook for ourselves. I already knew how to make a grilled cheese sandwich in a tiny square pan my mother bought me for this very purpose, but we didn't want to cook for ourselves. At night, when he left us alone, we mostly ate prepared foods: tuna fish out of the can, cottage cheese, salami sandwiches and our favorite meal, an invention we named bread soup, which consisted of pieces of sliced baguette floating around in bowls of milk.

Dad kept moving from house to house. He was experimenting with styles. A glass house, a white box, while, high in the Berkeley hills, Selz 2 was rising. "One day," he told us, "we'll have a view of the city, the bay, the Golden Gate and beyond that the great Pacific."

Like the world he was now part of, he showed art that was bohemian and irreverent. My father and Harold Paris invented the name for the art that was coming out of Northern California just then. "It's funky," they said, and called it Funk. My father put on the first Funk art show, mostly West Coast sculptors who were creating fleshy, erotic objects. Funk was unorthodox, like jazz. It was freewheeling art and nodded to the Beat culture of the previous decade. It was the opposite of Pop. Where Pop art glorified consumerist society, Funk put it down. *You just know it when you see it*, Dad wrote. Funk made us laugh, until it made us uncomfortable: a fur rat having a seizure, by Joan Brown; and Robert Arneson's soft-looking ceramic pieces: a typewriter whose keys were ladies' red fingernails, and *Call Me Lover*, a telephone made of clay. On close inspection my sister and I realized that the center of the telephone dial was a vagina, the mouthpiece a long pink penis.

Dad was the father with hipster friends. Cool cats like Bruce Conner, who was in the Funk show. Conner was as tall and gaunt

GABRIELLE SELZ

166

as the farmer holding a pitchfork in Grant Wood's painting *American Gothic*. He was already famous in underground circles for his experimental films made of collaged footage. *A Movie*, a twelve-minute collage of stock footage of comics and cowboys, and *Cosmic Ray*, a montage of fireworks, atomic bombs and nude girls. He was part of a pack from Kansas that included the actor Dennis Hopper. Later, Hopper said that he owed the improvisational style of his editing on *Easy Rider* to Bruce Conner.

Assembled and funky, silly, erotic, unashamed, political and free: that was art in Berkeley in the late 1960s.

One day Bruce showed up at my father's house with a black box as tall as a coffin. "What's that?" my sister and I asked.

"A sculpture," Bruce said as he grimly set it down in the hallway. We could see right away this was a piece of Funk. It was covered in black tar and wads of black and red lace, and inside was a female mannequin wrapped in nylons, draped in pearls, fur and more black lace. Bruce told us he'd been unable to come up with a name for his sculpture. Tanya and I pondered his predicament. We were intrigued by the costume jewelry, which reminded us of visiting Ossorio's studio in East Hampton, but the naked dummy inside with a nylon stocking suffocating her head was creepy. We couldn't think of any name that would be appropriate for her. "Never mind," said Bruce.

The sculpture loomed by the front door. In his inimitable way our father explained what Bruce was doing. "He is using all this collage and assemblage material to comment on the corruption of American beauty."

"You mean like Miss America?" Tanya asked.

"Exactly," our father said.

We thought we'd call her *Miss America* until a few days later the neighbor's pregnant cat Wednesday disappeared. She was an outdoor cat, used to roaming into our yard and sometimes our father's home. We searched the closets, under the couch, below the beds and eventually I gazed over and realized that there was a large tear in the bottom of Bruce's sculpture. Inside, Wednesday had made a nest among the lace and fur and was peacefully nursing her kittens. Afterward, Bruce christened the sculpture *WEDNESDAY* in honor of the cat choosing his sculpture to give birth in. The name stuck.

WEDNESDAY
Bruce Conner, 1960

Immersing himself in the art and politics "happening all around us," our father embraced the moment. Protests like Wednesday's kittens were being born in Berkeley practically on the door stoop. He was the father who handed us cardboard placards that read GIVE PEACE A CHANCE and told us to "be involved." On the weekends he took us to peace rallies in People's Park, to Be-Ins in Golden Gate Park, and to ogle the hippies along Haight-Ashbury, swarms of ragtag kids not much older than Tanya and me—with faces still plump with baby fat. Some played tambourines, had painted faces and flowers in their hair, some were half naked. "Aren't they beautiful?" Dad said. "They're so free." He loved the costumes, the celebrations, the ad-hocism

Ready for a sleepover in 1968.

of it all, art springing up in the streets like weeds. "Like Robin Hood and his Merry Men in Sherwood Forest, they band together and face down police pigs," my father said. But to me the hippies looked shabby and poor. They lived on the streets and slept in the park.

Soon I became the kid who was always, even at the last moment, ready for a sleepover. I was the child who sat at the friend's table and was congratulated by the parents on my surprisingly large appetite. I carried a little red box case wherever I went. Inside were my toothbrush, a nightgown and a picture of the front half of my fat cat, Nixi, that I'd taken with my Brownie camera. I was prepared.

I learned to make friends with everyone, even walking up and down the aisle on the airplane, introducing myself to strangers, when we flew back and forth for our summertime visits with our sometime Dad. The more people I knew, the safer I felt in the world.

Chapter 11

In the spring of 1969 my mother began working at an artists'
housing project under construction in Greenwich Village
called Westbeth. "When it's completed it will be the largest
home for artists in the world." Our mother's cheeks were flushed
with excitement as she told us about it over a rushed pizza dinner.
Pizza for dinner had been unheard-of before the divorce. Dad
had liked three courses when he was home, one of them almost
always consisting of potato, but now that he was gone and Mom
was juggling two kids and a job, we had pizza once a week. Though
she'd taught part-time in Chicago and California before she'd
had children, and done freelance editing and her own writing
since, Westbeth was my mother's first full-time job.

The idea of Westbeth was born back in the early 1960s as a
partial solution to the growing housing and studio problem for
artists living in New York. Spearheaded by the National Council for the Arts, the JM Kaplan Fund and the city's Housing and
Urban Development Department, funding was secured for this

ambitious renovation project that would not only provide afford-able housing for creative talent, but also revitalize the dying neighborhood along the West Side Highway. If Westbeth became a success, the model would be repeated in every major city in the nation.

By 1967 a location had been secured in a hulking complex of buildings comprising an entire city block at the intersection of West and Bethune Streets, hence the name Westbeth. The site was the abandoned old Bell Laboratories, once a great research center where the transistor radio, color television and stereo sound had been invented.

The JM Kaplan Fund formed an impressive board consisting of various heads of museums, art organizations and disciplines—from the Whitney, the Metropolitan and MoMA to LaMaMa Theatre Club and individual artists like the poet Stanley Kunitz and painters Robert Rauschenberg and Elaine de Kooning—and this group came up with the criteria and goals for what they dubbed "a pioneering new community." Open to all the arts, first dibs went to "primary" creative types: playwrights before actors, composers before musicians. Artists had to be committed and not dabblers; they didn't have to be "good," just serious. They had to be somewhat established, but not too established, had to have recommendations from peers and make less than $12,500 per year. The board wanted a mixture of old and young, locals and artists from the hinterlands. When I asked Mom, "Where are the hinterlands exactly?" she said, "Anything outside of Manhattan, dear."

However, because this prestigious board didn't want to do the tedious work of selections, they hired my mother and the writer and art critic Ellie Munro to make the final choices. Ellie had been married to the art historian and editor of *Art News* Alfred

Frankfurter until he died in 1965. Both Ellie and Mom were the perfect candidates: smart, willing to be discreet about their positions and having been married to high-profile men in the art world, they had sterling connections. Between the two of them, they knew just about everybody in the art community.

Down in a makeshift office at Westbeth, renovations going on all around them as empty labs were converted into live-work spaces, Mom and Ellie interviewed the artists who might get to live in the building once it was completed. With nearly four hundred low-income apartments to fill, half were specifically designated for families. Westbeth wanted to support the idea that an artist could have a career *and* a life. In the summer of 1969, my mother wrote Grammar:

We have made our major selections, Ellie and I, though we hope that everyone else believes that the impressive Board of Sponsors did the dirty work. Never have I been so glad to hide my little light under a bushel! Boy! But some marvelous people have now a more assured future and I feel like the Angel Gabriel and so does Ellie, I'm sure, or rather, like Michael, because it was he who stood beside the balance, wasn't it?, and the thought of the poor ones whom we misjudged or never gave a fair chance to . . . it does keep us awake, we find, and maybe that's a good discovery to make. It evens things up a bit in this most unfair life, perhaps.

Energized by the milieu in the Village, Mom began donning wild clothes—mini dresses with white zip boots, and her very favorite, a plastic pantsuit with a black-and-white-checkered pattern that she wore with a pair of huge white disc earrings that made her vibrate like an optical illusion. Whenever she walked out the door in this pulsating outfit, I was mortified. I was eleven and didn't want to be seen with someone—my mother— who looked like she'd stepped out of *The Mod Squad*. I got into the habit, especially when she went to my school for parent-teacher conferences, to beg her to wear "something normal, *please*."

"What's wrong with fishnets?" she asked.

"The other mothers don't wear fishnets," I whined.

"Well, *your* mother does."

My fishnet-legged and miniskirted mother had been working down at Westbeth for about nine months when she came home late on the winter afternoon of February 26, 1970, more than just tired from a hard day of placing tenants. Her face was ashen, her head sunk between her shoulders. Neither Tanya nor I had seen her this upset for a long time.

She sat us down in the living room. "Mark Rothko died. Topher and Katie's Daddy," she told us.

"I know who he is," Tanya said.

"Topher!" I remembered little Topher sitting on his father's lap. He must be six now. I thought, *Nothing could be worse than losing your parent*, until my mother said, "You'll hear about it, so I might as well tell you. Mark committed suicide."

At the word suicide Tanya pushed her hair behind her ears and became more attentive. "How?" She asked.

Mom bit her lip and shook her head. I don't remember her telling us the details, but we learned soon enough, for into the stunned silence of our living room the phone started to ring. The art world was already abuzz with his death.

Rothko had taken an overdose, a mixture of sedatives and antidepressants, and had gruesomely slashed his own arms just below the bend of the elbow. His studio assistant had discovered him that morning dressed in his undershirt, long johns and black socks, arms stretched over his head, a double-edged razor blade in his right hand, lying in a pool of his own blood, the same dark color of many of his last paintings.

There was some talk that foul play was involved. Rothko had been unhappy about his dealings with his gallery, Marlborough Fine Art, which had been scheduled to come and collect a number of his paintings the day he was found dead. Rothko was known to agonize over parting with paintings, and to have someone else make the selection could not have been easy. When his body was discovered, he was not wearing his round eyeglasses. His myopia was so bad that some wondered how he could have made the cuts without them. But eventually these rumors, too, died away. Rothko had been unraveling for the last two years.

At eleven years old I didn't understand the shock of suicide, nor the brutal desperation it required, but I sure felt the hysteria of the constant ringing phone. It frightened me, but in the way a horror movie did. I couldn't turn away.

On February 28 my mother, dressed in a conservative wool skirt that reached her knees, went to the funeral service:

This was awful, somehow: first, the terrible circumstances of his suicide, and then the gathering of birds of prey. I mean the conclave of dealers, sycophants, hangers-on, would-be artists, artists by association, all the hungry little ones. Poor Mark, slashed and given up to his despair, lying in that sealed oak box with Rosten reading a perfectly hideous poem written about his last black paintings. Who drew forth that little poet from the marrow of the fifties to squeak before the altar about a lot of things he couldn't possibly understand? Even the Mozart was ugly. All dead and without feeling. How many of those mawkish faces had ever felt any real feeling for him? I remember well those months prior to his separation from Mell, when he dragged her here and there to all dumb official things. To meet the Princess, for god's sake. When you live that life it takes away from you unless you've got a hide of tempered steel.

The only thing in which one finally found the man for a few moments was curiously enough in the most impersonal part of the service. Katie, his daughter, had insisted that someone say Kaddish for him, and in those few moments he became suddenly a real loss to us, one whose black grief in the last hours struck us all.

Then I left the chapel (what a misnomer!) I went down to work at Westbeth and worked hard for 1½ hours and that brought order into the world.

I did not read this letter until many years later, but I remember my mother coming home from after the service and her work at Westbeth, her hair shining with the hair spray that held the tight shape of the rollers around her head like a helmet. "People were pouring out of the woodwork," she lamented. "Nobody was really there to bury Mark, but to see de Kooning."

"Was Topher there?" I asked.

"Honey, of course, he was with Mell."

I was relieved. At least Topher still had his mother, though he had lost his famous father. I had quickly become obsessed with the story of Rothko's death, which seemed both horrible and mysterious to me. I envisioned Rothko being swallowed up by his pictures, or disappearing into one of them as if through a dark doorway, leaving Topher behind. Whenever I asked my mother why he had done it, she said, "Nobody knows, dear. Mark was very sad."

She told my father that she had seen Mark at a small gathering at his Sixty-ninth Street studio only two months earlier. She'd stood among their old friends, surrounded by Mark's gloomy paintings, *black like powdered cinders*, everyone drinking. At one point my mother had sat down next to Mark on his cot—he now lived like a pauper at his studio, though he was a rich man—and he'd placed his hand on her knee, in a gesture she thought more tired than flirtatious, as if *his hand with its skin as thin and white as tissue paper were clinging to me like a moth to a branch.*

My father, too, had recently visited Mark in January, and found him lonely, ill and sad. "He couldn't paint the way he wanted to," my father said. Rothko apparently told Dad that since his aneurism in 1968 he was unable to work on large paintings. His doctor feared that the exertion might increase his chance of heart failure or stroke. Then his financial adviser-cum-accountant, Bernard Reis (the same man who had oohed and ahhed over the excellent turnout at Franz Kline's funeral), told Rothko he was too prolific, and doing too many paintings at once would decrease their value. Mark, who was dependent on Reis for advice, told my father that Reis had urged him not to paint anymore after the end of March. "Of course, we all told Mark not to listen to Reis, and I don't think he did. Still, it bothered him. No wonder he killed himself at the end of February. He was very sad." There was that word again.

This seemed to confirm in my mind that Mark's paintings had killed him. My mother disagreed. In the last years Mark had become "alienated from other humans. Artists are permeable people," she said.

Apparently the scene of "hangers-on" at Rothko's memorial upset my mother more than any of us realized. A month after

Mark's death, she announced a decision. She said the uptown art scene was not her place. Dad had been the expert at navigating that world, not her. She much preferred the nitty-gritty bohemian crowd downtown where she'd been working. She was moving us away from our large Central Park West apartment into Westbeth. "I need a community," she said.

"Who is she kidding?" Tanya stomped off when she heard the news. "It's an artists' slum!"

Our father was equally opposed to our relocation. "Why does your mother want to give up a spacious Upper West Side apartment on a Central Park West location?" he complained over the phone. "You have four bedrooms for only a hundred and thirty a month. She has such a great deal!"

But not even my father's rational argument that we would be paying the same price for one-quarter the size could budge my mother.

Later that night I found Mom casting her eye around our apartment, deciding what we would have to leave behind. We were moving in two weeks, over Easter vacation. She wanted to be at Westbeth before the official opening in May.

"Are we low-income?" I asked.

She must have seen a furrow in my brow. She ran her hand over my forehead. "We're modest," she said. "Besides, it's like one huge family down there."

I wasn't thrilled about the move. The Village seemed like the edge of nowhere, far from my school, in a wasteland of neglected brownstones bordered on lower Fourteenth Street by derelict slaughterhouses and along the river by an elevated abandoned railroad track. With its cobblestone streets and a horse pasture only a few blocks from the Westbeth complex, the Village might as well have been in a foreign country. I was embarrassed that we were purposefully embracing "modest circumstances," worried my friends wouldn't travel out of their fancy neighborhoods to visit me among *permeable people.*

"Are you even an artist?" I challenged her.

My mother flinched. "I'm a writer, Gaby, and writers are artists, too."

Up until that point, when asked what she did, my mother had always replied, "I'm a woman who writes." Now, hand to head, she patted her hair as if she were adjusting a hat. Then she looked around our old living room. "Just think of those eighteen-foot ceilings and the view of the Hudson!"

LIKE THE DREAM of Bauhaus in the 1920s, Westbeth was based on the central utopian idea that art created a better world. If society supported the arts, the arts would in turn rejuvenate society. Paramount to both these visions was "the building." It was not just a place, it was an idea, a foundation. The Bauhaus had been a school aimed at bridging the gap between art and technology under one roof. Now Westbeth was going to be the home for the arts.

Fresh out of architecture school, Richard Meier had been hired to convert the buildings that made up the Westbeth complex into living quarters. In designing the compound, Meier channeled my Dad's old favorite, the inventor of standardization, Le Corbusier. It was this news that got my father on board with our move to Westbeth. "Open floor plans, industrial materials, modernity," Daddy sang to me over the phone. "Just like I'm doing in Selz Two!"

To accommodate as many artists as possible, Meier designed interlocking apartment units piled one atop the other, with identical kitchens and bathrooms and a raw "open space." Tenants were then given four modular closets mounted on rollers to use to partition rooms and turn their blank canvases into homes. Some artists, loath to give up valuable studio space, placed wooden boards between their closets, threw a mattress up on top, and presto, their kid had a bedroom.

We had a "duplex," a vast overstatement, as a duplex in "Modernist" vocabulary meant just two tiny spaces connected by a steep, raw cement staircase. Because Tanya was a teenager, she needed her own sanctum and was given the lower section of the duplex. She had a swinging red saloon door, à la *Bonanza*, between her closet and the wall to distinguish her bedroom from our little vestibule, and boy, did I enjoy tormenting her by swinging that door every time I went in and out of the apartment! My mother and I slept upstairs, where there were two main spaces: a kitchen/dining area separated by a thin wall from the living space, with an adjoining bathroom. Mom took the living section and put our couch and Knoll coffee table in one corner, her bureau in the middle and her bed up on a raised platform in front of the huge window—that part of the apartment was now our living room *and* her bedroom. Because our ceilings were so high, a carpenter was hired to build a sleeping loft for me. It cantilevered out over the dining nook and instead of walls for privacy I had a railing over which my mother draped her old black Spanish shawl with embroidered red roses. This thin membrane separated me from the rest of the house. A solution I found totally acceptable, as I had never liked having my own room. In my new accommodations, I felt like I was living in a tree house.

A labyrinth of hallways painted in psychedelic colors—neon yellow, electric green and florid pink—snaked through all the

Westbeth courtyard, 1970.

buildings. Ramps and passageways led to communal spaces that were designed for galleries, theaters, a co-op grocery store and a day-care center. Half-moon-shaped balconies overhung the courtyard and connected neighboring apartments—these were the emergency fire escape routes, my sister and I were told. Not to be used unless absolutely necessary, as in reality they were unstable for anything but potted plants.

And those eighteen-foot ceilings my mother had raved about—made of poured concrete, they waved in ripples and had been inspired by ocean currents and installed as part of an early experiment Bell Labs conducted in surround sound. They carried every creak, whisper, cackle and moan, literally around the block. Not only did I hear a composer working on his next symphony, but also the family down the hall sitting down to dinner and the drunk father next door yelling at his infant son. We developed our own Morse code, taps along on the walls and pipes to tell some noisy creator, *Keep the racket down.*

I loved Westbeth. At night, camped out in my loft like a bird in a nest, surrounded by the noises of five-hundred-plus artists busy at work, my fear of being alone in the dark abated and I drifted easily off to sleep to the humming, buzzing sound of people all around me.

Each day at the end of school, I waved goodbye to my private school friends on Fifth Avenue, and while they went off to ballet practice and piano lessons, I hopped aboard the cross-town bus, dashed through the complicated maze of subways where exhibitionists lurked at the turnstiles ready to expose themselves, tore down Eighth Avenue, book bag flying behind me, scooted through the wedge of Abingdon Square Park and along Bank Street, then up the elevator and into our apartment, banging my sister's door for good measure. Pulling off my private school clothes, I slipped into my orange plush bell-bottoms and canary-yellow T-shirt—because, just like my mother, I now had adopted my own downtown outfit that identified me as a member of our bohemian tribe. Then, taking off at a gallop, I roamed from basement to rooftop of Westbeth with an unruly band of equally unsupervised artists' children.

And because of the rule that half the units in the building be allocated to families, and most of those families turned out to have more than one child, Westbeth surged with children: crying babies in the arms of tired mothers, toddlers on tricycles zooming up and down the hallways, teenagers loafing in the courtyards, and my clan of overcurious, preteen mischief-makers. We were as plentiful as the weeds growing between the tracks on the railroad that ran through a tunnel on the third floor of our building. There were at least as many children as there were adults at Westbeth.

Sometimes, when I tore through the building, I wore my colored paper 3-D glasses. The 3-D glasses, with red and blue lenses, had been handed out to all the tenants at the grand christening in May when New York's matinee-idol-handsome Mayor Lindsay came and gave a speech about how we were pioneers revitalizing the area. Afterward he put his arm around me as he stepped off the podium. "I'll never wash again," I told my mother. Then we'd all trooped into one of the theaters to watch a 3-D experimental movie and roll around on the floor because as yet the theater seats hadn't been installed. Even when not viewing a 3-D movie I still liked how the glasses made the world look as if it had been dipped in different colors of paint.

My gang included between ten and twelve kids thundering through the buildings, up one elevator and down another. In Westbeth, it was common to be accosted by a poet quoting his latest haiku about the Hudson River, or a puppeteer on the roof prancing around with a dancer in tights. Our band of ragamuffins in colorful clothing and unwashed hair hardly stuck out. Impromptu performances and readings took place in the courtyard or gallery. Movie stars like Warren Beatty and Julie Christie lounged on beanbag chairs in the film center.

After we'd moved in, when my father came for his first visit to Westbeth, he walked through the building shaking hands as if he were the mayor. If Westbeth was the place to be, suddenly Dad wanted to be part of the mix. "This is an example of how great architecture can reshape the world. All this free-flowing space, people able to intermingle. Why, there must be two thousand people here, all against the Vietnam War. In Berkeley we'd be mobilized by now!" He immediately asked my mother if she could find him a space for his next sabbatical.

"I'll try," Mom replied coolly. Westbeth was her turf and she didn't want Dad to overshadow her. Though she no longer officially worked for the building—a board of tenants was forming to evaluate future residents—my mother still had influence. Even my self-absorbed father could tell who was steering this ship. The residents had christened her with a new name. "Mrs. Westbeth."

"Mrs. Westbeth," my sister and I teased. "If you're Mrs. Westbeth, then who's Mr. Westbeth?"

She scowled and pretended she didn't like the name, but she couldn't hide her secret pleasure.

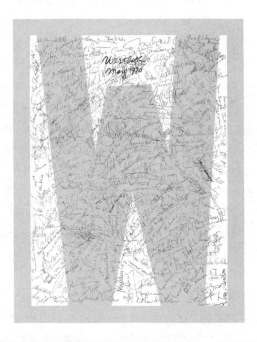

The official Westbeth poster that original tenants signed. Mom's was the first signature, smack in the middle.

The buildings were still under construction for the first several months we lived there. Every nook and cranny was open and available for exploration. On the thirteenth floor we discovered a majestic theater with a wall of mirrors at one end and rows of windows on the other. This was to be Merce Cunningham's dance studio, my mother explained. But since he hadn't moved in yet, it was okay to play there on its stage. Like most of the "penthouses," it had roof access. Forget the stage, out onto the roof we tumbled.

Some of the more earth-mother types planted a cooperative garden up on the roof, growing lettuce, tomatoes and herbs in milk cartons and soup cans. When they saw us scampering over the asphalt they tried to chase us off, but we knew our way around the roofs of Westbeth like a band of chimney sweeps.

On rainy days we moved inside and explored the lower floors. On our floor, the ninth, someone had brought a horse up through the freight elevator and into his space. If we knocked on the door and asked politely, the owner let us give the horse an apple, his soft nose tickling our palms. On the second floor sat a mystifying piece of equipment that turned out to be a huge printing press. And far below, in the basement, there was rumored to be a giant magnet that could control an airplane's flight pattern. And to this great kingdom my mother, Mrs. Westbeth, possessed the master key.

I discovered the key by accident about three months after we'd moved in. I was going through my mother's jewelry box, which sat atop her dresser. My mother was perched across the room on her high platform bed—her notebook open beside her, a black and white African coverlet thrown about her shoulders. She held her ivory-handled opera glasses up to her eyes and gazed out the windows. In the distance the World Trade Center towers were rising. My mother wasn't as interested in the towers, which she thought looked like two huge erections, as she was in identifying the boats that sailed up and down the Hudson River. Surveying the comings and goings on the estuary through her opera glasses was now a favorite pastime. That and waltzing up and down the halls of Westbeth in a flowing black velvet maxi dress with Juliet sleeves.

Underneath an amber necklace that had once belonged to my great-great-grandmother—the New England pioneer woman who had driven her wagon alone, from the Cape to Illinois—I saw the key. There it sat, with its special tag that read MASTER in bright red marker. I dropped the necklace and picked it up.

"What's this to?" I held the key out to my mother.

Turning from her investigation out the window, my mother focused her opera glasses on the key in my hand. It must have looked gigantic. "It's to Westbeth," she said. "I used it to show apartments."

A breath of an idea formed in my head. This was the magic key to the entire castle. "Do you still need it?"

"If there's an emergency."

"Can I have it? I won't lose it."

"Gaby, don't be silly. Put it back." And she pivoted her glasses to the window again. Outside, the sky was nearly white and a green barge with a red stripe running around its middle sailed up the river. She jotted a sentence down: *Like a great big piece of peppermint candy floating up the Hudson.*

My mother used the key once or twice when some distracted artist got locked out of their apartment. Though Peter Cott, who had recently directed the National Academy of Television Arts and Sciences, had just been hired as executive director of

Westbeth, no one really knew him yet. He was an outsider who didn't live in the building. When anyone needed a favor, advice or just an explanation, it was on our door they knocked. Could my mother help them get an apartment with a view? How about a communal darkroom in the building? And security? And someone had received a poison-pen letter because someone else was jealous of their space, their light, their extra rolling closet. And what about Diane Arbus, why did she deserve a duplex when neither of her daughters, Amy or Doon, lived with her?

And why did Diane get to hold her photography class in a vacant space, shouldn't someone get to live or at least work there?

Everyone had a friend who wanted to get into Westbeth. "It's just petty jealousies," my mother said, sounding like my father when he complained about her need to control his dating. "Diane has all that equipment to lug around." Diane, who lived catty-corner across the hall, was a tiny woman who wore a safari coat with a large leather satchel slung over her shoulder, and a big black box camera strapped around her neck. Mom called Diane a nocturnal flower because she came alive at night. She could be spotted most evenings darting across the courtyard, sometimes with her tripod, but more often than not it was just Diane, with that camera the size of her chest, going off alone into the gathering dusk.

"What do they all want me to do? I'm just a resident now like everyone else." Still, my mother felt protective of Diane, whom she thought very gifted. Mom had been introduced to Diane years earlier by one of the playground moms who had known Diane when she was just a kid growing up in the San Remo on West Seventy-fifth Street. Diane came from a wealthy Jewish family. As a child she'd had a maid, a cook, a chauffeur and a governess, but when she'd turned eighteen she'd married against her parents' wishes and left that world behind. Over the last ten years Diane had drifted through the downtown art scene, transitioning from a fashion photographer for *Glamour* and *Vogue* with her then-husband Allan Arbus, to a street photographer of tattooed carnival freaks, gypsy fortune-tellers, the disfigured and the perverse.

In 1967 Diane was included in a group photography exhibit at MoMA. And though some viewers were so outraged at her shots of nudists and transvestites they actually spat on her images at MoMA, photographers recognized her unique talent. Now her method of shooting marginalized subjects—looking where most were afraid to look directly—in a square format with a flashcube, was copied everywhere. But no one could quite capture the startling confrontation, the strange mix of curiosity, boldness and vulnerability, of an Arbus portrait.

Both Diane and my mother were dreamy and shy women, but while Diane could be called reckless—actively seeking out misfits whom she felt she could approach with her camera between them—my mother had a more cautious nature, preferring the world delivered to her door. Mom had recently gone to a party in Diane's duplex and returned describing Diane's bed, which, like hers, was up on a platform in the main room. Though, unlike my mother's bed, Diane's was not covered in an African throw, but in black satin sheets and furs. Soon my mother had purchased her own pair of satin sheets, not black, but silver.

Once my gang and I, roller-skating down the ramp in the central courtyard of Westbeth, blasted into the space where Diane was conducting her workshop. Black-and-white photographs were pinned to the wall and Diane sat cross-legged on the floor in a circle of students. At our interruption, Diane looked up,

Diane Arbus with Marvin Israel
teaching at Westbeth.

startled, then she put her hands together in front of her face and
applauded as we zoomed around the room and back out again.
When my mother heard about this event, she scolded me. This
was the only time Mom ever reprimanded me about my activities in
the building. When the first tenant meeting was held, my mother
and Diane went together. At the meeting my mother immediately
signed on as the secretary. Mrs. Westbeth was not ready to retire.

FIVE MONTHS AFTER we moved to Westbeth, in September
1970, our father called to tell us Mell Rothko had died. She was
forty-eight years old. In the span of six months, Topher had lost

both his parents. With a shock I realized that little Topher, whom I had known since he was born, was an orphan.

Only three weeks earlier, Tanya and I had seen Mell and Topher during our annual summer visit with our father in California. Visiting the West Coast, they had come over to see my father's new house. Selz 2 had finally been completed. It was not the house Tanya and I had dreamed of. The house we had dreamed of looked like the Bavarian castle of my father's childhood and had a connecting balcony between our two rooms shaped like the crescent balconies we had at Westbeth. Selz 2 was a large open space, in the center of which my father's office jutted out over the living room like a stage. It was bright and airy, with floor-to-ceiling windows overlooking San Francisco Bay. All except for the rooms designated for Tanya and me, which were located underneath the living room, in the basement, where it was murky, cold and damp as a dungeon. Accustomed to falling asleep at Westbeth in the heart of our home amid constant noise, I'd had nightmares during my stay in Berkeley. When Tanya let me, I dragged my blanket into her room and slept on the floor. When she refused, I curled up against her door like a dog until morning.

Even Topher had been uncomfortable down there. He was still pudgy, but much quieter than I remembered. He sat on my bed with his fingers folded under his chin and looked around my cellar and asked me if I was afraid of the dark. He was only six years old. I told him about my nightmares, which were fueled no doubt by my sister's delight in watching the horror TV show *Night Gallery*. It had an art gallery setting, probably the reason my father let her watch it. Unfortunately, in each plot a macabre painting came to life and the characters within it enacted some grizzly tale.

Topher nodded sagely. He stood up. He only reached my arm-pits, but he grabbed my eleven-year-old hand in his six-year-old one and said gravely, "I'll marry and protect you." As if he could fend off wicked paintings, loneliness, loss.

Later that afternoon we'd gone for a walk in Muir Woods, all except for Tanya, who wanted to stay behind and read her movie magazines. Under the giant redwood trees, while his mother and my father strolled behind us laughing about "our big engage-ment," Topher and I, back to being children, ran and darted through the forest.

Now he was alone. Dad told us Topher was the one who had found Mell. He'd been watching cartoons in the next room when he'd heard his mother collapse to the floor. "It was her overworked liver," Dad said. Mell was known to have a drinking problem.

The cause of Mell's death was given as a heart attack, and Mom wrote a condolence note to Topher and his older sister, Kate. Kate sent a card back, her script looking so grown-up across the page that it startled me. She was nineteen and in college. She said Topher was living with his guardian, the anthropologist Morton Levine. *I suppose your two girls are far too old to actually play with Topher, but we could still all do something together. I hope to see you soon*, Kate wrote.

"I'm not too old to play with Topher," I insisted.

Soon never came.

A WEEK AFTER we heard about Mell's death, the first Westbeth suicide occurred. A woman from "outside" came into the build-ing, took the elevator up to the roof, set her shoes on the ledge and jumped. She landed in the courtyard and lay there for a full day. My mother was asked to identify the body, but since the woman didn't live at Westbeth, nobody, not even my mother, knew who she was. Then someone in our building was mugged in the lobby. A girl was raped a few blocks away. "Greenwich Village is lawless," one of the muscular sculptors on our floor said. Discussions started about moving the building's entrance, which was through the courtyard, to a safer, more secure location.

It was the first winter at Westbeth and the snow and ice made the cobblestones slippery so that my walk home from the subway was slower and more circumspect. After the summer holidays my gang had disbanded. I was twelve now and going to dance parties in the posh apartments of my uptown friends. They had extra rooms for their maids and color TV sets, not Day-Glo walls. My schoolmates wore cardigan sets with pleated skirts, not silly 3-D glasses. Who cared if the two lenses brought the world together to form one solid picture, everyone knew they only did that when you looked at a 3-D movie. Tanya enrolled in an acting class for teenagers at HB Theatre. "She needs to learn to channel her emotions," my mother said. This of course backfired. At fourteen, expressing herself became my sister's great excuse for drama. With her long brown hair parted down the middle framing her heart-shaped face, she looked positively angelic as she practiced the lamentations of high-strung characters like Blanche in *A Streetcar Named Desire*. Her friends from the Upper West Side now came downtown to score the plentiful drugs available at Westbeth. In the courtyard, when she wasn't acting, Tanya and her friends sat in a huddle on cement planters smoking joints.

The building was changing, too. The first few months we'd kept our doors open, people coming in and out of each other's spaces with coffee and wine, but after a slew of robberies, dead bolts went up. The tenant with the horse was asked to remove his beast and a sad procession of children accompanied him down the elevator. I didn't ask where the horse went, maybe to the police stables a few blocks south. Paint began to chip from the walls and there was no budget for repairs. Everyone had begun to complain about all the noise at Westbeth. A noise abatement notice was posted in the lobby. My mother shook her head in disbelief. Those eighteen-foot-high waved ceilings we all loved had been specifically designed by Bell Laboratories to transport sound. The musicians began to turn down the volume of their instruments. Rock music no longer floated along the hallways day and night. Kids were forbidden to ride bikes and use roller skates *inside* the building.

After the New Year, four months after the unknown woman had jumped to her death, Sheldon Brody, a struggling photographer, leapt out a hallway window. Sheldon belonged to the building and had a little girl. His wife, Anne, came to my mother weeping, "Now the knot that he carried around all those years is in my stomach." I was up in my loft bed, right over the dining room table where they sat. Maybe they didn't know I was there behind my curtain listening.

As soon as Anne left, I climbed down my ladder and asked my mother what Anne's comment had meant.

"Her financial situation. She's worried about how she'll pay the bills now."

Later that evening, when my mother's friend Sonia Gechtoff stopped by, they hunched over cups of tea. "I carry their files around in my head," my mother said.

"Whose files?" Sonia asked. Sonia was an abstract artist who lived on our floor with her two kids. She was sharp and kind and levelheaded, and her pictures were full of bright-colored jagged shapes.

"All your files," my mother sobbed. "I know your lists of exhibitions, your publications and the names of your references. Christ, I even know your tax returns and statement of need. I'm your Mrs. Westbeth. The files I read when everyone applied are now in my head. Half the relationships in this building are lies told in order to garner more space. Some of the women who are now pregnant—I'm the one that told them if they had a baby they'd get additional room! I feel so responsible."

"Oh, no, Thalia," Sonia scolded. "If Sheldon lost his sense of possibility, that's not your fault. We're all struggling for our toehold here. This building has given us a chance."

A toehold? Was that all we had? Even though Sonia said the word reassuringly, I didn't like the sound of it, so precarious and unstable. That night when I fell asleep I dreamed of a great wind coming off the Hudson sweeping us all out to sea.

After Sheldon's death, roof access was blocked and the windows on the common hallways were locked.

I'm not sure how much my father knew about the events unfolding at Westbeth. Weeks could pass without our talking to him, and then the phone would ring and he'd tell us he was coming for a visit. In the early spring of 1971 he bounded up the stairs with tickets to take Tanya and me to the rock opera *Jesus Christ Superstar* on Broadway. Sitting down in our dining nook, he pulled out a photograph. "This is Donna." He proudly handed the picture around the table. We all bent over an image of a girl with the oval face and somber eyes of a Renaissance madonna. "We're getting married in the summer!"

My mother sucked in a long breath. "How *old* is she, Pete?"

"She's my student," my father said happily. "Twenty-one."

My mother frowned. Though she'd turned down Dad's requests to get back together, she didn't like the fact that he'd found another replacement. "Do you really want to get married, *again*?"

Chagrined, my father stuffed the picture back into his wallet. "We don't want to miss the curtain for *Jesus*," he said. Dad loved musicals, actually any spectacle, and Tanya had been walking around the apartment for weeks singing "I Don't Know How to Love Him" in anticipation. Kissing our mother goodbye, we left for the theater with our father.

He was so happy that day. "A new beginning," he said. "Everything is finally coming together." Five years after leaving us, he'd just opened his museum in Berkeley. He told us how he'd wanted a young Bulgarian artist named Christo, who had wrapped the Museum of Contemporary Art in Chicago in ten thousand square feet of tarpaulin and was planning on hanging a giant orange curtain between two mountains in Colorado, to wrap his new museum up like a present and then unveil it in a flurry during the celebration, but there'd been "too much bureaucratic bullshit and not enough time." Instead, he settled on enlisting a troupe of dancers to "christen" the building by rolling around naked on the floors. Some university regents suggested that Dad shouldn't allow this, but my impervious father replied, "It's not my desire to see naked people, but to see to the needs of the populace. It's the people's museum, too!"

I was never clear why Tanya and I missed Dad's opening. I remember pleading with my parents to go, but the trip never materialized. Perhaps it was the naked people, though I doubt my father had that much forethought. In any case, after all the fanfare of his departure from our lives to direct his own museum, we missed seeing the doors finally flung open. We missed watching our father along with western artist William T. Wiley, dressed in black cowboy outfits with holsters strapped around their waists, saunter up to the receptionist, pull out shiny toy pistols and demand, "Give us some art!" After that, Dad and Wiley ceremoniously downed shot glasses of ninety-proof whiskey, dancing girls climbed up on card tables and all of San Francisco's Beat poets came to read. Then my father led the whole rowdy group in a rendition of "To Dream the Impossible Dream." Tanya and I had missed that extravaganza, but not the wedding. This time we would be flower girls with garlands in our hair!

A month later, on a Saturday morning in the early spring, a letter arrived from our father announcing that, after *deep*

Anna Halprin Dancers christening the hard concrete with their soft flesh at the Berkeley Art Museum.

introspection and serious thought, he and Donna had decided to call off the marriage. Because of that, we wouldn't be flying out for the wedding, nor would he be taking a sabbatical at Westbeth this coming fall. Instead, he was going to Europe with Donna, his now-ex-fiancé. All Mom said, as she got ready to leave the apartment, jabbing her comb in her hive of hair, was, "Your father does things in a mixed-up, mind-changing way. That's the way he is. Talk to him about it."

That afternoon, with my mother and sister off to Tanya's therapy appointment, I wandered through the building in a miserable mood. I felt dejected: we'd missed the opening, Dad was jetting to Europe with Donna and now I wouldn't see him or get to be a flower girl. That's when I bumped into an older girl named Priscilla, a member of last year's gang. I didn't really like Priscilla but I needed some distraction. First, we set out to explore the basement, determined this time to discover the giant magnet that was said to be hidden in the building's bowels. But our search proved hot and fruitless. "A giant magnet," Priscilla scoffed. "I doubt it!"

Finally, giving up on our hunt, we wandered out to the courtyard and looked up through the grilled balconies and saw the roof. "I wish we could get up there and sunbathe," Priscilla said dreamily.

And just like that I remembered the master key.

Our apartment was still empty, the key in the jewelry box beneath the amber necklace.

Plucking up the key, we hightailed it to the thirteenth floor. Merce Cunningham had finally moved into the building with his company. We often saw him in the elevator, riding with a group of laughing young men in loose T-shirts and tight black tights that showed their calf muscles and made Mom grin. Unfortunately,

Priscilla and I soon discovered that we couldn't get through his space. He must have changed the lock. But we both knew that there was more than one access to the roof. Riding the elevator back down, we crossed over through the third-floor access hallway and back up the other side of the building. And sure enough the key fit in the locked door and we were outside.

We sat down on the gravelly rooftop and lifted our faces to the sun. "Let's play a game," Priscilla said. At fourteen she was nearly six feet tall and she still picked her nose when she thought you weren't looking.

"What game?"

"Dancers! We can play dancers balancing."

I thought of the dancers my father had said christened his new building. "Soft flesh against hard concrete."

"On what?" I looked around the roof. It was completely flat, with just a little narrow parapet running around the parameter.

"That," Priscilla pointed to the low parapet. "We can stand on that ledge."

"The ledge." My heart kicked against my chest. My ears buzzed. It was made of brick and was perhaps three feet high. No wider than four inches across. There was no railing.

"Sure, I dare you." Her hands on her hips. "Or are you still a baby in 3-D glasses?" I suddenly remembered how mean Priscilla could be to her fat little brother who looked like a mushroom. She was older than me. I didn't want word to get out in the building that I was afraid. Besides, I slept in a loft. I was used to heights and climbing up and down a ladder in the middle of the night in the pitch-dark to use the bathroom.

"Okay."

Priscilla did it first. She leaned against the building, hands clutching the brick face, and stood on the parapet, then she jumped down.

So I climbed up on the narrow brick ledge, too. Up there, thirteen floors above the courtyard, I did not think of the celebrating dancers in Berkeley communing with the stone surface, I thought of the unknown woman who had jumped to her death and stained the ground. Sheldon Brody, too, had leapt from a lower floor and died. Even knowing the danger, I could feel every inch of my being lean toward the open air. Empty space spun around me like a vast and transparent whirlpool. The ground below sucked like a magnet. There was darkness down there, into which people I knew had recently plunged. Yet standing so close to the edge felt hypnotic. I closed my eyes. Then, like a ballerina I lifted my foot, pointed my toe and, letting go of the wall, I stepped along the ledge.

"What are you doing?" Priscilla screamed.

With her words I fell down to the safety of the rooftop, scraping my knees on the asphalt.

Priscilla sat there, mouth gaping. I stood up and dusted myself off. I felt unsteady and sick, confused by what I had just done. But I didn't want Priscilla to see my fear, which as soon as I'd hit the rooftop had shocked me back to reality. *I could have died,* I thought.

We left the roof in silence, not even looking at each other in the elevator. On the third floor, Priscilla made her way in one direction, I ran off in the other, threading my way around Westbeth. Through the walls I could hear, almost feel, the throbbing of life.

When my mother came home I was sitting on the top of our cement steps, crying. "Where have you been?" I sobbed.

"Tanya had her appointment with Dr. Reich." My mother sat down beside me and put her arm around me. "What's wrong? What happened?"

Instead of telling my mother what had happened, I started writing poems about death. Suicides. Suicide became our regular dinner table conversation. I'd recite the latest stanza of my poem to my sister and mother, who would then weigh in with comments. "Kind of hard to kill yourself by stabbing," Tanya said. "How about drowning?" *He came upon her body, a-hanging from a tree. He came upon her body, as dead as dead could be*, my mother smiling as I delivered my lines, occasionally suggesting a word choice.

At first I wasn't even aware that my poems sprang from what was occurring around us. We were living together in this community where art and life were inextricably bound together. Spontaneous acts, not just of violence, but also of theater, music and dance, popped up in the halls all the time. When I walked along the parapet, I was imitating the grown-ups and their nightmarish grief. When I wrote poetry, I was also trying to do what they did, merge experience with art. I would come to learn that the body in all its manifestations was the favored medium of a performed piece of art. And not just at Westbeth, but early that year in California, Chris Burden had performed *Shoot*. This was a work of art in which he let himself be shot in his left arm by his assistant with a .22-caliber rifle in front of a small group of witnesses. Burden believed that the importance of art was not an object, but an experience. Everywhere I turned I bumped into the idea of an art form that was gradually encroaching upon real life.

The night I worked into one of my poems Anne's line about the knot in Sheldon's stomach that was now in hers—*And the knot that had been around her neck, was now around his own*—my mother's eyes widened.

"I wish you hadn't heard that."

"There's no privacy here," Tanya said. "We hear everything!"

The next evening Tanya came home and announced what she'd heard in the lobby: "Years ago Bell Labs created a noxious gas that was released into the air system. It makes people crazy and leap to their deaths."

"Don't be ridiculous," our mother said. "That's hearsay. Eat your carrots."

"Who cares if I can see in the dark if we're all going to go mad and kill ourselves?"

These conversations could have just been silly except that they weren't. My sister's friends had started avoiding the building, calling it Deathbeth. Tanya was hanging out uptown smoking pot and sometimes passing out from drinking too much. My mother sensed our life unraveling. She had not done the writing she'd hoped she'd accomplish at Westbeth. She'd given a reading in her black velvet dress at the White Horse Tavern—Dylan Thomas's former haunt—but most of her writing from that time consists of journals filled with descriptions of the vast dark blue funnel of the estuary, the flat barges, the bright tugboats and the seagoing vessels, chugging by our window. She began talking on the phone to Grammar about coming to live with her. "I can't handle two teenagers in the city all alone," she said.

Both Tanya and I vehemently opposed another move. Even if Westbeth had problems, our Grammar lived in a suburban neighborhood thirty miles northeast of Chicago. Not exactly the sticks, but as far as we were concerned, "Anything outside of

Manhattan is in the *hinterlands*." We hadn't been on board about the move downtown, but we'd adjusted. In the year and a half we'd lived in the Village, the neighborhood had begun to change. No longer a wasteland, it was a crowded circus full of "youths" attired in fringed vests and colorful hats wandering the streets spouting poetry and strumming guitars. We no longer ogled hippies, we wanted to be hippies. If we moved, we'd miss the carnival. All our friends were in New York. Tanya was so unhappy, she threatened to "split" and live at Bethesda Fountain in Central Park where the runaways slept under the arches of the tunnel arcade. But the choice wasn't really ours to make. Mom was tired and losing weight and Grammar was getting older. "In Illinois we will all be a family," Mom said.

Tanya was the first to go, already ensconced at Grammar's when I came home from sleepaway camp at the end of July to celebrate my thirteenth birthday, get fitted for my retainer and help Mom finish packing. It was muggy and we kept the windows open. When the tide was high a salty breeze blew in from the Hudson.

On the evening of July 28, the kitchenware boxed up, my mother and I went out for slices of pizza and Italian ices. We'd just returned and were washing up for bed—the next day would be the final push of packing and our plant sale and Mom wanted to get an early start—when we heard a commotion in the hallway. Mom went to see what the fuss was about. When she didn't return after a few minutes, I came down our duplex stairs and opened the front door. Peter Cott was standing in the hall in front of Diane Arbus's apartment with three other men, one of whom I recognized as Diane's friend the artist Marvin Israel, who helped teach her photography class. With his glasses on and his balding head, Marvin bore a striking resemblance to Mark Rothko, and for a moment I was so startled that I stepped back into our foyer. But I could hear my mother crying. When I next looked out our doorway, I saw her. She was next to Peter, running her hands through her hair, shaking. She must not have noticed me, because she bolted down the hallway toward her friend Sonia. I ran after her. When I caught up with her she had sunk down on her knees beside Sonia and was sobbing. I'd never seen her so overwrought. "I didn't believe her," my mother kept saying. I looked again at Diane's door. Two of the men had gone back inside and Peter Cott was talking to a police officer.

"Thalia, what has happened?" Sonia asked quietly. Unlike my mother, Sonia never got rattled except when you asked her if she was a feminist. Then she'd declare, "Man, woman, doesn't matter. I'm an artist!"

"Diane killed herself," my mother said.

"Jesus," Sonia gasped.

I was suddenly dizzy and squatting down, clinging to my mother, who felt very delicate in my arms. Sonia's daughter put the kettle on. We rose and gathered around her table. My mother explained that Marvin had been trying to reach Diane all day. "But her phone just rang and rang and he finally let himself in with his key." They'd been lovers, Diane and Marvin. "If he'd called me I would have been over there in a flash. I have a master key," Mom sobbed. Thank god Marvin hadn't called her, because when he found Diane she was fully dressed in her bathtub, her wrists slit.

"You wouldn't have wanted to see that," Sonia said.

Years later, when I read Patricia Bosworth's biography of Diane Arbus, I discovered that a few weeks before her death, Mom had

had a conversation with Diane. She told Diane that she was worried about her daughters, especially me because of my suicide poems. She was moving us out of Westbeth. Mom told Bosworth that Diane had then said she'd been considering killing herself. "But my work is what matters," Diane added. My mother admitted that she had heard the hesitancy in Diane's voice, but ignored it.

When I read that my mother had discussed my poems with Diane I felt a rush of love for both these women. I pictured them standing in the hallway between their front doors, my mother concerned about her children, Diane so vulnerably identifying and expressing her own confusion. Reading about my very small part in this intimate and tragic story made me feel again that intense connection I'd felt while I'd lived at Westbeth. We could practically hear each other breathe through the walls. Whatever was wonderful or sorrowful, we were all part of the experience together.

The next day was our last day in the building. We had a plant sale in our apartment, selling off the purple-leafed coleus, braided ficus tree, the leopard lily whose striped poisonous leaves we had been warned since we were babies never to put in our mouths, and the peace lily, with its blossoms raised like hands in prayer. Women trickled through the apartment all day, buying our houseplants and talking softly about Diane. It turned out Diane Arbus had mentioned to numerous tenants in the building that she couldn't go on and wanted to end her life. My mother must have been relieved to hear she hadn't been the only one Diane had confided in. Already there were requests for Diane's apartment.

Someone had brought over the May issue of the magazine *Artforum*, which featured a spread of Diane Arbus's pictures. She'd been hired to teach at Yale and show her photographs in the Venice Biennale. One of the poets said what she'd done was senseless and she was filled with a "hushed outrage at the wastefulness of what Diane has done." As with Rothko's suicide, I understood that Diane's death was more than just a personal tragedy. Everyone in that building wanted a chance at the kind of recognition Diane was gaining. To have someone among us on the brink of success end his or her own life was terrifying.

We bent forward and looked at the photographs. "So raw and distant." Mom turned the pages from the freaks, to the image of the Jewish Giant, an oversized child dwarfing his elderly parents, to the strange Identical Twins with their eerie and stoic gaze. Diane's shots of children always looked wise beyond their years, her adults like simpletons still playing at dress-up. Someone said these weren't pictures of other people so much as images of Diane. Someone else said, "No, they're us." Not literally "us" but, as my mother said, "foreign and familiar."

After everyone had left and my mother and I had finished packing, I told her about walking the parapet. We sat side by side up on her bed and my mother listened in silence, her eyes level on my face. "You could have slipped," she said.

I pulled up her African coverlet, though it was a warm July night. "Why do artists do it?" I asked.

"Which?" she asked. "Art? Or killing themselves?"

"Both, I guess." I felt very grown-up to be having this conversation with my mother. I liked the calm feeling that had settled down between us.

"Artists are suggestive people, like children, I guess. Sometimes they have a hard time distinguishing between reality and fantasy. That's a good thing when trying to create—to be able to see the magic in ordinary life. But you can't live there. Westbeth wasn't supposed to make artists famous, it was designed to give them inexpensive living and work space. But moving here, we all thought we were home free. Of course, we weren't. I want to believe Westbeth helped us."

"I think it did." I said.

"In what way?" she asked.

I said the simplest truth I knew. "At Westbeth I'm not afraid of sleeping in the dark."

My mother climbed down from her bed and went to pull her opera glasses out of the top of her suitcase. Standing in front of the window, she looked out at the estuary. It was a clear night and an ocean liner had pulled out of its berth and was sailing down the river.

"Can I see?" I asked.

My mother walked over and handed me her glasses. And, like it was with those 3-D spectacles that had made the world suddenly pop into high relief, as soon as I held the opera glasses up to my eyes, the ship in the distance was brought right in through the window. All the lights were on and the ship looked like a floating city.

"I wonder where it's going?" I asked.

My mother answered softly, "Towards the future."

Here at Westbeth we'd been part of a group of permeable people lost in the fog of a nearly impossible dream. In the last six months of her life, Diane had taken a series of pictures of mentally retarded adults dressed up in costumes, some of which were posted on the bulletin board in her apartment.

Unlike her earlier pictures of freakish dwarfs and tattooed men, which had a bold, anthropological frankness, these last shots are not crisp close-ups. They are deliberately blurred. One of these final images shows a group of five figures framed under the protective arm of a tree. With their faces hidden behind masks, these odd adults clasp hands, braving the unknown together. Haunting mystery envelopes these pretend pirates and princesses like a fine mist, as if the world in which they wander is under an enchanted spell that not even curiosity-seeking Diane wanted to break. Instead, even as she snapped their pictures, she chose to allow these truly disadvantaged people the grace of remaining unexposed.

In a strange distorted way, this last image reminds me of our first Halloween at Westbeth, when the building had mobilized, not for a protest against the Vietnam War as my father had wished, but for a celebration. Adults and children had swarmed out of every door and corner dressed in handcrafted costumes, bedecked like rococo monsters, glittering queens and joyous clowns, and paraded through the hallways and around the block.

Chapter 12

fter we moved to Illinois, we were separated more and more from our father. Our trips west shrank from one month, down to two weeks, then to ten days in the summertime. We were teenagers with our own lives. In the past Dad had traveled east not just to see us, but also to attend lectures, openings and art world meetings in New York City. What was there except us to bring Dad to Illinois?

To complicate the situation, Mom decided that she did not want Dad swinging through our home "seeking approval for every girl he meets." When he did come to visit, we met him at the end of the driveway and he took us out to lunch.

Grammar had sold Doc's experimental farm and moved to a suburban enclave near her son, my mother's younger brother. Deerfield was not Greenwich Village, not the home of jazz or the arts. It was the home of the Sara Lee Corporation headquarters, potato buns and cheesecake. A Republican community where, not so many years before our arrival, angry protesters had carried signs that read NOT NEXT DOOR, and shut down a neigh-boring development because of the proposed units for African-Americans. For a brief period during the 1970s, a "No-Kissing Zone" was established at the local Deerfield train station to avoid the congested traffic of farewells.

Grammar would have been fine with Dad's visits. Grammar believed in the mythmaking of great men. Doc's ashes were entombed under a slate-and-bronze shrine that sat on a bluff in the backyard of her prairie-style house, where, she said, "He faces outer space." Come evening, Grammar would totter out, a little tipsy from the bourbon and Angostura bitters she liked to sip, to pull the dead leaves away from his tomb.

We watched her through the plate-glass windows as she cleared the grave site. Mom shook her head. "Does he need an unobstructed view? I can just see him, his black hair crackling, welcoming the universe with a shout of self-approval!"

I really didn't mind having my grandfather only a stone's throw from my bedroom, his bronze plaque gleaming in the moonlight. I was in my gothic adolescent phase and so I thought graves romantic.

Mom was still toting around her own little grave relic—Mrs. Jemima Payne's stone fragment, now used as a rustic doorstop. In the spring of 1972 she began teaching creative writing part-time to continuing education students. Her mini- and maxi dresses, her slim bare midriff from our Westbeth days, completely vanished. Now she zipped herself into wool skirts with matching jackets buttoned up to her chin. In her notebook, right after we moved, she wrote, *I do not want to live solely in the land of art. I need to go back to real life to live. To take the long detours that will keep me safe.*

Deerfield was one of those long detours. Tanya, who'd inherited Mom's gift for sarcasm, dubbed it *Dead City*.

In Deerfield our life flattened out like the Midwest landscape around us. The heat in summer was stupefying and in winter the blizzards barricaded us indoors. We went to the local public school, where girls with straight hair wore baggy corduroys and army surplus shirts. Each morning we walked a mile and a half to the nearest bus stop. There were no more exhibitionists lurking in subway stations, no museums and no art galleries. We lived in the middle of nowhere, off a deserted county road, in Dead City. The only place to go in those days was the mall, where I stole a book from the local bookstore.

I maintained that I'd only done what the book told me to. It was Abby Hoffman's *Steal This Book*, which gave lessons in jailbreak, obtaining real buffalo from the U.S. government and making dynamite from toothpaste. I'd pilfered the book as a Christmas gift for my father.

Dr. Rosenbaum, the therapist my mother sent me to in order to correct my delinquent behavior, said, "Most girls steal lipstick for *themselves*. Not a gift for a parent who could question them about it."

"My father's a liberal," I replied, slumped in my chair.

Dr. Rosenbaum, a fat man who smoked Kent cigarettes—my father's brand since he'd exchanged his distinguished pipe for the more practical cigarette—sat behind a large wooden desk with a big glass ashtray smack in the middle of it.

His contention was that I had taken the book because I was desperate for attention from my father, who was, Dr. Rosenbaum boldly stated, a narcissist. This, he told me when I looked confused, was a person who thought himself superior to others and had an inflated self-image. "Like a big blown-up balloon," Dr. Rosenbaum said as he waved his cigarette through the air. To impress my father, I had selected, "an anti-establishment zeitgeist best-seller as both a plea and a protest to connect and separate from the archetypal, egocentric figure in your life."

Though I could barely understand Dr. Rosenbaum as he puffed his fancy words, I was fascinated. He'd called my father a name! And yet, wasn't it true? Didn't Dad mostly talk about himself and his life? "He talks about art and artists, too," I insisted.

"That is your father's life."

"You think I did this to get his attention?" I thought about walking the parapet at Westbeth.

"Did you?"

I shrugged, remembering my father's reaction when my mother had forced me to call and confess my theft: "It's a good book," he'd said. "And you were taking it for your renegade dad!"

Out in Berkeley, my renegade father was again running afoul of the UC regents regarding the museum. Aside from the fact that Peggy Guggenheim had pulled out of donating her large collection, Rothko had died before he'd been able to bequeath to Berkeley a group of paintings from the MoMA show. Now Berkeley had only one major Rothko painting. My father was not the best financial steward; administrative work was not his strongest talent and he was becoming increasingly disenchanted with his role as director. Perhaps that was why he decided, only a year after nearly eloping with his student, to marry a woman close to his own age.

My mother, hearing of the upcoming wedding, said, "He's just looking for a distraction." She wrote him a stiff little note of congratulations. *If this time you do manage to work out your relationship on a more permanent basis, I'll be wishing you full contentment and happiness.* After seven years, with my father about to embark on his second marriage since their divorce, Mom switched back to her maiden name.

The whole event happened so swiftly that when Tanya and I arrived a few weeks later for the wedding, we were in a daze. For the ceremony, I had packed the dress I'd worn for my intermediate school graduation and Tanya had borrowed one of our mother's old minis. When we descended from the plane, our father clapped his hands in the air and kissed the tops of our heads. "We're all going to have a wonderful time," he said.

Dolores Yonkers, the woman who was to be the third Mrs. Selz, looked like a schoolmarm, short brown hair going gray on top and thick glasses that magnified her eyes. She was a professor of Haitian art and culture whom Dad had known in his days at Pomona. He'd run into her again at a conference and asked her out to dinner, where, looking up from his soup—he told us—into her soft round face, her serious eyes, he'd thought, *What a nice companion she'd make!*

With her two cats in tow, Dolores moved into Regal House, the name my father had landed on for Selz 2, since it sat on Regal Road. Now her Early American antiques were scattered among his Day-Glo lamps, beanbag chairs, modern art and old European furniture.

Two days after our arrival, the wedding took place on my father's roof deck with its view of the Golden Gate. Tanya and I stood at the bottom of the staircase, handing out strings of love beads to arriving guests. Both Dolores and Dad wore full-length Moroccan tunics of royal colors: red, gold and purple. Someone played a flute while a minister with long flowing brown ringlets

Bride and groom, 1972.

talked about peace, love and freedom, then pronounced my father and Dolores husband and wife.

Later, all the guests sat on folding chairs around little card tables that Tanya and I had helped Dolores decorate with bright crepe-paper flowers. We drank champagne and ate wedding cake, and a girl I'd never seen before stripped off her clothes and climbed into my father's lap. Dad looked stunned but pleased as the crowd cheered. He wrapped a hand around her narrow belly. At first Dolores laughed, but when the girl settled in and began rolling a joint, Dolores rose and moved to sit across the deck with my father's old German cousins, Ruth and Ralph, under the shade of a sun umbrella. Ralph had his camera out, but discreetly screwed the cap back over the lens.

Tanya, stoned on pot, drunk on champagne, changed from

the pink mini she'd worn for the ceremony into a grass skirt and bikini top and belly-danced for the wedding party.

One of the wedding guests, a symphony conductor, rose up from his chair and lunged for the woman seated across the table from him. As the table between them toppled over, the conductor dropped his pants. He was naked from the waist down, bare-assed and big-bellied and, unlike the girl in my father's lap, ugly and fat and frightening to behold.

Everyone began to applaud again.

"Hold on there," I heard a voice call out. It was Harold Paris, my father's friend and the artist he was now showing at his museum. Harold, too, had risen from his chair, but he was not undressed, he was wearing a cape and a beret—Harold was a theatrical man—and he was pointing at me. "There's a child here." All eyes turned; even the girl in my father's lap stopped puffing briefly and glanced my way. I was sitting on the retaining wall. Until that moment, I'd been quietly observing the festivities. I imagined myself to be sophisticated for a fourteen-year-old. But even at Westbeth I'd never seen naked revelers before, not a young naked girl perched in my own father's lap, and certainly not a hideous naked man wildly grinning at the woman across from him. But until Harold called me what I was—a child—I'd been transfixed, unable to move. At his words, all the bewilderment and confusion of my adolescence surged inside me. I stood up and began threading my way through the tables, embarrassed to be exposed as a child, but also grateful at being dismissed. No one was telling the revelers to stop.

Just as I was heading for the stairs, the conductor vaulted over his little card table in pursuit of the woman fleeing his advances.

That cinched it. I ran and locked myself in my basement room.

Eventually they came looking for me, my father, Dolores and Tanya, banged on my bedroom door. "Come on, Gaby, we're taking the party down to the museum."

But by then I had buried myself in a book and refused to go.

Out my window I saw guests traipsing through the succulent garden, crepe-paper flowers, swiped from our centerpieces, pinned in their hair.

It was nearly dark before my father, Dolores and Tanya returned. By then I had grown hungry, stepped out of the house to look for their car and accidentally locked myself out. When they drove up I was perched on a boulder, finishing the last pages of my book in the fading light.

"You missed the party." Tanya skipped up the walkway. She was dressed again in the pretty pink mini dress she'd worn for the ceremony.

"We had a great time." Dad bounded up behind her, as happy as a puppy dashing into somebody's—anybody's—swimming pool. Then, almost as an afterthought, he cocked his head back toward Dolores. "Didn't we?"

She nodded slowly. What could she have said at that moment? Perhaps she blamed my father's friends or thought life would settle down now that the party was over. After all, they were about to honeymoon behind the Iron Curtain. What could be more sobering than a Russian winter?

It took me a long time to make sense of that afternoon. Images from that day stayed with me for years. My father with the nude girl in his lap, his third wife's unexpected grace, the camera with the covered lens, the bellowing symphony conductor, and most particularly the humiliation I felt to be there, the child sitting on the edge, watching the mayhem.

Later, I asked Tanya what had happened at the museum.

"Nothing much. You know Daddy, he gave us the grand tour."

We never saw Dolores again—their marriage broke up, as my mother knew it would, while they were still on their honeymoon.

Shortly after we returned to the Midwest, our father resigned as director of the museum he'd founded. He hadn't received the budget he'd needed to put on the shows he wanted. Nor was he particularly good at the diplomacy necessary for fund-raising. If his marriage to Dolores had been meant to stabilize him, it had backfired. "Don't worry," our mother said dryly when she learned the news, "your father always resurrects himself."

Even without his job directing the museum, my father still had a tenured teaching position at Berkeley and ambitions to write some major art history books. But multiple divorces had taken their toll on his income. He contended that his alimony to Mom should be reduced since his "change in status," and we were living on Grammar's nickel. My mother said a settlement was a settlement. Soon they were engrossed in a legal matter. My mother also wanted my father to agree that the art they'd collected together would be left to my sister and me. She was afraid he was bleeding his art to pay off departing wives. And he was. The little red Rothko that hung in his hallway was one of the first pieces to go. "Rothko works best on a large scale," my father insisted.

Mom filed papers on her overdue alimony and the next time my father came back from Europe he was detained at the airport. After that, his lawyer advised him not to enter the state of Illinois in case our mother decided to have him arrested, which she swore she wouldn't do. She didn't want to keep us from seeing our father. I only saw him once that year, when I was escorted across the Illinois-Wisconsin border by his girlfriend.

It would have been nice to have my sister as my ally in this battle between our parents. But Tanya was angry with our father for "being such a jerk." That year she refused to speak to him and even sent back his Christmas gift unopened. I missed my father and didn't see why Tanya had to be so stubborn. But she dug in her heels and refused to even talk to me about Dad. It took a year, and a compromise between our parents, before she would relent.

I'd begun cutting class. I had a friend, a girl who had spent a year living with relatives in Amsterdam and who smoked European tobacco from a corncob pipe. Together we rode the train into Chicago, where we hung out at the Art Institute, roaming the modern painting rooms. When my mother found out I was missing classes and where I was going, she didn't punish me. She called my school, said I was sick and drove me to the museum herself. In a quiet room off one of the long hallways we found a Rothko painting. It was bright orange and red, similar in color but much grander than the one my father had sold.

"Why did he sell it?" I asked my mother. We were sitting on a bench, staring into the painting.

"Your father thinks everything is replaceable."

I thought of Topher playing on his rocking horse and his father staring at the pink walls of his house and then disappearing.

Rothko, the artist who had been obsessed with creating paintings that thickened the space in a room until it felt as inevitable and unrelenting as a Greek tragedy, had exited the world leaving his children with very little.

Instead, he'd willed the bulk of his estate to the Rothko Foundation, a fund for struggling older artists. He'd named three friends as executors: Bernard Reis, his accountant; Theodoros Stamos, a painter and a dear friend of Mom's; and Morton

Levine, an anthropology professor and for a short time Topher's guardian.

My mother and I knew all this because, four years after Mark's death, the trial called *the Matter of Mark Rothko* was taking center stage in the art world. Her friend Stamos was being sued. So were the other executors, but it was Stamos who kept Mom abreast, sending our way every newspaper clipping and article about the trial.

Before she'd died, Mell had filed suit to challenge the foundation on behalf of her kids. After her death, at the instigation of Herbert Ferber, the dentist-sculptor Mark had removed from his will, Kate and Topher, joined by the New York state attorney general, brought another suit against the three executors of the foundation and his gallery, Marlborough Fine Art. They'd demanded the cancellation of contract with Marlborough to sell seven hundred and ninety-eight of Rothko's paintings, as well as dismissal of the three executors, Reis, Stamos and Levine, accusing them of wasting assets after they'd entered into an agreement with Marlborough to buy one hundred Rothko paintings for $1.8 million and take the remaining six hundred and ninety-eight paintings on consignment at a 50 percent commission. They'd also alleged that Reis and Stamos were guilty of self-dealing and conspiracy. Bernard Reis, in addition to being Rothko's accountant and executor of his estate, was also a director and secretary-treasurer of Marlborough Fine Art. Stamos had recently joined Marlborough's stable of artists.

The defendants countered that assets hadn't been wasted. In 1970 when the deal with Marlborough was struck the market had been depressed. The price negotiated included lesser Rothko paintings and works that needed restoration and might be difficult to sell. Since Marlborough had been Rothko's primary gallery, regardless of the fact that Reis worked for Marlborough, the defendants contended the contract with that gallery was the obvious choice.

To understand any of this, my mother said, you had to understand Mark's relationship with Bernard Reis. In fact, she said we were all indebted to Reis. "He hosted the art world and collected their work. Peggy Guggenheim, who could have stayed anywhere, stayed with the Reises when she was in town. He did all the artists' taxes for free, even ours, even after your father left." (Reis continued to do my mother's taxes until he died.) To Rothko, though, Reis was more than his accountant, he was his consigliere, his confidant, his friend. Mark didn't make a move without consulting Reis. Reis had handled Mark's mortgage and, when Mark went into the hospital for his aneurysm, it was Reis who not only suggested the doctor, but came to read to Mark each evening. Reis drafted Mark's will. Back in 1962, it was Reis who introduced Mark to Frank Lloyd, the head of Marlborough Fine Art Gallery, when Mark left the Sidney Janis Gallery over the scandal of the Pop art show. (Mark and the other abstract artists had been certain that if the Sidney Janis Gallery was showing Pop, it had lost faith in their work.) It was also Reis who had crowed to my mother about the lovely turnout at Franz Kline's funeral, "Just like an opening!" Stamos said Reis was like Mark's wife, and if Reis was the wife, then Stamos, the young Greek artist Mark had taken under his wing, was their child. Mark's style had greatly influenced Stammy (my mother's term of endearment for this fellow Greek). So it was with Mark's knowledge and support (however muddled by depression, medication and alcohol) that Reis had signed on to work at Marlborough and Stamos had sought representation there. Mark, who never trusted the business of the art world, would have wanted a full retinue of his people at his gallery. "The art world," my mother said, "is as entangled as a bowl of spaghetti."

Now this bowl of spaghetti was being untangled in court and in all the newspapers.

When I asked my father over the phone why Rothko hadn't left his paintings to his children, he said, "Mark didn't want to leave his children wealthy. He didn't believe in free rides. He lived like a poor man. He wanted to help support older, needy artists."

That was what the court was trying to figure out. What had Mark wanted? And what was the value of a Rothko? Was his work genius, or merely a passing fad?

In the meantime, Frank Lloyd was discovered spiriting paintings out of the country to Liechtenstein, England and France, in an effort to raise money to pay his legal fees. And it was revealed that in the winter of 1970, nine months *after* Mark's death, Reis had amended the certificate of incorporation of the Rothko Foundation. Originally the purpose of the foundation was to "*receive and maintain funds . . . to be used exclusively for charitable, scientific and/or educational purposes.*" Now the amended foundation provided "*individual grants-in-aid, awards and financial assistance . . . to mature creative artists, musicians, composers and writers . . . who should otherwise lack financial resources.*"

"But that's what Rothko wanted," my father said. "I heard him say it."

Kate Rothko and Robert Goldwater—one of the directors of the foundation—disagreed. What Rothko had wanted was the careful placement of his paintings in museums and collections to enhance their meaning and importance.

When the court went to recess in the spring of 1974, the *New York Times* reported, *Miss Rothko has insisted that she wants paintings as her share of the estate, and the Attorney General wants paintings, too. The Rothko Foundation wants cash . . . Christopher Rothko's guardian wants cash. Claims for damages and fraud are also involved.* "Nobody but Kissinger could negotiate a settlement here," one court observer commented.

"You're attaching too much of your own sense of loss to this trial," my mother told me. "Your father is still very much alive."

I was out in California the summer of 1974 when I learned about my father's involvement in the Rothko trial, at a dinner with my father and Harold Paris, the artist who had rescued me two years earlier from viewing the debauchery of my dad's third wedding. I had made the trip west alone; Tanya, having reconciled with Dad, had come for her visit earlier that year. For the first time in as long as I could remember, my father wasn't dating anyone and I was the woman on his arm. We spent our evenings together, dining with his friends, attending art shows and once sailing around the bay at a party on a yacht for the Czech film director Milos Forman.

Toward the end of my weeklong visit, my father took me down to Harold's studio: a long low building in the flats of Berkeley. Deep within the bowels of his studio Harold showed us an environment he was creating. A separate room, the walls and ceiling made of billowing white fabric like a tent or a bubble, the space filled with strange organic-shaped sculptures that looked like they held inside them colored, murky air: Harold called these objects *souls*. They were made out of vacuum-formed Plexiglas, and Harold told us these were the souls of artists.

I didn't know much about art then, not the real history, but I

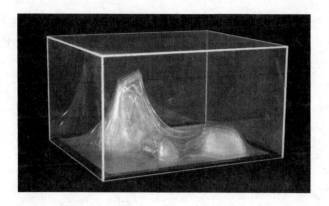

Homage to Boccioni #5
Harold Paris, 1971

didn't have to know the discipline to understand that everywhere
we went in those days, art was stretching out of its own skin.
Painting becoming sculpture, sculpture slipping into architecture or theater and performance. I thought I knew this had
begun with Jackson Pollock, who, in flipping the canvas off the
wall, had spun the world of art on its head and turned the act of
painting into an action. Rothko, too, had created environments,
rooms with paintings that when experienced together formed a
sacred space. More recently, Claes Oldenburg had created giant
comical installations of Pop objects, a hamburger, an ice-cream
cone, and a soft, sagging ice bag; and the sculptor Edward Kien-
holz had reproduced Barney's Beanery, a famous Los Angeles bar,
crafting a life-sized tableau that incorporated everything from
the odor of stale beer to the sound track of chatter and clinking
glasses. But looking around Harold's room, I thought maybe it
had begun long before that. All the way back to the Paleolithic era

when rituals designed to influence the spirit world had inspired people to produce cave paintings. Maybe the whole idea of art was to crack it out of a shell and bring something new to life. Like a cell, by turns unfolding, mutating, reproducing, art was constantly reforming into an entirely new creature. All it took was for someone to conceive of doing it.

Harold was such a crazy guy, all heart and passion, I could sense it even then, though I didn't know how wild he really was until a number of years later. Not part of the mainstream art world, Harold worked in the periphery. "There will always be people like your father," he told me, "who understand what I'm doing." That environment he took us into was hermetically sealed. We had to pass through an antechamber as if we were going into an operating theater, before we entered the art space. Inside, as if under a layer of skin, was every beautiful object Harold could conjure—soft, hard, transparent, solid, a world unto itself. A surreal playground. A reverent graveyard of artists' souls.

Then we left Harold's bubble tent and Harold fried us shrimp in the shell on his Bunsen burner and we sat at a makeshift table and ate with our fingers and drank beer from the bottle and my father and Harold talked about the Rothko trial.

"These are good men," my father said. "Not crooks. Reis was our accountant and Stamos is a wonderful painter. Levine wasn't part of the art world. He would have absolutely no reason to be in cahoots with anyone."

"Peter, I'm just not sure you should do it." Harold said.

"Do what?" I asked.

"Well, why not?" My father set his bottle down.

"I've heard things. That Frank Lloyd is a slimy bastard." Harold said.

"Noooo." Dad shook his head. "He's just an art dealer."

"What?" I asked again.

"Your father has been asked to testify at the Rothko trial," my father said, leaning back in his chair with a pleased smile.

"Why?" I asked.

"To put a value on the paintings, Gaby. Because at the end of the day, who else knows Mark's work better than me? I gave him his retrospective!"

Apparently, Frank Lloyd from Marlborough Gallery had contacted my father and asked him to testify and give an evaluation of the work. Dad had already flown to New York that June to consult on the case. Marlborough hoped that Dad's estimate would be lower than that of the other art historians and appraisers who had already given expert opinion, and consistent with their claim that at the time of Mark's death, nobody knew how high Rothko's prices would soar. If it was the case, as my father maintained it was, that "Pollock's prices dropped right after he died, so did Edvard Munch's and Auguste Rodin's," then the trustees had not wasted assets but had acted prudently in their negotiations, and the gallery had not depressed the prices artificially.

"But what about the kids?" I asked.

Dad shrugged. "They have plenty. They'll be fine. Mark wanted to help needy artists."

"Older needy artists," Harold corrected, tapping a cigarette out and handing one to Dad. Harold was fifty years old. He'd just gotten out of the hospital, but still smoked. His skin was copper-colored, weathered and tarnished like bronze patina. Sometimes he griped about being left out of the art world.

Now Harold's black eyes flashed at me, and he lifted his glass. "Your father has not abandoned the artist!"

"Never," Dad raised his bottle and then . . . I did, too. Who would want to abandon artists? Still, as I set my beer down I felt a hand reach inside and twist my heart.

Only a few weeks after my visit west, my father flew to New York and was cross-examined for three days as an expert witness. On the stand he gave his valuation, not a high one, but not a low one, either, insisting that his opinion on the prices of his dead friend's work was not tainted by the fact that Frank Lloyd had paid him a fee of $20,000 and his expenses to travel east. The decision, which a year and a half later found in favor of the children, stunned the art world. Marlborough and the three executors were convicted of fraud and ordered to pay $9.2 million; the executors were removed from the foundation; the children, who had become known as "the orphans," were now at least wealthy orphans. Kate was given control of the estate and won possession of the paintings. Mark's reputation, made all the more famous by the spotlight of press, trial and verdict, was solidified in history. The self-dubbed Prince of Painting rose to sainthood. Perhaps he could have been buried at Westminster Abbey, as he'd once long ago joked to my mother. As for Frank Lloyd, his canniness was legendary. He'd made up a past and a lineage, though he'd never shied from the fact that he was in the art business to make money. Facing three felony charges, Lloyd left the country. Stamos signed over his home to pay his debts but was granted life tenancy. Levine, who had distanced himself from the other executors—he had no conflict of interest—and hired his own lawyers, was hounded by both the IRS and the estate until he died. Reis, in his eighties when his appeal was denied, filed for bankruptcy. The Rothko Foundation, under new leadership, never reinstated the fund for aging artists but donated its remaining

Rothko works to museums. And for his testimony, my father was criticized, called an opportunist by some and disloyal by others. On the East Coast, he was vilified.

Paid by the wrong side, my father always maintained that he'd wanted to stand in solidarity with his friends: with Theodoros Stamos, an unselfish man who'd buried Mark's remains in his family plot, and Bernard Reis, the "surrogate" wife whom Rothko relied on daily. "Somebody had to do it," my father said. Perhaps my father needed to be the reigning expert and not relinquish center stage. Though he hadn't gone out and sought this role, an opportunity had landed in his lap like a beautiful naked woman. To be part of this grand drama proved too enticing. But nobody does anything for just one reason, least of all my father. Deep down Dad believed that he was defending Mark's dream, a dream that Westbeth had also championed, the belief that artists should have support; that especially old, unknown artists shouldn't be left in the dust. "That's what Mark wanted."

But in Berkeley that night, sitting with my father and Harold, as they discussed yet another piece of art, I felt heartbroken, as if somehow my father were leaving me all over again. "I don't want you to do it," I burst out, interrupting their conversation as if I were six and not sixteen.

He lifted his shoulders up to his ears again and let them drop, like Charlie Chaplin's little tramp, like a befuddled clown, which was not my father. He patted my hand. "Of course you do. You want your old man to do the right thing," he said.

PART THREE

The Fourth Wall

PERHAPS THE MOST POWERFUL FORCE OF ART, THAT THE
CHANGES MADE ARE NOT IN THE SITE, BUT IN US.

—*Jeanne-Claude Christo*

I'M GOING TO MAKE OTHER PEOPLE RECOGNIZE SOMETHING
IN THEMSELVES RATHER THAN ME.

—*Cindy Sherman*

Chapter 13

During the bicentennial year of 1976, while the rest of the
country was celebrating its independence from the Brit-
ish, I was celebrating my independence from Dead City.
I graduated from high school and pointed my compass west. I'd
been accepted into the University of California down at Santa
Cruz, only a bus ride away from my father's house.

Right before I left, I learned that Cindy Frankel was headed
for college at Santa Cruz, too. Cindy of the corn silk hair and dark
blue eyes, one of the crème de la crème of my high school and the
valedictorian of our graduating class. I'd only known Cindy in
passing, but as soon as I learned she was attending Santa Cruz
and that she longed to be an artist and play guitar in San Francisco, we instantaneously bonded over a passion for all songs
Californian. We sang about going to California, coming back
home to California, wearing flowers in our hair, having love in
our hearts and dancing under a sunset-pink sky. In huarache
sandals, swinging suede shoulder bags and lugging canvas duffel

bags, Cindy and I left Dead City and ensconced ourselves at my father's house for the week before college.

We tanned on my father's roof deck and shopped for records on Telegraph Avenue. My father promised us that on our last day before our college lives began, he would take us an hour north, up the coast to Petaluma to see the unveiling of *Running Fence*. "Girls," he'd told us, "it's a white fabric fence that will stretch for twenty-four miles, from the coast up into the hills. Wait till you see how magnificent it will be."

Dad had gotten to know the environmental artists Christo and Jeanne-Claude six years ago when the Berkeley museum first opened. He'd wanted them to wrap his new building, but the lack of time and money had made that impossible. Instead, after his resignation from the museum, he'd become the project director for what was to be the longest art piece in California and maybe even the world. Downstairs, hanging in the spot once occupied by the little red Rothko, was a collage by Christo, a drawing with a piece of the real fabric that would be used for *Fence*. At the bottom of the collage, a small map listed *Fence*'s statistics: It would cross fifty-nine ranch properties and fourteen roads including Freeway 101 and rise eighteen feet in the air. Starting at dawn on September 10, workers would install over two thousand panels of fabric. We were going to be there.

The night before, still in Berkeley, my father out on a date for the evening, I opened a bottle of his wine, spread pâté and Brie on crackers and Cindy and I carried this makeshift meal up through the open cavern of the house to picnic on the water bed that covered the lower roof deck off Dad's bedroom. A few years earlier the bed had been part of an art show in a gallery in San Francisco. Viewers were invited to lie on the water bed and gaze at art affixed to the ceiling. Dad said the sprawling bed was better than the art and the gallery owner gave him the bed after the exhibit ended. Huddled in the center, Cindy and I were buried under blankets, as if on a raft at sea.

Under the coverlet of dark, and with the buzz of red wine, we discussed sex. Cindy, who had been dating a wire-haired red-headed boy, confessed she regretted not having gone the "whole way yet," as if there were a finish line in sight.

"I have no regrets," I said nonchalantly, wondering if that was really the truth. I wanted to be regret-free, like my unfettered father.

"What about leaving Steve?"

Steve had been my boyfriend back in high school and the only boy I'd ever slept with. I shrugged. "I always knew I was leaving," I explained. I could hear—feel—the swish-swish as Cindy nodded her head in agreement and the responsive bed, too, gave off an echoing ripple of approval. Unlike us, Steve was never going to leave Dead City. Still, I'd pretended to love him, slipping into the emotion as if it were a new dress bought just for the season. *He didn't even know the real me*, I thought. I didn't know the real me, either, I just knew the person I wanted to become was not stuck in the Midwest.

In Illinois I lived in a houseful of women. Even our animals, four cats and a dog, were all female. The only male on the property was entombed. I loved my mother; I'd rarely fought with her growing up. I was proud of the life she'd built for herself. She was teaching, struggling to write a novel on her Greek-American childhood and she'd cofounded a literary magazine called *Story Quarterly* with two of her friends, Pam Painter and Tom Bracken. She'd even been interviewed on TV about the quarterly, so excited that on the way to the station she'd sung out the entire seventeen stanzas of the Alfred Noyes poem "The Highwayman." Still, it was a poem about a girl waiting and sacrificing her life for her lover.

The summer before, out in California, I'd caught a glimpse of the life I wanted. My dad had thrown a party for the Christos after an opening at the Oakland Museum to celebrate *the Fence that was to be*. I'd been lying on this very water bed wrapped up in the arms of an artist ten years older than me. He'd studied sculpture with Harold Paris and now he was studying painting. He had wide, solid hands and a flirtatious grin and somehow I'd ended up floating on the bed intermittently kissing him and puffing on his joint. He smelled of turpentine, he smelled of Westbeth. There were people all around us, drifting, smoking, drinking, laughing and gazing at the stars. At one point, I'd spotted my father on the deck above me. He was talking to Christo and Jeanne-Claude about the next set of court dates to gather the permits required for *Fence*. Christo kept enthusiastically calling Dad "Le Professore." Dad was aglow. Then I heard clapping, and through the crowd my father's girlfriend de jour emerged triumphantly bearing a giant cake that she'd baked in the shape of *Running Fence*. It was resplendent with green icing hills, a buttercream fence and tiny bride and groom figurines to represent Christo and Jeanne-Claude standing by the edge of a blue-food-dyed ocean. We'd sung, "Happy birthday, dear *Fence*, happy birthday to you," though it was a year off. After I returned home to Illinois, whenever I closed my eyes I could still transport myself back to that night: remembering the gentle roll of the bed beneath me, the man's strong but relaxed arms holding me, the burnt popcorn smell of pot, the sugar-sweet taste of cake and icing, the singing of off-key voices and the crackling expectation in the air.

"WHAT DO YOU think of the museum?" my father asked.

We were standing on the top tier, overlooking the huge central space. Truthfully, I'd never liked the Berkeley Art Museum, not even when I was little. It was no Frank Lloyd Wright or Le Corbusier. To me it looked like a parking garage, cold and drab gray and full of cement ramps.

My father thought it was beautiful. "So modern! Everybody wanted it built with wood, but why cut down a forest?" Then he pointed to the far wall where the Hans Hofmann paintings hung. "Come look at these."

Cindy and I impatiently trudged behind him. We were eager to get to *Fence*, to see what my father called "the moment of completion." But though we were already running late, Dad was caught up in displaying his acquisitions at his former museum.

There were still three levels of art to examine. I'd seen this museum dozens of times, and though there were pieces I loved, I didn't love the Hofmanns. But he'd been an important figure in the forties and fifties, teaching Lee Krasner, Joan Mitchell and Helen Frankenthaler, and my father had succeeded in securing a major body of his work for the museum. "See how he eliminates the unnecessary, so that only the necessary speaks." Dad quoted Hofmann while we stared at the blocks of contrasting colors. Then he spun on his heels and practically skipped down to the next level.

Following behind, Cindy and I exchanged smiles. It was hard, nearly impossible, not to be swept up in his enthusiasm. He was like a kid at a carnival. Art made him happy.

We caught up with him in front of the large Rothko, a blood-red rectangle hovering over a dark blue one. My father walked toward it, reaching out his arms as if the painting were an old friend he was greeting. In a way it was. "Ahhh," my father said with a sigh. And again, "Ahhh!"

Cindy laughed.

"Do you think Rothko eliminated too much?" I asked, thinking about how in his last majestic paintings Rothko had reduced his palette down to hushed nuances of black, before he obliterated himself.

Dad charged right past that unpleasant thought. "Well, some people have a hard time with the late paintings," he said. "They think them too austere and depressing. But my god, those last dark canvases were breathtaking!" Dad stepped back to take in the whole painting. Then slowly walked toward it again. "It was such a coup to get this one."

Finally we were finished with the museum and on our way to *Fence* in Dad's tiny blue Fiat. From the backseat Cindy asked, "Weren't you disappointed to leave the museum?"

"Well, no," my father said. "I have the time to write my books now and I'm still paid the same." He chuckled as if he'd gotten away with something. Since his contract to direct the Berkeley Art Museum had included a tenured teaching position, Dad was still gainfully employed but "less hassled." He had this trick of smoothing over any bumps in his road. He'd done this with the Rothko painting at the museum, I realized. The fact that he'd only gotten one and not the whole suite he'd hoped for was no longer a disappointment, it was an accomplishment.

He switched on the radio and spun the dial, but couldn't locate a channel that wasn't distorted by static. We were in the hills now, all golden and dry from the summer sun. Then all of a sudden he slammed on the brakes and yelled, "There it is! Look, girls, look!"

In the distance, up over the tops of the hills, patches of white were opening like sails into the wind. It looked like a fleet of ships crossing the earth toward us: *Running Fence*.

"Wow," Cindy and I said in unison. Billowing fabric rippled and caught the light. I turned to my father and said, "They're like flags scattered over the hills." He nodded and with his free hand rumpled my hair, and I leaned toward him. In that instant I was back in my childhood looking at art with him, the smell of his sweet eau de cologne mingling with the burnt, earthy odor of pipe tobacco.

"You girls are witnessing the largest piece of art in California history," he told us. "Of course, that's not the point."

"What's the point?" Cindy asked.

"That it's good," my father stated simply.

And we all smiled. I could feel goodwill flooding the car. Dad pulled the Fiat over and we watched as the fleet of white sails merged into one long, continuous, flowing ribbon. *Fence* looked like a line tracing the earth's surface.

We drove on, at one point passing through the town of Valley Ford where *Fence* ran right alongside the U.S. post office, leaving a passageway for cars, cattle and pedestrians.

We found the main crew near Highway 101, gathered around a series of posts, some agile teenagers swinging up ropes, strapped into holsters and securing cables that held the nylon fabric to the poles. Cindy and I stood under them with our heads lifted skyward. I thought, *I'd give anything to be up there, flying around in the folds.*

My photo of the *Running Fence* installation, 1976.

A film crew was making a documentary and cameras flashed. Luckily—typically—Dad had arrived just in time to answer the reporter's questions about the meaning of *Fence* and why it was so important.

"It's public art. Think of what's gone into creating it. All those permits and court battles, the money and time spent. Christo has brought us into the creation process. Christo's art isn't about working alone in a studio. He has united us by bringing us into the collaboration, like theater, like politics. This structure is impermanent, only the memories, the film and the photographs will last. It changes color. Imagine, a twenty-four-mile-long work of art! There's no need for a canvas to depict the landscape, because now the canvas has become part of the landscape. Look how it follows the hills like a caress over the earth." He moved his hands for the camera, imitating the curve of the hills as if he were touching the body of a giantess. "Can you believe it?" We watched as gusts of wind billowed and expanded the material and *Fence* undulated with life. Shadows danced and trees were silhouetted on the rippling white fabric. Dad said, "The *Fence* is meant to energize and underline the existing topography." My father looked around and asked, "Where's Christo?"

Nobody knew. He'd been spotted here and there along the fence line. Finally someone said that he had to go to court; a new injunction was being filed against *Fence* going into the ocean. "That's not good"—my father shook his head. And so we drove down to the water to see what the fuss was about. We found Christo and Jeanne-Claude standing thigh-deep in the surf. They wanted *Fence* to merge gradually into the sea, but a committee had appealed their permit, claiming that the nylon fabric might hurt the ecosystem. While everybody else was in court arguing the pros and cons, Christo was busy installing the last segments anyway. Up on the crest overlooking the scene, we couldn't hear what he was saying (Christo and Jeanne-Claude were now tiny animated figurines in the roiling blue Pacific), but it was obvious from his gesturing hands that *Fence* was going to go into the water no matter what the judge decreed. His intentions, his vision, would not be swayed. My father beamed and waved, rebel to fellow rebel. "This," Dad told us, "is an important, historic moment." Sure enough, soon the last piece unfurled and the white *Fence* slipped over the cliff and like a capsized sail, floated on top of the water, then diminished until it had slipped beneath the surface.

Later that evening we attended a party for the Christos at a collector's villa set into the hillside. The floors were tiled in copper-colored terra-cotta and hanging on the walls were several preparatory drawings of *Fence*. Stacked on a table were samples of the white woven fabric. Cindy and I each put one in our pockets.

Guests mingled around sculptures: a large abstract David Smith, a curvaceous Henry Moore, a kinetic George Rickey whose long, thin, moving steel rods reminded me of a tuning fork. My father poked one of the tiny steel arms, moving it back and forth with his finger. "Isn't it delightful?" He laughed.

My photo from our vantage point of *Fence* going into the ocean, 1976.

"Hey, what happened to your Rickey?" I'd just remembered the delicate kinetic Rickey that had sat on his coffee table. I hadn't seen it all week.

"It was small. I sold it," my father said. Before I could protest—I liked that Rickey, it *was* delightful—my father disappeared into the crowd.

When Christo and Jeanne-Claude entered, they stood back-to-back like two sides of a coin, surveying the crowd. With her thick red hair, my father called Jeanne-Claude "the fiery pragmatist to Christo's good-natured intellectual." You could tell they knew, with the unveiling of *Fence*, that they were the new art world power couple. This was years before they became identified under the single moniker *Christo*—yet they might as well have always been one person. They were both forty-one years old, born on the same day, in the same year and were so united that I'd never seen them apart. Two years earlier over Easter break, my father had taken me to visit them in their SoHo loft. I'd left the table and gotten lost on the way to the bathroom. There were so many twists and turns. Finally, I'd opened one door and discovered not the bathroom, but their fourteen-year-old son Cyril, sitting at his desk, pinning dead butterflies to cardboard. It was creepy, finding this skinny kid alone with his bugs while my sister and I, barely older than he, ate a fancy meal with the grownups at the other end of the loft. But he seemed happy to be alone, working. He looked like a mini-replica of his father, with his dark flop of hair and long narrow chin. We'd sat and talked for a while. He had tons of equipment in his room—a microscope, little tweezers—I could see that he was diligently trying to make a collage of yellow wings and emerald green scales. He told me that he wanted to be a botanist, to live in Africa and to write poetry.

Then he said that sometimes when he came back from school he'd find that his father had wrapped up a piece of furniture just to discover its hidden shape. Like his parents, Cyril, too, was enveloped in his own world. Eventually I'd left and gone back to find the grown-ups. When I later told my father about the kid in the back room he'd said that Jeanne-Claude and Christo, in true European fashion, were raising Cyril to be "truly independent."

Tonight, both Christos looked exhausted. They had just come from *Fence* and hadn't even changed their clothes, but were still wearing their blue jeans and matching windbreakers. As Cindy and I inched closer we heard Christo tell my dad that they'd just learned they'd been slapped with a $60,000 fine for installing *Fence* in the water. "No, no, Professore, it wasn't illegal," Christo insisted. "We had the permit, but it was to become effective only *after* the date *Fence* was going to be taken down." He shrugged in amused bewilderment.

Huddling with Dad, they discussed the possibility of wrapping the Reichstag in Germany, a project that had been on hold, but now, with *Fence* up, suddenly interest in it was revived. "That would be fantastic!" my father exclaimed. "What a gesture, sitting near the border between East and West Germany!" Christo nodded and Jeanne-Claude explained that both governments would have to be involved in the political and artistic process. "This piece will join the opposing sides of the world," she said.

Cindy listened, her mouth slightly agape. I could tell she was bewitched by the status of standing close to the celebrated artists of the time. The Christos were ostensibly unglamorous, they were dressed in drab work clothes—but they had a magnetic quality about them, as if they existed in their own energy field that no one could actually penetrate but everyone wanted to get near. Tonight, watching as cameras clicked and people hovered ever closer to shake their hands, and drinks and appetizers were offered, I wondered where their son Cyril was. I hadn't seen him at *Fence*, nor even, I realized now, last year at his parents' opening.

At just eighteen, I was still learning to navigate around creators and their dreams, as an observer and an occasional participant. "So this is your daughter," people often said, as if they were surprised to learn my father had offspring. Some of the artists my father knew asked if I drew or painted. Some of my father's girlfriends wanted to take me shopping, and others preferred that I wasn't around. Watching Cindy's rapt and eager expression, I felt the uncomfortable shock of recognition. *Why doesn't my father introduce us? Acknowledge we're in the room?* I caught my father giving Cindy that appraising glance of his. His eyes narrowed, he took stock of her: good listener, pretty blond girl. I wasn't sure, of course. How could I be sure of a look? Maybe he just liked Cindy. And why not? She eagerly ate up everything he said. She'd been valedictorian, and though I was a good student, my father had always said, "You can do better."

It was in this state of uncertainty that I found myself turning away from the crowd and wandering out the French doors into the garden beyond. It was a warm California night, the air heavy with the scent of lavender. Amid beds of perennials rose a marble fountain, water trickling from a carp's mouth into a glistening pool below. I sat on the lip and dangled my fingers. Over the barren honey-colored hillside the moon hung halfway up the sky. In the distance I could make out the gliding silver lifeline of *Fence*.

Four years to complete, I thought. *The time it will take me to finish college.* It seemed like an eternity.

I hadn't told Cindy the whole story about my boyfriend Steve, I'd left out the ending. Two weeks earlier, right before I'd departed for California, he'd suddenly taken off on a camping trip. I'd been surprised that he'd choose that moment to go hiking—and all the way up in Canada! But the day before I was due to leave, he'd reemerged from the wilderness and had come to say goodbye. There, in Grammar's driveway, he'd pulled a baby pine tree out of his car, told me he'd dug it up in the Canadian woods and transported it back. I was touched. Even though it was a scrawny little tree from a boy I didn't love, it was the kind of gesture that up until then I'd only read about in novels and seen in the movies. The kind of gesture an artist would make. No one had ever given me anything like it before.

And suddenly I felt I understood *Fence* and why it was so important. Not because it was big, but because, like Steve's tree, it was a simple declaration of love. Christo and Jeanne-Claude had set off on a journey, too. In the end, they'd done the same thing. They'd gone off into the unknown wilderness of their imaginations and returned with a gift, a gleaming line of light upon the earth.

"Here she is, I found her!" Cindy called. She stopped in front of me, in a bright yellow sundress with a ruffle on the bottom. "Your father's sent me to find you. He wants to introduce you around."

Behind her I could see my father standing at the French doors. He was beckoning at the threshold, that big huge wave of his stroking the air. "Come join the party," Dad called. "What are you waiting for?" From all around him, music and laughter and the clinking sound of glasses spilled forth.

Chapter 14

The University of California at Santa Cruz was a liberal school overlooking the blue waters of Monterey Bay. Founded in 1965, eight separate colleges were scattered across a mountainside covered each morning by thick fog. By midafternoon, when I emerged from my art history class, the fog had dissipated, revealing rolling green meadows and redwood forests. This idyllic setting was home to numerous professors who claimed, at least according to my father, to have fled the tyranny of the East Coast Ivy Leagues for the radical West. Santa Cruz was the sort of school that gave science credits for classes in wine tasting and women's gynecology. It was the sort of school, I discovered, where the more rebellious coeds sunbathed topless in the quad during lunch, declaring their feminist independence by baring their half-naked bodies while munching alfalfa sprout sandwiches. "Like *Le déjeuner sur l'herbe*," my father said happily when he dropped me off, referring to the painting by Manet, scandalous for its time, that depicted elegantly dressed men in top hats picnicking with naked ladies in a Paris park. "Santa Cruz," my father opined, "is a veritable paradise."

My father and I had agreed that Santa Cruz was a good choice for me, a way for us to be near each other, and yet a way for me to have an independent life while I was at college. In reality, this arrangement turned out not to be so very different from my childhood. Instead of half the continent between us, we had sixty miles. I should have been ecstatic to be in such a sumptuous and beautiful landscape—far from Dead City. But the truth was, what disturbed me most about Santa Cruz right from the start was its hippie tranquillity and isolation on a mountaintop. I wanted to be where the action was.

Down from Berkeley came my father's compelling voice: "Come on up and see your old man." I'd hop on the bus and within a matter of hours we'd be going to a round of openings and parties. I would drink scotch, my father's drink, and bum his Kent cigarettes. In November I voted in my first presidential election twice, because when my father found out that I was accidentally registered both in Berkeley *and* in Santa Cruz, he told me it was my patriotic duty to break the law for the benefit of electing a Democrat. When Jimmy Carter won, we celebrated my minor crime with champagne for breakfast.

Sometimes I attended my father's packed lectures at the Berkeley campus, where students sat enthralled by his eyewitness account of the history of art. Standing up at the podium, excitedly gesturing at the images that flashed behind him on the screen, his hair sticking out of his head as if he were plugged into an electric socket, my father seemed to be the very embodiment of the idea that the experience of art wasn't static. That it was alive, constantly changing.

In January I fell in love. His name was John Good and he was a junior, a psychology major whose parents were divorced, too. John was six feet four inches tall, had pale green eyes with long, curly eyelashes and his shirts were always too short. Within a matter of weeks I had moved into his dorm room in Beard House. We tossed out the furniture, except for a desk and chair crammed into a corner, then plundered the dorm for spare mattresses and laid them across the floor with blankets and pillows so that the whole space became a cushioned nest. It was like Westbeth all over again, funky and makeshift. Peeking in the door, our friends giggled. No one could even step inside without climbing aboard our bed.

John had other ambitions besides psychology, though he didn't realize exactly what they were then. He hadn't grown up in a world of museum-going, but he loved art and the crazy characters who produced it. He'd taken an art history course and now, with me, he was taking another.

The first time I brought John up to Berkeley he'd walked around my father's house with his mouth ajar. My father fixed us cocktails and John sipped his drink, settling into Dad's Italian couch. "This place is amazing," he said, craning his neck to look at the portraits hanging above him, Jean Arp, Willem de Kooning and Max Beckmann. Dad called them his Row of Heads, but I thought of them as his audience. In the corner, on the far side of the couch, was my favorite picture, a delicate Matisse drawing of a woman with squiggly hair whose face was turned in profile and gazing out a window. The dreamy quality of her look reminded me of my mother.

My father finished off his scotch. "It is a great house," he agreed. "It's perfect for me."

On the coffee table was my father's new book, a monograph on the artist Sam Francis, who once said he envisioned himself as a bird painting the sky. Years ago, when he was still at MoMA, my father had planned on doing a retrospective of Sam's work, but since then the idea for the show had morphed into this large coffee table art book.

"Isn't this beautiful?" My father already had a book signed and ready for me. While John and I flipped through the pages, Dad watched attentively.

As a teenager coming out to Berkeley, I'd met Sam dozens of times. He was a short, round man with a big Marlon Brando leer and the oversized personality to go with it. He'd been a pilot during World War II until a crash had landed him in the hospital, where, stuck on his stomach convalescing, he'd begun to paint. For a while, in the 1950s, Sam's abstract, lyrical paintings had fetched the highest prices in the world. He had homes in Paris, Tokyo, Switzerland and Los Angeles. In 1965 Sam had been commissioned by a Tokyo newspaper to do a "sky painting." Five helicopters had trailed colored smoke over Tokyo Bay, realizing Sam's dream to actually paint the heavens magenta, yellow and blue. That same year, in an effort to convince the woman who was to be his fourth wife to marry him, Sam rented a P-38 and flew it straight at her home like a heat-seeking missile, threatening her father that if he didn't relent and agree to their union, Sam would crash the plane into the house, killing everyone. A terrifying performance, but also a grand and beautiful way to embody his love. For Sam, art and life were as entwined as light and dark, space and matter, they defined one another. The girl's father, who happened to be one of Japan's wealthiest oil barons and Sam's biggest collector, relented.

Even by Expressionist standards, Sam was a high-flying man, indulging in drugs, wives, children, homes and airplanes. But his pictures, often large white canvases with stains of shimmering, gemlike colors, were breathtaking. As self-aggrandizing as he was, Sam could be gregarious. When I was fifteen Sam showed me how to make paper from pulp, impressing flowers and butterfly wings into the spongy surface. Now Dad told John and me that Sam was giving him a painting. "A very big painting." It was due to arrive soon and would take up the central wall of the living room.

"Your father is intoxicating," John told me after we returned to school. Though I was flattered, I was also slightly unsettled by how seduced John was, not by me, but by my father.

IN THE SPRING my mother flew out for a visit. I found her sitting on the bench outside my dorm room in Santa Cruz waiting for me to return from class. Next to her was John's father, a huge man with a face like a sheer cliff. Mom looked lovely, though out of place on our casual campus dressed in an elegant gray shift, a pink Pucci scarf and silver hoop earrings. "I don't know why I still dress up for your father," she told me when I asked about her fancy outfit.

"You saw Dad?"

"He made me lunch. He wanted me to see his house and meet his new girl. So I thought, *I'll show her.*"

John's father chuckled. "Oh, you women."

"I can't believe you said that, Mom! I like Catherine." Catherine had recently moved in with my father. She had dimples and a hearty laugh and was the first girlfriend of his I'd liked in years. When she wasn't cooking or talking politics, she read novels. She'd introduced me to the works of Nancy Mitford, whose eccentric characters, Catherine said, lived in a world of superlatives, like my father.

"Catherine wasn't there." My mother gave me a mollified smile and pulled her big Jackie O sunglasses over her eyes.

Beside her Mr. Good said, "I have a lot of girlfriends, too. I'm strong, like an ox." I couldn't tell if he was flirting with my mother or me or both of us.

Now that my sister and I were both attending college—Tanya was a freshman, too, having taken a year off before she enrolled in a state school in Illinois—my mother was finally free to do what she wanted. And what had she done, but come in search of our father. Perhaps he had encouraged her to visit. He was prone to encouraging women. He'd recommended and booked her hotel room in San Francisco and invited her to his house. Catherine had been conveniently absent when he'd picked her up at the Bart station and driven her up the hill:

Pete meets me in his black turtle-neck, flat black gondolier's hat clamped on his head, wearing the Nigerian coin necklace I'd once given him around his neck, curly long white sideburns and white halo of hair. "How do I look?" Pete asks me.

"Like a good-natured vicar. Are you happy?"

"They keep moving in with me. I can't help it." He pounds the steering wheel. Then he sighs . . . All afternoon he lies beside me smiling and sighing. Watch out girlie!

When I was little and my parents reunited, I never thought beyond the fact that they were getting back together to be *parents*. I didn't consider the "lover" aspect. In particular, I never thought of my mother as a sexual being, though she'd had plenty of boyfriends. But now that I was in love and sleeping every night with John, I recognized that warm glow in my mother's cheeks. I noticed the relaxed way she tossed her head back and smiled at the setting sun. It irritated me in the same way that John's adoration of my father rankled me.

"You're too territorial of your father," John diagnosed. "Because he left you."

Regardless of my mother's visit, my father continued to live with the vivacious Catherine. That summer they went to Europe and John and I stayed in the house, John ensconcing himself at my father's desk to work on his thesis. When they returned, the Sam Francis painting arrived and Dad hung it in the place of honor. Sam hadn't known what to name the painting, but after seeing the white-as-snow center with all the colors shifted to the corners, Dad suggested, *Iris*. "Like an eye"—my father pointed at his own pupil. "But also for the Greek goddess Iris who descended from the heavens on a rainbow." Dad pointed toward the skylight in the ceiling. Sam thought the title perfect. Rainbows painted the sky, and like an artist, the goddess Iris was a messenger. She traveled as fast as the rushing wind, streaming a multihued communication behind her as she linked heaven and earth. Sometimes Dad invited students over to the house and projected art slides onto the big white surface in the center of *Iris*, a layer cake of art on top of art.

In the fall of my sophomore year John and I moved off-campus into an apartment and enrolled in a modern art history lecture together. Sitting in the dark theater with the slide projector whirring, the slides blazing to life in front of us, I couldn't help but blurt out the names of the artists and paintings to John, as I had done with my father when I was little. At the front of the hall, our exasperated art history professor would clear her throat and say, "Gaby, this is my class."

On weekends I was still drawn north toward my father's life, frequently going for visits to Berkeley alone. I'd developed a crush on one of my father's students. He was eight years older than me, smoked French cigarettes and drove an Alfa Romeo. I didn't tell John that I was going to Berkeley in the hopes of running into this man, so John just thought I wanted to keep my father to myself. Perhaps I did. Between John and me, a certain discord started to grow.

On a Friday evening in the fall of 1977, a little over a year after I'd moved to the West Coast, nine months after Catherine had moved in, I walked into my father's house and noticed something was amiss. Catherine was slamming pots and pans around the kitchen and my father, head hanging between his shoulders, had a chastised-dog, please-stop-making-a-scene frown on his face. As soon as he saw me he hustled me out of the kitchen, then grabbed me in a big hug. I loved his fierce bear hugs, those few minutes when I felt like the most important person in his world. "I'm having an affair," he whispered. "I'm going to take you to meet her after dinner. Don't tell Catherine." He released me.

I was stunned. Not by the news, but by a tingling thrill of conspiracy I felt as my father invited me into his private world. His eyes sparkled as his arm reached out and enveloped me again.

By the time Catherine strode into the dining room, my father and I were seated quietly at the table. Thumping a bowl of fettuccine between us, she let out a loud sob and ran for the stairs.

Above our heads we could hear Catherine rummaging around

in the closet of the spare bedroom. "Do you think she forgot the sauce?" Dad asked earnestly.

I glanced into the bowl. No butter, no cheese, no vegetables, not even salt. "I think this is it. What's going on up there?"

"Shhhh." He put his finger to his lips and we both listened as Catherine tore through the closet. I wondered what I should do. Eat, stay with my father or flee. A few minutes later, Catherine reappeared wearing a brilliant fuchsia and green kimono. She was partial to long gowns with exotic sleeves. Her face was red. In one hand she held a glass of wine, in the other a small vial.

Placing both the wineglass and the vial on the table, Catherine said, "White food is good for depression. Mashed potatoes, pasta, oatmeal. It's soothing and good for the nerves."

I twirled strands of pasta around on my fork. This wasn't going to end well for Catherine. Still, she was plucky. She was making a stand and my heart went out to her. "Rice pudding, vanilla ice cream, warm milk," I chimed in.

"What's that?" My father pointed to the glass vial in front of Catherine. It was emblazoned with a single word, RUSH, and a lightning bolt.

"It's what they do in the discos," Catherine said, "to keep dancing. You inhale it. Watch. It's fun!" She held the bottle up to her nose, titled her head back and snorted.

I'd seen all sorts of crazy events around my father's table, naked people, people smoking pot, but no one had ever done an inhalant in the middle of dinner before. "Oh, please," Dad moaned. And to me, "I'm sorry you have to see this."

Me, too, I wanted to say. And, *Poor Catherine*, though after her snort, she seemed in a much better place. Her face turned beet-red, and she began laughing. Then she bolted up, and again fled for the stairs.

Later that night my father told Catherine we were off to the movies, father and daughter. In the car I noticed that he was freshly shaved, his sideburns defined at crisp angles along his jawline, his cheeks smelling of eau de cologne. "How's John?" he asked.

"Fine."

He nodded, patting my knee. "People like us need stimulation," he said.

And again, that jump, like an electric shock. Had my father guessed about my secret crush on his student? Had he sensed my need to escape living with someone, too? In Santa Cruz, John and I now shared an apartment far larger than the little mattress-covered dorm room. Why, then, did it feel so cramped? Maybe I was like my father. The thought hovered, a scary and enticing possibility.

At the top of Grizzly Peak, my father pulled the car over. We were on a crest, teetering high above Berkeley. The view made me giddy. In the distance the city lights sparkled. San Francisco glowed like an emerald ready to be plucked from the bay.

"Come on in and meet Deirdre." My father trotted off through a bed of glossy ivy, up a staircase made from recycled tire treads.

Deirdre was in her early thirties, as thin-hipped as a preteen girl, with no waist and high, large breasts under a tight V-necked sweater. A dome of strawberry-red waves framed her heart-shaped face. Into these red waves my father immediately buried his big gray head. "Peeeter," she said drawing out his name in an exaggerated style. "You've brought your daughter. So I'll set an extra place. I've made sushi!"

"Thanks," I said, "but I've already eaten."

"Nonsense." My father pushed me into the house, over toward a coffee table that was set with two bamboo place mats and an assortment of small china dishes. "Sushi sounds good!" As soon as Deirdre bustled from the room to get my place mat, he said. "Try and eat some." Then, louder, he called out, "Deirdre, where's Brad?"

"He's with his father for the weekend," came Deirdre's response.

Brad? My father was dating a woman with a child? A new girlfriend was one thing, they were always nice in the beginning, but making friends with their bratty or sullen or, worst of all, exceptionally brilliant kid was not something I looked forward to.

I flounced down on the couch just as Deirdre came back with a large plate of sliced raw tuna and an extra place mat. Leaning over my father, she ran her hands over the armchair he was sitting in. "I just finished it this afternoon. Like it?"

It was upholstered in denim and embroidered with a series of curving black lines like the waves of a Japanese landscape. In fact, all of Deirdre's pillows and seat covers, even the lampshade, were decorated with intricate embroidery. The room felt as claustrophobic as a cobweb.

Popping a slice of fish into his mouth, my father swallowed. "It's a veritable arts-and-crafts piece," he announced.

Deirdre was obviously a "crafty" woman with a talent for making things. My father had dated a few—a macramé artist and a ceramicist who'd embedded imprints of her tits in the bottom of coffee mugs. At least Catherine hadn't made kitschy crafts. "Real art is not utilitarian!" Catherine had said.

"Have you told Gaby yet?" Deirdre asked as she poured each of us a thimble of tea.

I raised my eyebrows at my father, but I already knew what he was going to say.

"Deirdre and I are getting married!"

And Deirdre, setting her teapot down, leaned across the coffee table and pressed my father's cheeks between her manicured fingers and kissed him.

Later in the car I asked, "Why her?"

"Oh, she's lovely!"

I shook my head. I wanted to tell him this was the most ridiculous thing he'd ever done, but it probably wasn't. "Why do you have to *marry* her, though?"

"She has a young son, Brad, and she doesn't want to just live together." After a moment he added, "We have the same timing; we like to get up early and go to bed early; we run on the same clock."

What could I say? *You are a crazy fool flying your kamikaze plane into someone's home?* As we pulled into his driveway he looked so elated, his face round and satisfied, as lit up as the full moon that had risen and now hung over the house. I couldn't help but hope for the best.

We found Catherine waiting up, a book open in her lap, a wineglass at her feet, sitting under *Iris.* She looked small and vulnerable beneath all that white space, as if the painting were about to swallow her up.

My father had explained to me that the point of Sam's white voids was "*ma,*" a Japanese word for a gap or a pause, and that by pushing all color to the side, Sam was trying to create blanks not full of empty space, but of consciousness. That white space, Dad said, was heavy with possibility.

Well, tonight Catherine certainly looked pretty weighed down. Her face flushed with wine, grief and maybe a little more RUSH. I wanted to jump into the white void behind her.

I couldn't face either Catherine's heartbroken gaze or my father's deft evasions. While Dad pulled up his Barcelona chair and leaned over to see what Catherine was reading—Anthony Trollope—I fled upstairs to the spare bedroom. The air was fragrant with the scent of Catherine's spicy perfume, which clung to her long silk gowns and seeped from her closet door. Within a few minutes, I'd found the bottle of RUSH in the top drawer under her

Iris

Sam Francis, 1965/67

pink bra. There was that telltale lightning bolt and in tiny script the words *Amyl Nitrate Liquid Incense*. Just a whiff, I thought, and inhaled. I felt a surge as I collapsed on the coverlet and the room expanded above me. My heart pumped behind my eyeballs. The air liquefied into an unblended mass of water and oil, color exploded at the periphery of my vision, then seeped toward the center. For five seconds or five minutes a herd of antelopes stampeded by the bed. The rush was over very fast, subsiding first into waves and then into ripples as the room again congealed.

In the morning when I came downstairs I stood in front of *Iris*. Like my father, Sam had been an absentee parent who, in an effort to make his presence felt, had also taken his daughter on his escapades, though they had gone to the Moulin Rouge in Paris, not the hills of North Berkeley. He'd introduced his young daughter to pot when she'd been thirteen. Dad hadn't introduced me to pot, he'd just let me smoke it at his parties, claiming marijuana was harmless, like giving your child a sip of wine at the dinner table. I was a little envious of Sam's daughter. Apparently she was wildly sophisticated, a half-Asian beauty gallivanting around the world instead of attending a boring college on the top of a mountain.

Once Sam had actually painted a whole mountainside of snow. (For what is snow but crystallized sky fallen to earth?) He hired a group of professional skiers to zip down the slopes at a resort in Japan while projecting colored paint from canisters. He'd used the same color palette as he had in *Iris*. Brilliant swirls of vermillion-red, midnight-blue and citrine-yellow that had settled on the pristine canvas of the mountain. Like my grandfather Eugen Selz, who'd once placed a peach on a slope as a declaration of love, Sam Francis, too, had left the mark of his passion in the

Ski Painting
Sam Francis, 1967

snow. In the early seventies Sam suggested a proposal to NASA to send jets of ionized colored compounds up in rockets to paint outer space, but adequate funds were never raised. I couldn't image what colored paint would look like out in the emptiness of space. Would it shower down on some distant planet like multihued raindrops, freeze into crystals or gather in dust clouds of color? Sam was oversized in every sense of the word. Looking at *Iris* now, I decided Sam's work was safer when contained on a flat canvas.

Chapter 15

Within a few weeks of my father's split from Catherine, Deirdre and her son Brad moved into Regal House and I cheated on my boyfriend John with my father's student. He was dark-eyed and witty and knew about art and literature. He gave me books to read by André Breton and Baudelaire and he scrawled a list of must-see films on a paper napkin, with the Spanish Surrealist Luis Buñuel's *Un Chien Andalou* at the top. He bit my lower lip when he kissed me, and talked about the pagan Pre-Raphaelites and the intellectual carnality in Marcel Duchamp.

It was heady and sexy, but down in Santa Cruz I was living with John. Confused by my own lies, by my own secrets, I grew distant from John, with his goofy smile and too-small clothes. At first John interpreted my behavior as mysterious. I was perpetually running late. I wore silk blouses and pencil skirts now instead of peasant dresses and clogs. I peppered my sentences with superfluous phrases like *au currant* and *de rigueur.* I knew I was cheating, but I thought that made me sophisticated, a desirable woman of the world. I hated myself, but this new person emerging from under my own skin also thrilled me. Who was she and what would she do next? My father, who suspected I was sleeping with his student, kept telling me that being faithful was provincial. He seemed intrigued by my relationship. Once, this student reported to me, my father had asked him, "What's my daughter like?"

I wondered uneasily how my father meant that question: What was I like as a person or as a lover? And were they in fact separate identities? For my father, it didn't seem like they were.

In Santa Cruz our art history professor gave us the assignment to "get out of the lecture hall and write about real paintings instead of slides." I wanted to write about Richard Diebenkorn, who was about to open with a retrospective at the Oakland Museum. Diebenkorn had been a West Coast painter in 1959 doing figurative work when my father had put him in his *New Images of Man* show at MoMA. In the sixties he'd moved into Sam Francis's old studio in Santa Monica and abandoned the figure, focusing instead on the background, the landscape behind the form. He'd begun the *Ocean Park* series, which he'd named after the neighborhood outside his door. Some 145 paintings, all flat and geometrical, with an aerial perspective—though not focused on the sky as Sam Francis's were, but on the ground below—and bisected by intricately veined lines that Diebenkorn had erased and repainted again and again. Ghost strokes from earlier images still showed, a residue of impulses recorded in paint.

When I mentioned to my father that I was writing my paper on Diebenkorn, he said, "He's magnificent. He's so relentless in his willingness to show on canvas his mistakes along the way."

He invited me up to the opening. John, asking to come with me, said, "Don't be afraid I'll steal your father's attention." My fear was only that my two lives would collide.

The show covered three levels of the sprawling Oakland Museum. On the walls, Diebenkorn's barren vistas opened up, the colors reminiscent of Matisse or Bonnard, but without the jazz and decorations.

Together, John and I moved through the packed rooms, clinking against each other like ice cubes in a narrow glass. My father was there, enthusiastically introducing Deirdre around. I drank too much and my body darted away from my head. Disentangling from John, I ran over to say hello to my crush. John, following behind me, reached out a long possessive arm and pulled me in under the shelter of his shoulder. He gave me a hard squeeze. My father, standing near us with Deirdre, chuckled with approval.

The next morning I woke up blurry and hung over. John was gone and my father told me that he'd just received a call that a Diebenkorn painting had been stolen from the Oakland Museum sometime during the opening.

By midday the stolen painting had been returned. A confessed prank by an art student who'd slipped the small still life under his coat on a dare. He'd wanted to "spoof" all the people around him who said that since it was an early example of representation, it was an unattractive painting and wouldn't be missed. "He just walked off with it?" my father asked, baffled. "In plain sight?"

Apparently I hadn't been the only one doing something stupid right in plain sight.

That afternoon, alone in my father's house, I sat on a beat-up old black leather beanbag chair, a relic from the sixties that none of my father's girlfriends or wives had succeeded in convincing him to part with, and worked on my Diebenkorn paper. Whenever I shifted, the beanbag chair coughed up little white pellets where the seams had split. I'd chosen to write on a painting titled *Woman in a Window* (1957): an earlier semi-figurative work, done ten years before Diebenkorn began the *Ocean Park* series. In *Woman in a Window*, the figure was still central to the picture: a girl sat in profile to the viewer, her head in her hands, deep in thought. It was a painting of simple, vivid forms, with the red triangular shape of the girl against geometric planes of mustard-yellow, pale and dark blues. When I'd seen the painting last night, I'd thought it was luminous. The girl's solid but simple shape held two worlds together, the abstract world of color and the figurative world of form. She was the painting's focal point, her red intensity its locus. But now, thinking about the later *Ocean Park* paintings, I wondered if perhaps they hadn't abandoned the figure entirely. Maybe the point Diebenkorn was making in his later work was that the figure hadn't vanished, it had just moved outside the frame. Like Rothko, Diebenkorn had been influenced by the colors of Matisse, but where Rothko had gone into the picture and toward the color, eventually removing everything (the furniture, the decorations, the people, even the lines) until only color was left, Diebenkorn went in the opposite direction. He'd retreated above the surface of his paintings so that the viewer felt like a detached spectator flying over a distant landscape. I knew in my heart I felt closer to Rothko, closer to even the earlier Diebenkorns. I didn't want to be far above art, only a witness to a painting. I wanted painting to overwhelm me. I wanted to get inside it.

Back in Santa Cruz, John said he knew the truth about my affair. "It was just the one time," I pleaded. We broke up, got back

Woman in a Window
Richard Diebenkorn, 1957. Oil on canvas, 59 × 56
(149.9 × 142.2 cm), Estate #1225.

together, fought more and broke up again. Sometimes when we made up we had angry sex that felt both passionate and like a fight at the same time. Once John threw an entire bowl of apples at me, across the room, without hitting me, though I know he had perfect aim. Then we made love on the floor, both of us crying, amid the sweetly fragrant, mushed apple pulp. Eventually we broke up for good.

My father said, by way of consolation, "Better to leave them before they leave you."

But I hadn't left John; we'd left each other.

I was juggling not just places and boys, but my father's women.

Over one weekend, while my father was out of town, I met first with Catherine and then with Deirdre. Catherine and I arranged to meet for lunch at the Washington Square Bar and Grill in San Francisco. I'd called her because I missed her. She knew everyone there, the waiter, the maître d', all the city politicos and the bartender who let me sip white wine even though I was two years under the legal drinking age.

We talked about whether I should change my major to English literature; we talked about my favorite book, which at that moment was *A Portrait of a Lady*. Finally Catherine rested her chin in her hands and asked, "How's your father? I heard he's getting married."

"He's ridiculous that way."

"He wouldn't marry me." Her green eyes flashed.

"You're so lucky!" I laughed.

Catherine only swirled the wine in her glass and said thoughtfully, "You know, people warned me about your father; even one of his old girlfriends warned me." When I didn't answer, when I just nodded my head wisely, sympathetically, Catherine brightened and her dimple showed. "But let's talk about you."

By the time I headed for home I was drunk. Intoxicated not just with wine, but my newfound power as the holder of confidences. Skipping through the streets of San Francisco, I was the giddy girl in the middle, the keeper of secrets, the guardian at my father's gate.

A day later, Deirdre and I had lunch at a dark restaurant on the Berkeley side of the bay. It was the kind of place with concealing leather booths and swivel chairs at the bar, where middle-aged men met their mistresses for a martini in the afternoon. On that day it was all but empty.

Deirdre and I scrunched down into a booth and watched the waves crash into the rocks and disappear. She was eager to meet Tanya, she said. And maybe next summer we could all go to Disneyland together. Brad had never been to the Magic Kingdom.

"We did Disneyland with Nora," I said, remembering my father bellowing: "Look at the awful *kitsch*!" I was into my second scotch and feeling pretty risky. "Deirdre, don't marry him."

"What? Why not?"

A look flew across Deirdre's face that encompassed surprise and recognition and everything in between. It was the same look I had seen on my mother's face on the airplane back from California after her failed reunion with my father. "I knew we shouldn't have had kids together. I just knew it in my bones." Then my mother had smiled at me, hugged me and added, "But then we wouldn't have had you or Tanya."

"I don't know. I just know," I said into my scotch.

Deirdre brushed a piece of lint from her sweater. "Well, silly you," she said. "You don't need to worry. We're all going to have a lot of fun."

She meant it, too. She wanted us to become best friends . . . sisters. She offered to teach me to sew. It was a project we never had the time to embark on, although one afternoon a few months later, while my father was sleeping, she did teach me how to drive stick shift. We practiced in her maroon Honda Accord. It was no easy trick, driving stick up those steep hills in North Berkeley. Deirdre liked to lend me her clothes and to buy us matching outfits: knee-high black leather boots, sea-green silk blouses and red berets. Even then I understood that in her desire to cast me as her younger sister she hoped that I might solidify her marriage to my father. But she seemed sincere. She was a sweet woman, as nice as John, but maybe a little boring. I halfway understood why my father was marrying her. There was something uncomplicated about Deirdre. She wasn't a wild Irish lass like Catherine, nor was she one of Dad's crazy artist girlfriends who cast their body parts in bronze and clay, nor was Deirdre remotely like my mother, envious, unable to compete and still trying to step into the sphere of her own importance. Deirdre merely adored my dad.

In the dark restaurant, that windy afternoon with the waves hitting the shore, Deirdre told me not to worry. "Your father's just a sweet, big baby. I can take care of him."

Chapter 16

Unrolling a piece of paper from his typewriter, my father cleared his throat and called out, "Listen to this." I lifted my head from the couch where I was reading *The Awakening*. Earlier that week, I'd come up from school and moved back into my father's house with the "new family" for the summer. A few feet away, Brad, Deirdre's son, was rearranging the parts of his bionic doll—a miniature replica of the character Lee Majors played in the TV series *The Six Million Dollar Man*—trying to play quietly in my father's loftlike open space. One level down, Deirdre was in the kitchen, busy ripping up the black-and-white linoleum kitchen floor and replacing it with terra-cotta tiles. Married to my father six months now, Deirdre was putting her stamp on his house. Even though I wasn't fond of Deirdre's decorating style—those embroidered throw pillows!—I had to give her credit for her industry. That morning she'd mixed and poured her own cement.

Hearing Dad's voice, Deirdre bounded up the stairs. Tanya

had recently pointed out to me over the telephone, "She's only ten years older than me."

Dad began to read from his manuscript. *"If one general statement can be made about the art of our times, it is that one by one the old criteria of what a work of art ought to be have been discarded in favor of a dynamic approach in which everything is possible."* Dad looked up, "That's very good, don't you think?"

"Wonderful, Peter," Deirdre agreed.

"Yeah," Brad echoed. Poor Brad, he was only nine, his body still as soft as a pillow. He didn't know what to make of my father, this professor with flying white hair and a booming voice who didn't like the boy's choice in TV shows—*The Incredible Hulk*, *The Bionic Woman*—and who sat all day in the middle of his house like the Wizard of Oz making stern proclamations: If Brad wanted to learn about Superman he should read Nietzsche.

My father cocked an eyebrow in my direction. "You want me to show you some pictures?"

What I wanted was to finish my book. I had just gotten to the part where the protagonist, Edna, decides to drown herself in the sea in an effort to liberate herself from the restrictions of her gender. But reading was now impossible.

The house was a hive of activity, students and research assistants in and out every day. Dad was working on two books simultaneously: *Art in Our Times*, his magnum opus history of art book that would span the twentieth century, and *Theories and Documents of Contemporary Art: A Source Book of Artists' Writings*, which he was coauthoring with a former student, Kristine Stiles. This was the third volume of *Theories*, an encyclopedic anthology of the writing and statements by artists, a mammoth undertaking that would take a decade to complete. Dad was excited because both books would be sold as textbooks—"Where the money is," he said. My father had been planning these books for years. He saw the study of art as a three-tiered enterprise consisting of pictures, documents and interpretation. So while *Theories and Documents* was a compilation of the artists' own words and quotes, *Art in Our Times* was pictorial. It would include over sixteen hundred illustrations arranged by decade in what my father called *a revolutionary format that relates the arts to the social and political worlds from which they spring and on which, in turn, they comment*. There were sections on bridges, churches, visionary designs, landscapes, heads, collages, films, erotica renderings, nudes and more. Right now his desk was littered with pictures of still lifes from the 1940s. He held up Picasso's *Skull and Jug*. "Look how somber and simple. This was painted during the German occupation when Picasso's friends were being killed."

I picked up the transparency. The skull and jug sat side by side on a table. "It's a man and a woman." I handed it back to my father. "The skull head is male, the curvy jug is the female form."

"That's very good." He beamed. "What do you think of this painting? It's by Paul Klee, *The Last Still Life*, same period."

I looked at the green teapot and the strange organic shapes placed all around it. I wanted to think of something smart to say, but nothing came to mind.

My father jumped in. "These are flowers." He indicated the middle section. "This is the angel of death. It's an allegory. The angel represents the eternal nature of history which wrestles with the objects—Klee's transient present, the teapot from his breakfast, a vase of flowers—on the table of life."

"Who wins?"

My father laughed. "It's a very unstill picture. Klee wasn't breaking up the space like the Cubists, or filling it with vivid patterns like Matisse, he used this format to comment on the struggle between motion and inertia, the tussle of life." Together my father and I bent our heads and gazed at the images Klee had chosen to place on the black surface of his table: a small sun disappearing into the top corner, a large moon rising in the center, a vase of flowers spilling over, at the very bottom an angel of death battling with life to carry a cross offstage.

Then my father added thoughtfully, "I suppose history always wins."

Years later I read that when Paul Klee created this final still life he was dying of scleroderma. As he'd painted, his tissues were turning to stone, his body becoming as hard as a piece of statuary, stilling into art.

Dad at work.

That day, standing next to my father, I'd flipped through the images for *Art in Our Times*. "You have a lot of portraits of women, but where are the women artists?" I'd asked.

"There are some," my father had said. "More toward the end of the book. I can't help history."

I found a summer job working at the Floating Museum for one of my father's old girlfriends, an artist named Lynn Hershman (Leeson). I was learning that the art world, at least our corner of it, was a nest full of my father's former flames. One of my art history professors had had an affair with my father while he'd been married to my mother. Lynn was soft-spoken and brilliant. Her hesitant way of speaking masked a forceful personality. She wasn't afraid of creating a life and occupying its center. The Floating Museum was Lynn's idea. A museum without walls where, for a brief two months, performances and exhibitions sprang up all over San Francisco. Or, as Lynn said, hands flapping, "Outside." The idea was art could exist anywhere.

By the late 1970s, the physical boundary between the artist and the viewer had disappeared. That boundary point had, once upon a time, been obvious. The art object was a painting in a frame or a sculpture on a pedestal. But once the barrier between painting and sculpture had been broken down—Robert Rauschenberg's *Combines* in the 1959s were messy, often vertical and horizontal at the same time, fearless and breathtaking in their simultaneous embrace of painting, sculpture and collage—it had become wildly important for artists to question not just the making of objects, but the threshold between themselves and their viewers. They referred to this boundary as "the fourth wall." They wanted to find another dimension for art to exist in, one that ran like a direct conduit from their imagination to the audience's. Art was no longer just in galleries and museums, it was on the streets, in store windows, out in the desert, in the middle of a lake, running across the hills, melting into the snow and up in the sky. Robert Smithson created *Spiral Jetty*, a monumental landmass formed by hauling 6,550 tons of rocks, dirt and salt crystal into the middle of the Great Salt Lake, and Christo briefly transformed even the public space we all moved in.

But these large-scale structures were usually more the domain of male artists, who liked moving tons of earth around with bulldozers and tended to create big happenings that involved orchestrations of vast numbers of people. In the late seventies a lot of women artists made, or at least showed, much more auto-biographical work. Influenced by feminism, they were claim-ing their bodies as an arena in which to practice art. I saw this at school, too, how the feminists at Santa Cruz, while seeking equality, also sought differentiation, sometimes even the exclu-sion of men. Those half-naked girls lying on the grass in the college quad baring their breasts were establishing ownership of their bodies. Lynn told me that feminism had "raised con-sciousness" and one of the elements women artists were now conscious of was that the subjects of their lives, often the banality of their daily existence, wasn't represented in a male-dominated art world. Taking me under her wing, ushering me through the city by her side, Lynn warned, "You have to find a way to hear yourself." I knew she was implying that I do this not just against the backdrop of this male art world, but specifically against the backdrop of my father.

Lynn herself dressed up in a blond wig and became a work of art, an assumed character named *Roberta Breitmore*. *Roberta* was a performance piece that Lynn had started in 1973. This alter ego of

Lynn's existed for five years. Real things happened to *Roberta*. She rode the bus and saw a therapist. She even had a driver's license. She attended Weight Watchers meetings and checked into the Dante Hotel in North Beach where visitors came in and saw the trail she'd left behind, the empty glass by the bedside table that had *Roberta*'s lipstick marks on the rim. Sometimes Lynn lived as Lynn, and sometimes she was *Roberta* in her blond wig and a red polka-dot dress and very specifically applied makeup. This was what performance art was all about: the membrane between art object and reality thinning. Between the thought and the final object, there was the performance of the act. These artists wanted the audience to be there with them in the moment of creation. That was what they were trying to capture, that split second in which their art came into being. It was the same moment that scientists searched for when they talked about the Big Bang. Before that, time itself was at a standstill. Then came the singular moment when all the mass in the universe began to expand into being. A painting or an object already possessed a certain form, but an artist embarking on a performance was stepping into a space still full of possibility. These artists were seeking moments that embodied the origin of creativity: a first breath, a first word. To perform a piece of art was to inhabit this instant of birth, to incarnate expression.

It was my job to ferry Lynn's visiting artists around the city to and from their impromptu performances. I drove around a band of European artists who spoke broken English and only wanted to check out where to buy cheap sound equipment in San Francisco. I escorted a woman from Los Angeles who gave me a long soliloquy about why she was thinking of changing her name to an astrological formation. One artist sailed three beautiful straw pyramids on barges down the bay. Another, Suzanne Lacy, a feminist artist in her early thirties, dressed up as *The Bag Lady* and exhibited the garbage she collected.

Quite rapidly these artists realized they needed documentation for their actual performances. Photography, video, film were the means they began to employ to record and later sell their work. Lynn was embracing all this technology and displaying it under the banner of the Floating Museum. It was there where I first saw an exhibition that included an image by a young photographer named Cindy Sherman.

Sherman had just started taking self-portraits dressed up as a 1950s B-film starlet. These pseudo-film-stills shot against black-and-white city backdrops looked both haunted and naïve. She was twenty-four, a year out of the University at Buffalo. She'd only been studying art for four years and picked up her camera just two years earlier. But she'd always loved dress-up. At college she'd decked herself out as Lucille Ball and then went about her own life. People, she said, were entertained but confused and she liked provoking that mix of emotions. At some point she'd made the choice not to transform into a famous, recognizable person, but into her own creations. I had never seen anything like the odd way that Sherman transmuted, with a little makeup and some tricky camera angles, into a fictitious person, the archetype of the teenage girl or the heroine of a B-movie. But Sherman's work was not about the performance, not about what her character did in the real world. Instead, she'd jumped right past performance to a finished product: a photographic record of a moment that never existed. I went back again and again to

Untitled Film Still #21
Cindy Sherman, 1977

look at the picture. In her still photograph she linked a shared cultural memory bank (that ingénue B-starlet we thought we recognized) with her own re-creation. You couldn't tell where memory ended and imagination began. Influenced by Diane Arbus, who'd documented "flawed" people, Sherman was casting herself as peripheral character. Inserting herself in history, she was a chameleon, giving herself not just one additional life, but two, three, four, a hundred lives.

Many of the performances during the summer of the Floating Museum weren't very good: artists playing snare drums in museum courtyards, dressing up as hobos and muttering, sitting in circles and stating how little they knew about the world. The artists would bring props in a paper bag—a mop, a wad of rags, a ball of yarn—like a child toting a favorite toy to a birthday party. The sparse audience gathered in a semicircle and the artist placed the object on the ground, recited some words, eerie music might play to signify the importance of what we were witnessing. Sometimes the artists were deliberately silent, letting their bodies speak. Sometimes they were naked and usually moving in excruciatingly slow motion. I'd watch impatiently for the next twitch of a big toe, the nod of a head. They were expressing the spontaneity they felt in the moment, they were finding themselves, pinpointing the triviality of all our existence within a complex universe. But a lot of it was silly antics or, worse, boring.

One afternoon I watched a muscular artist I had a crush on because of his bulging deltoids shoot an arrow through a row of Plexiglas slabs in the rotunda of the San Francisco Museum of Modern Art. The piece felt more like a staged circus act than art, but I hung around and introduced the guy to my father, who was there for the event. After my father excused himself, the performer turned to me and said, "Why didn't you tell me your father was Peter Selz? I would have asked you out."

"What do you mean?" I stammered, backing away. I shouldn't have been surprised. I had used my status with my father's girlfriends, withholding and delivering information as I chose. I'd had that affair with one of my dad's students. But this artist had been so direct that I wondered if that was all I was, an access to my father. I walked away feeling like one of Lynn's erased women, or a marginal character of Sherman's with only a minor role to play.

Still, even after that encounter I liked being part of all the activity. I liked being in the driver's seat with my kooky charges en route to some artistic event. Maybe I wasn't ushering around the next great artist, but I was on the scene and part of the mix. Deirdre and my father would often show up at one or another of the performances and then we'd all carry our wine in plastic cups through the pearlescent light of a San Francisco evening, off to more openings and eventually to a dinner in Chinatown or North Beach.

At the end of summer, right before I returned to school, I flew to the Midwest to drive cross-country with my sister. With Deirdre's encouragement Tanya was transferring to San Francisco State to finish college. "She's so nice," Tanya said. Our mother looked dubious: nice was not a trait my father valued. But she wanted Deirdre to embrace us. She was off to Columbia, Missouri, to take a one-year teaching position at the University of Missouri. After that, she didn't know. She hoped her novel would be published. "It's my lifeline," she said. I knew she was scared. Spreading her wings and leaving the nest was something my mother did in fits and starts.

IF I HAD been introduced and charmed by performance art in the summer of 1978, the following summer I became acquainted with its seamier underbelly. By then I'd declared my major in art history, though I still couldn't focus on staying in one place. Santa Cruz, Berkeley, I ricocheted between them, unable to remain in either for long.

My father and Deirdre had flown to Europe, leaving Brad behind with his own father. Tanya had moved to Haight-Ashbury and sometimes we met at the coffee shop where Tanya operated the espresso machine and fretted about Brad. He was downright resentful of our father and had been caught stealing a bottle of rose perfume for his mother at the local pharmacy.

"At least he's not being dumped in a Kinderheim," I said.

"Don't even mention that word," Tanya barked.

In Europe Dad was curating a show, *Two Decades of American Painting, 1920–1940*, that was opening in Dusseldorf, then traveling to Zurich and finally to Brussels. According to my father, Europeans were unaware that America had produced any art before Abstract Expressionism. Dad wanted to remedy this ignorance. "You'll be happy to know your old dad included the work of women artists in his show, Georgia O'Keeffe and Florine Stettheimer!" he'd told me proudly before he left.

I moved up to Berkeley for the summer, enrolling in a film studies class at the university, and found a room in a student co-op. While he was away my father had rented his house. Tanya believed that he'd done this because he needed extra cash. "Can't you tell he's getting ready for another divorce?" she said.

With a sinking feeling I realized she was right. There was nothing to do but wait for another family to fall apart.

I'd run through most of my allotted college money for the year and I found a part-time summer job working in a small, no-name art gallery that is now defunct. I sat behind a pristine desk waiting for someone to enter the gallery, but no one ever showed up except, eventually, Dale. He was a short man with a Burt Reynolds mustache and a belief in himself I'd only ever encountered before in the form of my father. We started dating. Dale pretended to be in the import-export business selling Turkish rugs and gold jewelry, but he was actually a drug dealer. He did collect underground comic book art. Eager to be where the action was, and to fill the void of my father's absence, I fell under Dale's spell. Most nights and quite a few days I escaped into Dale's world. Dale sold "happy dust"—cocaine—to the art crowd. Sitting on a bed covered with an embroidered silk Chinese dragon, he held court with a pile of joints on one side and a plate of cocaine on the other. It was 1979, and just about everyone was doing coke. Politicians and professors (particularly in the Art and Science Departments), *Playboy* centerfolds, famous photographers and their super-skinny models, they all came through the doors and sat down on the rug-strewn floor around the silk-covered bed. Gonzo journalists showed up, sculptors, painters, actors, producers, rock musicians (the blues and jazz guys preferred the dreamy effects of opiates). Art dealers brought their wealthy clientele, and future financial wizards stopped by at six a.m. so that they could be fueled up when the market opened at nine-thirty New York time. Even a few suburban housewives dropped by to pick up drugs to take home to their hot tub parties in Mill Valley.

I recognized quite a few faces from my father's world. The carefree hippies in flowing clothes I'd known a few years ago were now clad in shimmery spandex waiting to score in Dale's dark apartment. For, in a familiar but distorted way, this drug world shadowed the art world like a dark twin. People on drugs were obsessed in the same way artists were obsessed. They both sacrificed time, friendships, family, money, life into the black hole of an obsession. I'd seen this at Westbeth, how artists could disappear into another world that wasn't quite reality, and lose all touch. The same thing happened with drugs. It's just that drug users never brought anything back from that other realm, and artists, if they were lucky, did.

It was at one of these gatherings at Dale's that I learned from a photographer that Harold Paris had died of a heart attack. Harold, the artist who'd made those vacuum-sealed environments and saved me from the sexual mayhem at my father's third wedding. While the party swirled around us, the photographer and I talked about Harold and how he'd experimented with everything from ceramics to sculpture to performance to installations, but never found his true medium. "Maybe it was sex," the photographer suggested. Then he told me he'd been to one of Harold's events, a Happening-cum-orgy where my dad had been one of the decorated bodies on the scene.

"Happenings?" I asked. "You mean like art?"

"Naked bodies lit up under fluorescent blacklights. Harold had his students there. It was sort of a heaping, glowing blue-violet art orgy and everyone was high," the photographer said.

Not my dad, I thought. He wasn't high. He swore drugs didn't affect him.

The next morning I woke up gulping for air. Dale was wandering around his penthouse barefoot looking for someone to party with. Dale could be intense. Once, after I'd told him about Cindy Sherman, he'd called up the local bookstore and ordered every monograph and history book on women artists to be delivered to his penthouse for me. Today I declined the drugs, put on a skirt and heels and headed to Harold's memorial service being held at the Faculty Club on the Berkeley campus.

I don't remember much of what was said at the service. Mostly people got up and talked about Harold's zest for life. He used to say, "Gaby, we are so lucky. We get to live art."

I thought about this cri de coeur as I was leaving the service. I was angry that Harold and my father had used art as an excuse to have sex with a crowd. They couldn't just commingle art and life indiscriminately. Though I understood, from growing up in a world where all the boundaries had come down, how easy it was confuse the two. That was one of the attractions of taking drugs, it let me hide from reality, slip under a coverlet I could call experience or even art, yet deep down I knew this was a lie. On some level art always critiqued life, observed life. Duchamp had understood this, so had Tinguely. My father, who had brought Tinguely to the garden at MoMA to burn up a sculpture, and participated in a Happening hold-up for the opening of the Berkeley Art Museum, enlisting a troop of dancers to roll around naked on the floor, had always wanted to get into the creative act. He was a rule-bender, answerable only to himself. Still, he must have known that stripping off his clothes and having sex with a bunch of co-eds under purple-colored lights didn't make him or Harold performance artists or turn what they were doing into a Happening.

Outside the Faculty Club, Debbie, Harold's widow, was standing under an oak tree shaking people's hands. I walked over and hugged her. "I wish your father could have been here," she said.

"He's in Europe with his fourth wife."

Debbie, who had once been Harold's student, had participated in those wild sex scenes. Now she was Harold's widow. She nodded knowingly and kissed my cheek.

Later that day I called my sister and asked her if she knew about the orgy/Happenings, and without hesitation she said, "Sure, and what do you think was going on at Westbeth?"

"What?"

"Acid parties, wild sex up on that stage before Merce Cunningham moved in. I didn't do it, but I knew."

I'd thought I'd known everything that had happened at Westbeth, it had been my palace. Now my sister told me that she and my mother had agreed to keep the seamier elements secret from me. "You were so innocent," Tanya said. "We wanted to protect you."

Three weeks later Dad returned from Europe and announced his breakup with Deirdre. The marriage had lasted two years. Maybe leaving was Deirdre's idea. Tanya maintained that Deirdre realized she was "too good for Dad." More likely Dad was ready to move on to his next encounter. In one fell swoop, Deirdre and Brad disappeared from our lives. When she left, Deirdre took her sewing shears and cut her own image out of all the pictures. I understood why Deirdre might not want to be just another ghost in Dad's photo album.

Chapter 17

I graduated in the spring of 1980 with a degree in art history and no plans for my future. I'd spent four years looking at art slides, reading novels and mingling at cocktail parties. I felt unequipped for a career or making a home for myself and I could feel the real world pressing in on me.

"You have a good mind but you aren't using it," my father said. "Get some discipline." We were sitting out on his deck, my father under the shade of a sun umbrella, a straw hat on his head. Leaning back in his director's chair, he looked like a bather at the French Riviera.

"For a career in the arts, total dedication is a minimum," he continued. Though his home environment was in a constant state of flux, my father maintained a very disciplined schedule. Up early every morning, he was at his desk either writing or conducting business by nine a.m. "Work hard during the day, play hard at night," was his motto.

He'd recently met a "splendid woman." Her name was Carole.

She had two daughters close in age to Tanya and me. Dad and Carole met at La Peña, a Latin American restaurant and cultural center in downtown Berkeley. He liked that she was politically active and concerned about the environment. When I asked my father what she did, he said, "She likes plants." Carole also held a volunteer position as the park commissioner in Berkeley. She was going through a divorce and had just started designing some of her friends' gardens. Soon Carole would find out that Peter Selz was her full-time job.

The first time I was introduced to Carole she strode up to me, a big-boned woman in a long skirt, flat sandals and mismatched earrings, and looked me straight in the eye in a way that unnerved me. She must have known I wasn't keen on another woman taking up residence, let alone another family. She was in her mid-forties, fifteen years younger than Dad. Dad told me when he'd asked Carole out she'd refused, she'd heard about his reputation. He'd thought she meant his reputation in the art world. Undeterred, he finally won her over.

"Why don't you just live alone for a while?" I suggested now.

"That wouldn't be any fun, would it?" He shrugged and snapped his red suspenders. The sun shone down on the deck; he rocked up to his feet.

I resented that my father was wrapped up with another family. He was already suggesting that Carole and her daughters, move into Regal House and take over the rooms my sister and I stayed in. I'd inherited $700 from my great-uncle and I decided to go to Europe. I would take a year off to work in an archaeology pit in Southern France and look at art on the Continent. My mother had written my father in a letter that I'd confided to her that "I always get along better with Daddy when he isn't married." To which she added her own postscript. *Your constant remarrying and my never remarrying reminds me of the nursery rhyme about Jack Sprat and his wife—only we seem to do it in reverse, don't we?*

> *Jack Sprat could eat no fat;*
> *His wife could eat no lean.*
> *And so betwixt the two of 'em*
> *They licked the platter clean!*

In all this time my mother had never even come close to remarrying. For the last three years she'd had a serious boyfriend, a journalist for NPR. After she'd moved out from Grammar's and began teaching in Missouri, they tried living together. But he was too skittish, Mom said, from living in all the war zones he'd covered. And perhaps, she admitted, she wasn't willing to go through "all that again." Now she was finally, completely on her own. "I don't even own a plant!" she bragged over the phone. The only thing she missed, she told me, was a good bakery in the neighborhood.

I'd never expected my mother to love anyone else but my father. And I guessed she hadn't, either, because, though she'd dated many men, I'm not sure she tried to form a lasting bond with any of them. Once, she'd told me by way of explanation, "I had a doll when I was a little girl. After dolly burnt in one of the fires in Doc's lab, I never wanted another doll. That doll was mine and that was all there was to it."

In Europe, I traveled over my parents' long-vanished footsteps. I went from museum to museum standing in front of painting after painting. I wanted to see the original art that I had only seen projected on the walls of my art history classes.

In those moments, standing in front of a Titian, a Rembrandt or a Vermeer, I could hear my father's voice rhapsodizing, feel him beside me pointing out the details of the brushstrokes, the qualities of lights and darks of these masters, and how they had inspired the artists he'd known, the artists I'd known. Like my mother, I wrote in my journals about what I saw. Paintings like signposts on a trail, though I had no clear idea where this trail was leading me. During the year of my sojourn abroad, I circled Austria and Germany going to Denmark, the Netherlands, Belgium, France and Italy. I couldn't bring myself to visit the country where I'd been left in the Kinderheim or the land that my father had been forced to flee.

I wrote my father about what I had seen; art had always been the mainline to his emotional heart. He wrote me back begging me to return to California. Isolated first in a wet tent at the archaeology dig, then in dreary youth hostels, and once even sleeping on a bench in the Arles train station in France—to me, even "hello" would have sounded like a plea. *I miss you*, he wrote. *Wouldn't it be wonderful if you were here? Perhaps you'll come back.* From the moment I'd first set off on my journey and left his domain, he'd begun suggesting I return. "That's the way it is with him," my mother said, when twelve months after I'd left I told her I was heading back West. "Look how many times he's reeled me in."

After her stint in Missouri, and the failure of her novel to sell—an event that left her gutted for a year—my mother had picked herself up, begun another novel and was now the writer-in-residence at Trinity College in Hartford, Connecticut. "You can come here," she said.

"Hartford? No way!" Though I had never actually been to Hartford.

We're all here now, my father wrote, meaning Carole, her two daughters and my sister across the bay in San Francisco. *Come and join us.*

Tanya had graduated with a degree in theater, but when she didn't immediately find work as an actress, she gave up. *Maybe I'm not any good or I just don't have ambition*, she wrote me. She'd found a job working for Williams-Sonoma taking phone orders.

Art in Our Times had been published to good reviews, and Dad had completed two shows and accompanying books on his original fascination: the turmoil, fragmentation and transcendence of German art on the brink of disaster. One show had focused on German and Austrian Expressionism—Egon Schiele, Kandinsky, Franz Marc—for the Museum of Contemporary Art in Chicago. The other, on the successive movement, German Realism of the twenties—George Grosz, Otto Dix, Max Beckmann—for the Minneapolis Institute of Arts. Just as I was returning to the home of my father, he had again returned to the art of his fatherland.

Though my father and Carole hadn't married yet, the signs were all there: her furniture mixed in with his, her daughters where his had been. Carole had torn out all the hens-and-chicks and succulents I'd once planted with my father—true, they had never done particularly well. No one had tended the garden consistently until Carole came along. She put in long tendrils of prostrate rosemary, species geraniums and a towering princess flower plant with purple flowers and leaves as soft as velvet. Regal House was veiled behind an enchanted realm of flowers. She was opening up the kitchen, replacing a wall with a sliding glass door. Strangest of all, Carole had cut my father's hair. The wild mass, which for years had sprouted from the sides of his head like a pair of matted but magnificent wings, was groomed for the first time since his New York days.

Together with a girl I knew from college, I moved into a place in the vibrant and cheap Mission District in San Francisco. Meredith had straight brown hair and owlish glasses. She'd studied photography and poetry in college and I'd always thought of her as a calming presence. Now she worked as a secretary downtown. Soon I found a job at a company that produced gourmet food and wine shows. First as a receptionist, then writing brochures about herb-infused vinegars and fennel fern salads.

After I moved in, a crate arrived from my mother. It was my delayed graduation present. Inside was a bubble-wrapped picture. I peeled away the layers of wrapping and leaned it against the wall.

"What is it?" Meredith asked.

It had discolored so badly over the years, the paint darkening with time and neglect, that I could barely make out the image. Something lay beneath the dark pigment. Then, in a heartbeat, I saw a spindly body like a chemical beaker and the attenuated limbs. It was Marcel Duchamp's *The Bride*.

"It's an aquatint, a collaboration by Marcel and his brother Jacques Villon. See?" I pointed to both their signatures at the bottom. "Villon did a print of Marcel's painting *The Bride*, and then Marcel painted his own painting on top of the print. Isn't it beautiful?" I said triumphantly.

We were both thrilled. We had a piece of real art to hang on our wall.

"You should have it restored," my boyfriend Michael said when he saw it. Michael was a blond California artist who looked like a surfer. We'd met at a party within a week of my return from Europe and started dating casually. Michael said he didn't believe in commitment, he believed in the freedom to paint. The transient quality of our relationship gave our time together a heightened glow. I was nostalgic for him even when he was there. Like Duchamp, Michael painted shapes that resembled machinery, though Michael's colors were more intense. His paintings were not the part of Michael I loved. I loved the way he rode his motorcycle up to my window and stretched out his hand into the lamplight while I dropped my apartment key into his hand, then bounded up the stairs, springing and somersaulting into my bed with the grace of a gymnast. I loved how he slept with his palms open as if he were waiting for dreams.

But he was right about the painting. It needed work. I found an art restorer who said she could wash and bathe it until it was newly born. Like a baby, I thought, handing over all my savings. Sure enough, a month later, when I picked it up, I could see the colors. Soft yellows and beiges, smoky gray-blues and the pinks of *The Bride*'s vulnerable flesh parts. I remembered from my art history classes that *The Bride* was a motor, an apparatus whose role in Duchamp's world was to seduce men—*the bachelors*. I hung the restored bride back into her place on the wall. Then Meredith and I invited my father and Carole over for dinner to celebrate. I wanted my father to see that I had brought a work of art back to life.

As he burst through our apartment door, my father's eyes were sharp and warm at the same time. "This isn't such a bad place," he said after he had caught his breath and looked around.

Carole followed, her step more circumspect. She handed us a small jade plant and a dish towel. "Housewarming presents from your father and me."

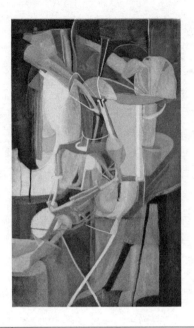

The Bride
Jacques Villon & Marcel Duchamp,
1934

Dad made a beeline for *The Bride*. Any piece of art within smelling distance, and he was upon it like a hound after a fox. "Ohhhh," his voice thick with longing. "Isn't she lovely? Perhaps this should hang in my house?" he suggested.

"Why?" I asked, stunned.

"It's so beautiful," he said, as if that were reason enough. Then, shrugging, he sat down at the head of the table.

Meredith and I served coq au vin. Carole talked about the Shakespeare Festival they'd been to in Ashland, Oregon, then Meredith talked about her desire to get back to taking pictures.

"Good, good." My father nodded approvingly. Finally, my father began to gush about, of all things, Disneyland. He'd told us that he'd just been hired by the Disney Corporation to create a Kinetic Island Theme Park for the Magic Kingdom.

He leaned back in his chair, his voice booming, speaking as if he were addressing an audience of hundreds and not three attentive women sitting just a few feet from him. His hands darted and zipped through the air as he demonstrated the flips and turns the sculptures would make. "A ride on which people will be able to enjoy all these moving sculptures. Finally they're doing something interesting. Instead of cartoons, we're going to educate the masses on Kinetic art."

"Educate the masses, how perfect! Shades of the Bauhaus," I said. Only Carole laughed.

At the door my father twirled his yellow scarf and kissed all of our cheeks wetly, even Carole's.

Meredith's face was flushed with wine. "He so sparkly," she gushed after they left. "It must be wonderful to have a parent you can share so much with."

Meredith had never really known her own father. He'd died of cancer when she was very young. "He lay in a bed that was constantly rocking," she'd told me, "up and down, up and down. I had to wait until the bed rocked down before I could climb up and see him." Her mother had worked as a seamstress and used to sew all Meredith's clothes in stiff forbidding fabric, which Meredith dutifully wore until I convinced her to jettison them.

I used to invite Meredith along when I went out with Michael to dive bars to hear slippery jazz. Life, like art, was open space and meant to be explored. Our world was fluid; we exchanged clothes, shared books, split the food in our refrigerator. In college, Meredith and I had even shared a sexual romp with a man, a tumbled threesome that we both chalked up to reading too much Colette.

A few mornings after my father and Carole's visit, the phone rang, and when I picked up the receiver and said hello, I heard a grunt and then the line went dead. This continued to happen for a few days. Meredith shrugged it off. But the calls kept coming.

I thought at first that it might be Tanya trying to reach out to me. She never liked to be the one placing a phone call. She thought it made her look needy and so she'd devised an elaborate method to get me to call her. She'd tell our mother that I owed her a call and Mom would tell me to call Tanya. Maybe Tanya was trying something less time-consuming. But when I asked Tanya, all she said was, "No, and why haven't you called me until now?"

And still the calls kept coming.

I was a snoop and a sneak when I was little. I'd roamed through Westbeth, I read my sister's diary, raided her closet and, when I was a teenager stuck in Dead City, I snuck bottles of my grandfather's ancient bootlegged alcohol to parties down by the slough. My father always pretended that everything was out in the open. He didn't have any doors on his rooms, let alone on his cabinets, until Carole moved in and tried to change all that. But when I came home and heard Meredith cooing on the phone, I was suspicious. I picked up the hall extension, certain that I'd hear my boyfriend Michael on the other end. It wasn't Michael. It was my father. "When can I see you again?" he asked.

I slammed down the receiver. On her end, Meredith did, too. In less than a minute she was standing in my bedroom doorway uttering the words, "He wants to take me out."

"Are you crazy? He's engaged! He's my father!"

"I think he's charming. He sparkles."

Then she told me that he'd kissed her in the kitchen the night he'd come to dinner with Carole. I could picture them standing by the refrigerator, Meredith in the folds of my father's embrace. It was so easy to see my father kissing her, like the image had been there for years waiting to come to the surface. Just as Meredith finished telling me this, the phone rang again.

"You can't pick it up!" I yelled, and we both immediately sank down on the carpet and stared at each other. Meredith pushed her glasses up her delicate nose. She told me my father had invited her to his annual New Year's Day party.

It was a tradition. The first day of the new year, all the artists, literati and politicos in the Bay Area stood around slurping soup and looking at my father's art collection while nursing hangovers from the night before. Meredith said she wanted to go.

"Carole's making the soup this year," I told her. Had she really thought a haircut would transform Dad?

"I can come as your friend," Meredith suggested.

The strange thing was, I wanted Meredith to still be my friend, my father not to have done what he'd done. I wanted the image of them kissing erased.

"It was my father hanging up on me, wasn't it?"

She nodded.

"Do you think this is a game of musical chairs?" I cried. "This is my life."

Behind her thick glasses Meredith's eyes were wet. She was crying. She shook her head as if she didn't believe me.

I couldn't say any more and slammed out of the apartment.

Down the street, I called my father from the pay phone. As

soon as he answered I blurted, "You're crazy, she's not coming to New Year's Soup!"

"Who?" came my father's bewildered but guarded reply.

"Meredith."

"Ohhhh." Neither an admission nor a denial, but I heard it all in his voice. Thick with the same mix of desire and contrition that he'd expressed on the night he'd come to dinner and I'd pulled him away from my refurbished *Bride* painting. *Why not give it to me?* that voice said.

And then I said, in a voice I recognized as not my own, but my mother's when she was at the end of her rope with my dad: "I don't care what you do in your own life, but don't come and dump your shit in mine."

I DIDN'T BLAME Meredith, I blamed my dad. All the same, I felt uncomfortable living with Meredith. I moved into an apartment a few streets above Chinatown and began a long, awkward hiatus from my father, interrupted by moments when he would try to break through to me. He called me up to proclaim, "I'm so busy these days. I'm working on a Max Beckmann show for the St. Louis Museum. He defies classification—" Before my father could go any further, I told him I had to run. I was busy, too. Dating Michael on and off, zipping around food shows on a golf cart with a walkie-talkie in my hand at work. I became closer to Carole, often helping her in the garden. She was a smart woman who seemed to have her head on her shoulders. Once, while we were digging in the dirt, I asked her why she was marrying Dad; after all, she knew his reputation. "Because I need to make a commitment in my life," she said gaily. So be it, I thought.

They were married in the nave of Grace Cathedral at the end of 1983. No naked hippies, no drunk ugly men this time, just us four girls, with our feather haircuts, wearing such thick shoulder pads adhered with Velcro inside our dresses, we looked like a row of linebackers.

I gave my father and Carole a bottle of Armagnac as a wedding present, though I was still avoiding my father's attempts at reconciliation. As a thank-you, or just because he couldn't help himself—he had to share—my father sent me a copy of his Beckmann catalogue. When I sat down to read his essay, I began to understand why Beckmann was a touchstone for my father. He wrote that Beckmann was an artist whose paintings veiled *a deep anxiety and despair that responds to his own inner turmoil and the turbulence of his time*. And yet, my father added, *he affirms life*. My father had come of age in the same inferno as Beckmann. He, too, rose above the rubble.

One night, a few months after the wedding, Michael and I went to see a performance by Survival Research Laboratories. On the outskirts of the city, underneath the freeway in an abandoned junkyard, an artist named Mark Pauline staged battles between gigantic motorized robots. The audience sat in bleachers watching as Pauline's mechanized creatures smashed into each other in machine sex and then consumed each other in the process like an enactment of Duchamp's *The Bride Stripped Bare by Her Bachelors, Even*. Dynamite detonated, spears, sparks, flames, and spiked balls flew through the air, and dead animal carcasses were hurled across the arena, all in the name of art. It was a gladiator battle of art objects. Pauline saw art as a vehicle that gave viewers the intense experience of danger without real risk. This, despite the fact that he had a mutilated hand. Half his fingers had been replaced by some of his toes when he'd blown his right hand off during one of his performances. Michael thought Pauline's mangled hand was a perfect metaphor. I thought it was just plain stupid.

Pauline had come to San Francisco by way of Florida. He'd been a teenage hell-raiser in the late sixties, a self-confessed juvenile delinquent who had repossessed billboards by covering them with spray paint in the middle of the night. He saw technology as the tool man used to remake himself as a god. San Francisco, with high-tech Silicon Valley nearby, was the perfect environment for Pauline and his repurposed warrior machinery. He incorporated Survival Research Laboratories and bought used equipment. His shows, often in large parking lots, had begun to gather audiences of thousands.

That night with Michael, I watched as the crowd placed bets on which robots might couple, which might succumb and which might survive the event. It was far beyond kinetics. It was apocalyptic art. A cannon shot was fired out of the mouth of a giant painted Medusa's head. The mob cheered and shouted throughout the spectacle and the raw energy in the air carried me away. It was easy in that moment to understand how crowds could get stirred watching a matador battle a bull to the bloody end. Afterward, stepping gingerly around mechanical anatomy strewn in the dust, I thought of my father. How so much of his life was about rising out of debris. Did he need to create destruction in order the surmount it? I wondered.

On the way home Michael and I stopped at a bar for some shots and chasers and argued. Michael compared Pauline's spectacle to the movies *Mad Max* and *The Terminator* because of their violent robotic battles. I said no, Pauline was following the tradition set by Marcel Duchamp and Jean Tinguely, who had each claimed the machine as an art object. Juiced up from the violence of the battle we had just witnessed, we didn't realize we were actually in agreement. Both examples dealt with the idea that out of destruction, creation was born.

"I want art to take me somewhere," I said.

We left the bar and I climbed onto the back of his bike. The night was cold. I had no helmet, no coat, even. Michael and I never rode with a helmet or protective gear, which we thought was for sissies. We liked speed and the heady recklessness of hurtling through spaces, unshielded. With my legs gripped around the body of the bike I felt like I was part of the machine. I tucked my head into the back of Michael's neck and closed my eyes. I felt kinetic and alive. I heard a car engine, the rev of the bike's motor underneath me, and then nothing.

One minute I was behind Michael on the bike, the next minute I was catapulted into the air by a distracted driver who cut us off at the intersection. I bounced off the hood of the car and landed in a split. When I came to, one of my legs was pointing north, the other south. I could see Michael running toward me. Instinctively my hands went to touch my face. I thought I was okay, too, and tried to stand up. That's when I started to scream. I couldn't make my legs move.

In the hospital I became a long, thin, horizontal object. I was told that I had a hole the size of a fist through my left femur, a torn kneecap, four broken toes and three broken fingers. They had to stabilize me before they could operate. Never immobilized before, I lay in a morphine haze, in traction, for a number of days dreaming of the robots. I felt as if I were transforming into one of Pauline's creatures with attenuated, twitching legs and a fiery scream pouring out of my mouth.

My father called from New York. "Oh, I hate to hear you like this, it hurts me so much," he wailed over the crackling line of the phone. A day later my mother materialized. Right after they wheeled me out of surgery, with a long metal rod hammered down through my thighbone and a prosthetic flange in my knee, I heard her soft voice in the bright, fluorescent room. "I couldn't get a plane out of Athens."

She explained to the nurse that she'd been visiting her boyfriend in Greece when she'd heard I'd been injured in an accident. She was wearing her strand of long jet beads, clad in my clothes, my gray cotton jacket and white linen skirt. Except for that necklace and a fancy dress, her suitcase, she told the nurse, had been full of beachwear.

The next time I woke, my sister was glaring at my leg. When she saw me watching her, Tanya said, "Did you do this to get attention? You're just like Dad." Then she walked out.

Beside me my mother passed off my sister's comment as older sister envy. She was eating the candy that friends had left by my bedside. Offering me divinity fudge, my mother told me she'd just finished writing a list of all the things I was going to need: *toothpaste, shampoo, tampax, lotion, soft socks.*

"Birth control pills," I added.

"You're wasting your youth and beauty on that man. He'll kill you if he gets a chance."

"Mom, don't start." I reached for the little button that released the morphine.

"I will, too, start." Hands on hips, she leaned over me. "For once you just have to lie there and listen to me. That man almost killed you."

"But it was the other driver's fault."

"You were drinking shots and chasers and Michael was drunk. It's the sort of thing your father would do, too, get behind the wheel drunk."

"Michael didn't mean to hurt me!"

"Of course not, and he won't mean to hurt you the next time, either. Look, there are some people, and your father is one of them, who never get hurt. Maybe they are just born under a lucky star. They are always more careless than the rest of us. They can afford to be. But mark my words—be very careful. Because what happens is that the people standing next to them are the ones that take the bullet."

Her eyes as black and sharp as two little pellets, her hair like a helmet, a warrior mother. She frightened me. I knew she was right.

Because my mother had to return east to teach, because I was unable to support any weight on my leg until my bone grew back together, I returned to my father's house to heal.

It had been a long time since my mother had seen my father, and she had never met Carole before. All three of them stood in a row at the foot of my hospital bed the day I was released. The two women shook hands across my father, whose eyes skipped back and forth from one to the other as if he didn't know where to rest his gaze. I think my mother was happy that Carole wasn't a bombshell, but a solid-looking person.

All stairs and jutting levels, my father's house was not designed for the impaired. I was trapped up on the third floor in the little guest bedroom where I had once snorted RUSH. During the time

I was there, Carole came into my room almost every night with her long list of grievances. By now her daughters were gone, one off to college, the other living across town with her boyfriend. My father, sitting in that open space, but so closed off in his own realm, often left the people around him stranded in the busy thoroughfare of his enthusiasms. When Carole was in a good mood she'd say affectionately, "Too much is never enough for your father." When she was unhappy she'd reveal that he was unable to show intimacy, but that his cheating was okay just as long as he didn't lie. "I don't like sneaks," she'd warn, eying me suspiciously.

Eventually my father, too, would appear at my door, curious as to why Carole was taking so long to come to bed. He wanted to know what we were talking about. Shuffling in his slippers, scooting around Carole, he'd sit on my bed. "You're here," he'd say, thumping my leg—almost always the bad leg. When I hollered, "OUCH!" he'd moan an echoing cry of pain, of solidarity. "Ohhh," he'd say, grabbing his own, perfectly fine leg. Then he'd tell me, "I hurt when you hurt!"

As they both left my room, I'd swallow down my pain pill with one refrain echoing through my head. *I have to get out of here.*

Within six weeks I moved back to my apartment in San Francisco. I was still a "gimp," as my father called me, limping around on a brass-handled cane, one limb flesh and bone, the other held together and repurposed with a metal rod and flange.

Chapter 18

Eight months after the accident, over a breakfast of croissants and coffee, my father's friend the artist Carolee Schneemann described a piece of art she'd performed way back in the early 1970s: *Up to and Including Her Limits*. Carolee had suspended herself naked from a harness and, with crayons clutched in her hands, she'd drawn randomly over sheets of paper adhered to the walls and floor of the gallery. She was a human drawing machine. With a flourish Carolee waved her napkin delicately through the air and told us in a singsong voice, "My entire body became energy in action." Carolee was a statuesque woman with a pile of light brown hair wound like a crown on top of her head. I'd audited a seminar on body art at UC Berkeley while I'd been recovering, given by Kristine Stiles, my father's former student and coauthor of *Theories and Documents of Contemporary Art*. She'd shown slides of Carolee dangling naked like a female version of Jackson Pollock marking a canvas. In this piece Carolee described herself as a "human crayon." I knew that part of the point of her work was to appropriate the "Boy" world of action painting by using her body as an object and a tool. Carolee Schneemann had started as a painter in the fifties, but then in the sixties she'd became interested in Happenings, film and performance. When my father had told me she was staying at his house, I'd eagerly driven over from the city to meet her. That was the thing I continued to love about my father's life, even years after I left. I never knew who was going to show up for breakfast. As my mother once said about her own father as well as mine, *He brings the world in the door.*

I liked Carolee. She had a regal beauty, and her art, though often graphic and physical, was also elegant. Even hanging upside down naked, she'd managed to look like both a trapeze artist and a displaced queen.

Like Pollock, Carolee Schneemann's wall and floor drawings were not meant to depict an illusion but to record her bodily motions. Tethering herself in a harness, documenting her performance with three video cameras, Carolee was not only a mark-making tool—an artist—but a subject to be gazed upon—the work of art itself. Integrating her nude body with her art was her way to take possession of the male gaze. I knew this made my father nervous. In place of a wedding ring he wore a thick silver band with a ceramic eyeball in the center. He was married to art, or at least to looking at it. Gaping, gawking, scrutinizing, regarding, this was his territory. That was another reason I was here. I wanted to see how my father would handle this audacious woman.

Now she sat at the head of my father's table telling Carole and my father about the appearance and disappearance of women's art from history.

Dad wolfed down his croissant and grunted in agreement.

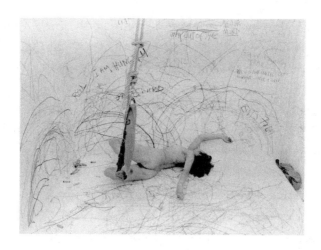

Up to and Including Her Limits
Carolee Schneemann, 1973

"Peter, you're not a feminist," Carole, his wife, said. She turned to Carolee. "He just likes women."

"I'm a feminist!" My father insisted. "I always include women artists in my shows."

I squinted at my father. He was getting better at including women. This was partly due to Kristine Stiles having convinced Dad to include Carolee in *Art in Our Times*. Kristine loved my dad. "He changed my life," she'd told me. "He gave me the honor and opportunity to do this great book with him."

"Good," Carolee said now. I wasn't sure if she was saying good Dad's a feminist or good he likes women. But the simple word resolved the debate. Then Carolee turned to me and said, "That's a nice cane."

I was having a protracted recovery, still unable to walk without a cane or, on my weaker days, crutches. I had what my doctor referred to as a "nonunion." My thighbone, the major weight-bearing bone in the body, refused to knit together. I would need another surgery. The only advantage, I told Carolee, "Is that whenever I go out, men bend over backward holding doors open, bringing me glasses of wine at shows. It seems I'm more desirable injured."

"No." My father shook his head. "Not true." But dad had treated me differently, too. Right after the accident, when I was immobilized and unable to even hop on a crutch, he'd pushed me through the Legion of Honor in a rented wheelchair to see the Renaissance drawings. As we moved slowly from image to image, from compassionate madonna to languishing pietà, if someone dared to step in front of me to look at the art, Dad shooed him or her away with the words, "Can't you see my daughter's here? Don't block her view."

Now Carolee said in her syrupy voice, "You're probably right. There is nothing men like more than a damsel in distress." Then she asked if we all wanted to go to a party for Hunter S. Thompson at the Mitchell Brothers Theatre.

The year 1985 was just a few years before the dot-commers and Silicon Valley techies claimed San Francisco for their sporty, upscale lifestyle. The city was still a Wild West town, infused with the flavor of sexual liberation left over from the hippies and Haight-Ashbury. When the Democratic Convention came to town in 1984, they partied with local pornographic comic book artists like R. Crumb. Hunter S. Thompson, the original gonzo journalist, was writing dispatches for the *Examiner*, the local paper. He was also apparently writing a book. I had no idea what the book was about. (Later I learned it was titled *The Night Porter* and it was never published.) All I knew was that Carolee had invited me to his book party taking place that afternoon in the Tenderloin District, the seedy neighborhood notorious for speakeasies and gambling dens in the 1920s. While I had been bedridden I'd begun to write stories, and though nothing beautiful appeared on my pages, I persisted, trying to hear myself. Now I wanted to meet the author of *Fear and Loathing in Las Vegas*.

I went home to change, though I have no memory of what I wore. I took my cane and hobbled down to O'Farrell Street. Back then the Mitchell Brothers Theatre had a mural of joyful blue whales painted on the side of the building and over the entranceway, a flashing sign advertising the naked, sinful dancing girls to be found within. I had never been inside before.

I spotted Carolee right away, standing next to Warren Hinkle, the former editor of a defunct, hip, leftist journal *Ramparts*. Warren had interviewed Huey Newton and John Lennon. He wore a pirate patch over one eye—he only had one eye—and shiny black dress shoes. Warren knew everyone in town, but it was still a small town. My father had briefly dated Warren's sister, and I'd gotten to know Warren a little. He reminded me of his dog, a basset hound, which I think was probably why he had the dog. It was a sort of mascot. Like the dog, Warren was endearing in a droopy-eyed way and always sniffing around for a story. A few years later he ran for mayor of San Francisco and joked that the dog was his running mate. He was a serious journalist, and one of Hunter's closest friends. Now Warren was leaning on a cane, too. He had bad feet, he explained, pointing at the splitting seams of his polished party shoes. Neither he nor Carolee knew where my father was.

I wandered around, seeing who else was there, and looking for my father. I wanted to find Hunter S. Thompson, too. For the event, they must have dredged up every underground personality in the Bay Area, but mixed in with the newspaper guys and artists were topless girls in G-strings serving champagne and fruit. In the ladies' bathroom one of the Mitchell Brothers—Art or Jim, they looked alike to me—was laying out lines of coke along the sink. Dale, the drug dealer I'd dated in college, was there, on the arm of a woman in a black stretch body stocking. I felt nervous seeing him, but not surprised; he was part of this circus, too, perhaps even the supplier. San Francisco was such a small, tight corner of the world.

Eventually I found my way into a dark theater where a girl was pole-dancing onstage to the Eagles song "Hotel California." She was naked except for a bow in her hair. People were seated around her in the plush but decaying old theater chairs and I sat down, too. She slid to the floor and opened her legs and because I didn't want to look, I turned and glanced around the room.

A few rows back I spotted Carolee. She was wedged between Warren on one side and my father on the other.

We'd both been invited to the same party, which I'd understood was being held at a porn club. I just hadn't expected a porn show. The Mitchell Brothers Theatre was known to be decadent, but in a wholesome way. Their claim to fame was producing the first feature hardcore film that had a semblance of a plot. *Behind the Green Door*, starring Marilyn Chambers, the girl from the Ivory Snow commercials, was also the first X-rated movie widely distributed in America. The brothers even supported the arts. They wanted to bring back burlesque, though what was happening up on the stage—the girl now upside down on her pole—was more than I understood burlesque to be. Carolee, Warren and my father all seemed to be enjoying the show. The girl did a scissor kick and bounded off her pole. Bowing to the audience, she glanced up, smiled, lifted her hand and waved. "Hi, Professor Selz," she called out. "I was in your art history class."

My father applauded.

The crowd loved the moment, clapping and laughing, but I felt embarrassed. The naked girl was probably younger than I, and that made me feel quite unexpectedly mature and protective. I wanted to throw a coat over her, shield her. Not because I thought she was in danger—Warren often wrote about how well the Mitchell Brothers paid their girls, and she seemed to be enjoying herself—but because I understood how easy it was to get caught up in fun, to make the wrong turn, to stay too long, and not find your way out of the circus.

I didn't think my father had noticed I was there. At that point, I didn't want him to see me. Sitting there, watching him relish being recognized at a porn show, the other thing I'd realized was that if I stayed, in one way or another I'd always be his audience.

By the time I got to the lobby my head was spinning. It was slow going with a cane, the halls were crowded and I was upset, not with my father this time, but with myself. For years I'd been so in love with the sense of possibility that surrounded my father, as if any moment might explode into a symphony, that I'd kept coming back for more. But at twenty-five, I wasn't a child mistakenly entering a grown-up world, I was a grown-up knowingly entering a childish one. That brass cane that Carolee had admired didn't make me more vulnerable, which the men who had held open doors and brought me cocktails imagined. It gave me distance, pause, space. It made me stronger. I don't know what Carolee felt sitting in the theater watching the show. Maybe by being there she was appropriating a male space and claiming it for her own, but I'd noticed Carole, my stepmother, wasn't present that afternoon. Perhaps she'd been busy, or perhaps she'd just recognized her limits and declined to come to the party.

On my way out, I got lost, of course. The place was a maze of one secret room after another. Each wrong door opened to crazy sights—a group of Japanese businessmen shining flashlights at a naked girl; something that looked like a shower scene; finally, I reached the lobby.

I was making my way toward the entrance when I nearly collided with Hunter, the man of the hour, the writer I'd come to see. He was barreling across the room, looking like a character out of *Gilligan's Island*, wearing his trademark khaki shorts, aviator glasses and a sailor hat, but oddly, he had no shirt on. He stopped at the front desk and began to pound with his fist, screaming, "You promised me a girl! Just give me a girl." Then he turned his head and his gaze rested on me. Through his tinted lenses I saw his eyes, like little rolling roulette balls, looking for a place to land. Backing up, I crashed into my dad.

"Where are you going?" my father asked.

As we both watched Hunter being led off behind a door, I told him. I was tired, my leg hurt, I was headed for home. Later I would tell him more, that I thought it was time for me to move, I was ready to leave the party, but for now this was enough. He thumped me on my back and said, "This is a marvelous party! Everyone seems to know me here." Then he, too, lumbered across the lobby, disappearing behind a door.

It was dark outside. I guessed I'd been inside the theater for hours, years, maybe.

PART FOUR

Entering History

I BELIEVE THAT ART IS THE ESSENCE OF LIFE, AS MUCH
AS ANYTHING CAN BE A TRUE ESSENCE. IT IS EXTRACTED
FROM EXISTENCE BY A PROCESS. ART IS A REFLECTION ON
LIFE AND AN ANALYSIS OF ITS STRUCTURE. AS SUCH, ART
SHOULD BE A GREAT MOVING FORCE SHAPING THE FUTURE.

—*Agnes Denes*

Once, still in the early stages of my recovery from the motorcycle accident, when I was laid up at my father's house, my stepmother Carole came into the room with one of her complaints about my father and told me the story of the *Liquidambar* tree. "Your father wanted to get rid of the tree," she said.

"What tree?"

"The beautiful *Liquidambar* outside the big window in the living room. He said it spoiled his view."

I knew the tree. It grew in the neighbors' yard, tall and glorious, and when it was in leaf, blocked out the silver line of the city, the shimmering bay and the Golden Gate.

"He asked the neighbors to cut it down," Carole continued. "And when they wouldn't, he paid someone to sneak over in the middle of the night to poison the tree."

"But it's still there," I pointed out.

"Well," Carole snapped, "whoever he got to do his dirty work poisoned the wrong tree."

By then my dad had followed Carole and was standing behind her in my doorway. He was listening intently to the story of what he had done with a hungry look on his face. He loved being talked about.

"Is that true?" I asked him.

He nodded. "It wasn't there when I built the place twelve years ago."

"You just didn't notice it," Carole said, "until it grew up and blocked your view."

"Precisely." My father dug his hands deeper into his bathrobe pockets.

"Can you believe he would do such a thing?" Carole didn't wait for me to answer, but pushed around Dad and out the bedroom door.

I looked at my dad leaning against the doorframe. He was chortling. He thought Carole was making a fuss over nothing. He'd engaged in mischievous behavior before when as a child he'd dangled purses of money out his grandfather's window. Why shouldn't he poison the tree? He wouldn't want anything blocking his view. I could almost understand it. The view outside the picture window of the water, the city and the bridge like a giant harp strung from bluff to bluff was magnificent. My breath often caught in my throat while I sat transfixed watching the light fold into the horizon.

A few years later, my father's neighbors topped the *Liquidambar*, hacking off the tree's head, and ruined its shape, but saved Dad's view. All the same, the night Carole told me that story was the night I began to think seriously of leaving California.

AT THE END of the summer of 1986, I moved to New York. By then I'd had a second rod inserted down my femur. I'd spent nearly six months in physical therapy learning to walk, step by cautious step. I could fall without freezing up. I could even run half a block. At the least, I'd be able to hail a cab.

Though I'd visited New York twice since we'd moved away from Westbeth, I was not prepared for how much the city had changed in the intervening fifteen years.

When I first arrived I went looking for my past memories, as if, just by walking down a street and turning a corner, I would find the rows of fur coats lining the hallway outside our apartment door, the women with their coiffed hair sitting in cinched dresses on the playground benches, the Boys huddled over their amber drinks ranting about art: what my mother still referred to as *That Life*.

I visited our old building on Central Park West where Roz, the old Marxist friend of my parents, continued to hold her Sunday brunches serving lox and bagels. The building had gone co-op, which meant that everyone talked not about art, or even the price of art, but about the value of their apartments.

For the first time in my life, I *paid* admission to get into MoMA so I could walk through the modern galleries and sit in the Philip Johnson sculpture garden under the birch trees by the reflecting pool. Aristide Maillol's giant female sculpture *The River* was still dipping her head into the water. She'd been there since 1953. As a little girl I climbed up her naked back. Later, I'd heard that in 1969 she'd inspired the Japanese avant-garde artist Yayoi Kusama to mastermind an impromptu Happening. In *Orgy to Awaken the Dead at MoMA*, Kusama had enlisted eight people to tear off their clothes and wade into the pool. I knew those innocent, sculpture-climbing days for me, and maybe also for art, were over.

One afternoon I took the subway over to Westbeth. Life hadn't changed so much there. The psychedelic colored hallways had been repainted white, the roof was caving in and the half-moon-shaped balconies were rusted, but the resident artists still relentlessly pursued their dreams. Tanya had called Westbeth "an artists' slum." It wasn't a slum then but it was badly in need of repair. Merce Cunningham had been the biggest name in the building and now he no longer lived there. My mother's old friend Sonia, who was still on our floor, told me that after we left, there were more suicides, maybe nine in all. Across the hall in Diane Arbus's old apartment, a friend of my mother's, a painter, now lived and worked. She had Diane's old furniture, which she proudly showed me, including the bathtub where Diane had died. No one wanted to leave the building or change anything, ever, just so long as they could continue to work living in their own interior worlds. They were allowed to stay as long as they remained poor. Many lied about their income, as they always had. The residents of Westbeth hadn't become the next great wave of creators.

That wave was in SoHo. And by the time I moved to Thompson Street, in the winter of 1987, that wave had almost reached its high-water mark. Before SoHo, artists didn't live and work in the same areas where they exhibited, mostly because they couldn't afford the fancy neighborhoods that housed the galleries. Not even Westbeth, with its small cooperative gallery, had been able to change that practice. But after new zoning resolutions were passed in 1971, legalizing what artists had been doing for years—living where they worked—they flocked to the large, naturally lit loft spaces in the old cast-iron buildings South of Houston Street (SoHo). The galleries quickly followed. Before SoHo, one of the appeals of buying and selling art had been that it was secretive, and completely unregulated. But SoHo changed that, too. It had become the new Mecca for the art world. The place of pilgrimage where art and commerce deliberately merged, where on a Saturday afternoon the streets were packed with crowds of gallery-goers as well as shoppers, and limos cruised up and down the wide boulevard of West Broadway while wealthy consumers bought art in broad daylight. Openings, which in the past were traditionally held on Tuesday nights, were now held on Saturday afternoons to accommodate the crowds. The art world was booming, earning big bucks alongside the Financial District. This was no longer my father's realm but the realm of men like my old boyfriend John Good, who, after studying psychology at Santa Cruz, had moved to New York, where he'd operated Leo Castelli's gallery on Green Street for a few years. He'd married Wendy Burden, the granddaughter of William Burden II, who had been the president of the board when my father was at MoMA. Now John had his own gallery and referred to himself as "Mr. West Broadway." Art was no longer elitist, John said.

He was right. That had begun to change as early as 1962 when Andy Warhol created his famous replica of thirty-two Campbell's soup cans and, a year later, his stack of Brillo boxes. Fine art for Warhol was a commodity that could be mass-produced.

Over the years my father had softened his views on Warhol. Dad now understood that Warhol was not a quintessential Pop artist. He'd only appropriated the language of Pop to question society's notions about value and identity. More importantly, Dad had always opposed the critic Clement Greenberg's insistence that art must resist any intrusion of commerce or politics. Greenberg had advocated that after abstraction, art was compelled to abandon representation—no figures, no faces, no soup cans. Dad's definition of art—like his personality—was more expansive and inclusive. He didn't believe that art followed one mainstream, progressing from figurative to abstraction to pure painting. He believed that the history of art was made up of many tributaries. Warhol, whose art embraced not only representation, but also commerce and politics, did not flow out of Greenberg's mainstream. Underlying all of Warhol's posing and slick indifference was the belief, an essentially Bauhaus belief, in the revolutionary power of a well-designed product. A can of soup could be as beautiful as a Hellenic vase.

At the MoMA retrospective in 1989, I stood under Warhol's camouflaged self-portrait, done a few months before his sudden death in 1987. There he was, full frontal as if finally ready to reveal himself, yet his pale face and spiky trademark wig were masked by a silkscreen of camouflage. The pop icon had cloaked himself with an abstract pattern. The fabric of military camouflage fascinated Warhol because of its dual effect of concealing as well as identifying the wearer. America's abstract past merged with its current fad of representation across this man's ghost-like face.

Up until this point, my experience of art had mostly been filtered through my father. Even in Europe I had mainly visited the paintings I'd heard him speak about, or those I'd studied in my art history classes. Now I began to look with my own eyes: SoHo was awash with postmodern art, the art of appropriation, a recycling of past styles with contemporary images layered with texts. Rolling out my door on a Saturday night, I'd join the throng of gallery-goers, a current that swept me from gallery to gallery until my mind was riddled with images: brazen David Salle's mix of the pornographic with the ornamental; Julian Schnabel's

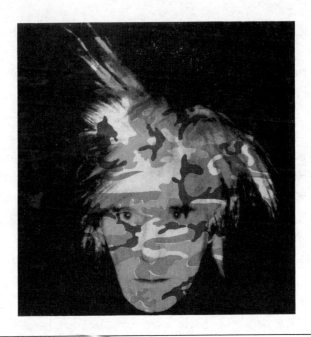

Camouflage Self-Portrait
Andy Warhol, 1968

big, crockery-encrusted canvases; Barbara Kruger's billboard-sized collages. Kruger had studied with Diane Arbus and merged photographic imagery with pithy text: a silkscreened image of a hand holding up a red sign that read *I shop therefore I am.* The landscape of art had become a many-branched delta with no dominant style. "It's just a big grab bag," my father said on the phone. At Mary Boone's gallery on West Broadway, I gazed at Eric Fischl's canvases, mysterious and anxious scenes that portrayed the ennui and sexual habits of suburbia. "He's reintroducing the figure and emotion back into painting," my father said. "He's wrestling with Beckmann."

Dad's Kinetic Island Theme Park had not panned out. The Disney Corporation decided to invest the money into reviving its animation studio instead. "Cartoons!" My father wailed. Dad was sixty-seven, his monograph on the Basque sculptor Eduardo Chillida had just been published by Abrams. Chillida was another artist my father felt hadn't had his due. He was as great as Henry Moore, David Smith or Richard Serra, "but undervalued." His work, made of stone or iron, was monumental and site-specific and integrated architecture with the environment. But it was often located in faraway places like San Sebastián. Because Chillida's sculptures were in the public arena, my father said his massive abstract forms connected man with nature—with space. *Like Duchamp, who insisted it is the viewer who completes the work of art . . . Chillida's work calls for this discourse.* Dad didn't think the art that was on view in SoHo created much of a dialogue with the viewer.

I found a job working in television production, as an assistant producer on commercials for products like soda, beer and deodorant. My father had taken my decision to leave California personally. He sulked and would ask, "Why do you want to be in New York?" I saw him occasionally, visits when he blew into town and we'd meet for a quick dinner. When my father retired from teaching in 1988, I did not fly out for the big splashy party Carole threw. I was working, I told him, though that wasn't the whole story. I was finding my footing and was rigid in my refusal to turn away from my own life to gaze at the prestige of my father's.

At night I went to City College and began working toward my MFA in creative writing, a choice that initially my father didn't support. "Your mother has had such a hard time in this profession," he said.

"What about you?" I asked.

"Academic writing is different. I'm an author, not always a writer." It was one of the most humble sentences I had ever heard him utter.

In my tiny apartment on Thompson Street, I covered the bathtub that sat in the middle of my kitchen with a plywood board and used it as my writing desk. I ate standing up, gazing out my window into the alleyway, where pigeons, their wings flurrying aggressively, battled for position on the windowsill. By 1990 I had published two short stories—both of which included a female character with a dynamic father—in small literary magazines. My father came to town and suggested that instead of writing fiction, I should write a profile of him. "For *The New Yorker*." He wanted his fifteen minutes of fame to last forever. We were sitting in Fanelli's, the local pub and burger joint on Prince Street. I was flattered that he'd asked me. I didn't believe *The New Yorker* would take the essay, but who knew what I'd learn, and perhaps the piece might be published elsewhere. If the piece was about him, Dad was sure they would want it.

"You can ask me anything you want," my father said.

Dad roped his old friend the author and art critic Dore Ashton into the mix, insisting that if he was engaged in a conversation with Dore, who, like him, had been around back in the heyday of Abstract Expressionism, the piece would be more in demand. We met in Dore's narrow yellow brownstone. Dore served us a Spanish frittata, then sat at the table chain-smoking thin cigarettes as my father told the story of the time he and Dore had sponsored an art auction and raised the money for the first Freedom Bus for the Freedom Rides in 1961. This was an interracial bus ride sponsored by CORE (Congress of Racial Equality) with the purpose of traveling across state lines to test the prohibition of racially segregated bus travel. Intending to go all the way from Washington, DC, to New Orleans, the Riders rode down through Atlanta, where they met with Martin Luther King, Jr. However, after the Ku Klux Klan firebombed the bus in Anniston, Alabama, the Riders were forced to fly the rest of the way. Though Dore and my father had not been on the buses, their involvement caused quite a stir. "We nearly lost our jobs," Dore added, tapping out another cigarette, meaning Dad's at MoMA and hers as the art critic for the *New York Times*. "Your father is a very impassioned man." Next to her my father pounded the table and they both sighed in synchronicity like old comrades.

Then they told me about their recent visit to East Germany to curate a show, *Twelve Artists from the German Democratic Republic*, which was exhibited in museums from Germany to Harvard, Los Angeles, Michigan and finally Albuquerque. This was the work of artists who were being sponsored by the GDR, a sign, my father said, that great artistic freedom had been allowed behind the wall. "People think that good art can't come out of a socialist regime, but it can! None of these artists are known outside of Germany."

I couldn't locate my father behind these stories of art and politics. When I asked my father about family, about us—my mother, my sister and me—he deftly avoided the topic, turning the subject back to his work. "Why do you want to know about that?" he asked.

"Because without any family background it's just a long CV," I tried to explain.

Beside him Dore let out a stream of smoke.

What I didn't see then, because I was too close, was that he was revealing something crucial about himself. That in seeking out the tributaries in the art world, he'd been following his own mainstream: the undervalued, the bypassed, the art of those working on the periphery. This inclination flowed back to his own childhood in Germany, when he'd first been excluded and labeled "other." True, Rothko hadn't been unknown when my father showed him at MoMA, but Mark, too, identified himself as an "outsider."

The fact was, I felt tongue-tied with sharp-eyed Dore sitting there. When I asked my mother what was it about Dore that was so intimidating, she said, "She's brilliant, tough as nails, too." Then she told me that Dore had been the *smart girl* whom she'd accused my father of having an affair with back in 1960. The woman she'd approached at a party and confronted, and because of whom she had written to my father and threatened to leave him.

"I can't do it," I told my dad on the next day. He frowned and grunted.

"This is something I should do with Peter, not Dore," my mother had said firmly over the phone. "After all, I was there. I want to write the story of us."

ON AND OFF over a three-year period, my parents met in either my living room or, when my mother traveled west, in the central space of my father's house. A small recorder on the table in between them, they talked, sometimes to each other, sometimes addressing the recorder. They talked about how they met, the places they traveled, and whom they'd known. *Bob Motherwell thought he was the centerfold of the art world.* And, *Poor Rothko was a man in constant conflict with being an outsider and an insider.* They even mentioned Andy Warhol: *He shrewdly made himself into an* enigma, my father said. They talked about who was still alive: *De Kooning, suffering from Alzheimer's, was rumored to be painting abstractions in East Hampton.* Mostly they talked about themselves, what they had given to the art world and what the art world had taken from them.

These were the tapes I found and listened to after my mother became ill. My mother asked my father on the tape, *When did the art world become the center of your life?*

Maybe when I met Stieglitz, Dad said.

I didn't realize it was that early. Then she added, *When we moved to New York I thought it would go on forever, the light flooding in the door, but there was a moment when our life hinged.*

It went on for a long time, Dad said.

For me it was about a year and a half, she corrected. *I was in love with the social whirl, it was much less tiring than mothering.*

My mother pressed my father to talk about family. *It was as though your wife and children fell into a black hole. What the hell happened to us?*

Oh, God! My father must have thrown his hands in the air, because on the tape I heard the slap of his palms landing on his knees.

We put together a unit that worked as two, Mom said, to herself as much as to him. *We could not do more . . . Until now, I didn't see how clearly, immensely, your professional life meant to you . . . But the destructive impact of that life on me, on your marriage, made childrearing virtually impossible.*

The children were occupying you and I didn't like it, Dad admitted. *I regret to say I was selfish. This is what really happened.*

I was too close, you were my center . . . Even after the Kinderheim when Tanya was three, the center of my life was you, she told him.

But I continued feeling tied to you, too. My father's voice was ardent. *I still feel that our relationship was the best thing that ever happened in my life. You could look and discuss the work with me. You helped me write . . . You just made too much of my affairs and then of course I felt angry and had more.*

I had an affair, Mom said softly.

You never told me. Why are you complaining about mine? I didn't complain.

How could you complain, Pete, if you didn't know? she snapped. *You said you didn't care, and that insulted me.*

Often my mother talked of envy. Sitting in his house, she pointed up to his study and addressed the recorder. *I see two long shelves, each about five feet long and aligned with publications. All his own stuff. Books and catalogues, and what I feel when I look at them is a real stab of jealousy, admiration yes, but Pete was always far more directed than I. I got my direction very late. I didn't fight for it early on.*

Why is that? My father asked.

It's very hard to grow up in the shade of a very large tree. I grew up in the shadow of a very productive tree, my father. Then I married one. And my father was competitive. After I published my first story I realized he was competitive with me.

Well, I'm not like that! Dad asserted loudly. *The nicest thing that happens to me is when people say, Are you Gabrielle's father? Nothing makes me prouder than that!*

Hesitating, my mother said, *Well . . . that's very nice.*

Again and again on the tape my father asked her: *What are we going to do with this material? What kind of book do you see?*

We must let it show us its form, my mother would reply vaguely.

Though I let them use my apartment, at first I was uncomfortable with my parents being together. Not since I was seven had I had much real experience of them as a unit, and yet, while I listened through the wall of my bedroom as they talked in my living room, their mingled voices felt familiar. They depended on each other for meaning. How could I not want them together, if only on a spool of tape? During the three years of taping, Tanya moved from California to Colorado. She was a waitress, then a baker. What Tanya liked was sports. She took up dance and hiking. She did not have any interest in what our parents were doing or in the art world. I dated, was engaged and then, briefly, married. At one point I even waltzed into the living room in the middle of a taping, and told my parents to stop talking so they could look at my big, poufy wedding dress. Instead of marching down an aisle, I was wed in a circle of redwood trees out in California, and when my father walked me through the meadow he whispered in my ear, "I don't want to give you away."

I married a loud, demanding, boyish artist who wanted to paint like an Expressionist, but merely ended up drinking like one. The marriage lasted a little over a year. Before my parents finished their taping, I'd filed for divorce. I realized that I had never taken marriage seriously. I had never known a successful one. Along with my parents, none of the artists I'd known as a child stayed married long enough to count as a success. My college and post-college friends hadn't fared much better. Yet despite the failure of my first marriage, I continued to believe it was possible to find that one person who could go from playmate to coparent to coworker and on to aging partner.

I've been married five times. I've made a lot of mistakes, my father said on one of the tapes as if these, too, were accomplishments.

My parents put aside the tapes and began roaming through galleries and museums together. My father was visiting New York, curating a series of shows for the Gagosian Gallery (Sam Francis's *Blue Balls* paintings and Max Beckmann's self-portraits). He wrote my mother, *Gagosian is now the fanciest of all New York galleries. Strangely in the space where Cordier & Ekstrom used to be and where we rode up in the elevator with Salvador Dalí and Gala for the Duchamp show and Dalí, even with that mustache, wasn't recognized. So many stories.* When he was in town, my mother drove down from Hartford, where she was still teaching, and they met to look at art. She refused to go to the MoMA, she hadn't set foot on that block of West Fifty-third Street since he'd left our family in 1965 and she wouldn't return even with him. But the Met, with its long marble galleries of European paintings, its sculptures of Greek and Roman torsos, held safer memories.

Pete is enthusiastic and questioning and enormous fun in a show. We spark ideas in each other and I really enjoy the hell out of that. Though I find myself exhausted by the end of the afternoon. I'm on every minute—yet I relish the role or I wouldn't play it. So exhausted was my mother by her outings with my father that one evening, while I waited for her to arrive and join me for dinner and sleep on my fold-out futon couch, I received a phone call instead. "Darling," came her distracted voice. "I'll be a little late. I'm taking a nap first with your father in his hotel room." I could hear giggling in the background.

"Do you really want to do this again?" I scolded when she finally appeared at my front door. "He's old now. Do you want an old man?" My father was seventy-six, Mom about to turn seventy.

"Maybe I want a man." My mother had a smug look on her face as if she'd just devoured a hearty meal. "Once I hook, I never unhook. And by the by, your father was the one who mentioned divorce."

But I wouldn't hear it. My father considering divorcing Carole, his fifth wife, to reunite with my mother! Five years had elapsed, four while they made tapes and one year of art viewing. My divorce was now finalized. I'd met a solid man who restored old houses and wanted what I wanted, a baby and a home. I was in my first trimester, about to leave the city and move to the east end of Long Island to live with him, not far from where my family and the artists of my childhood had frolicked in the summertime. I wanted to shake my mother awake, to tell her it was time to move on. She'd been the one who warned me in the hospital not to get too close to men like my father or I'd be collateral damage. Though sometimes I envied my parents' rapport and their continued devotion. "Are you serious?" I burst out at my mother. "Divorce again. Then what, remarriage?"

Soon after our fight my mother wrote my father a letter:

An hour ago I felt very bad for a bit. I came home and I saw an old house I'd lived in when I'd first moved to Hartford, before I bought this one. It was on fire. A huge stinking mess, fire trucks everywhere, I felt so bad for the family that lives there, but for myself, too. How could it happen to my old home? Then I remembered suddenly long ago when we first stepped off the train in Munich—that first time you'd gone back. We stepped down from the train onto a broad platform with a lot of pillars standing around in a sort of grayish daylight, and you looked up with a startled, puzzled look on your face and said, "But there was a roof."—And that was pretty much how it was for the next 4 days. Much of the city resembled a stage set for a nightmare. It was hard for me to imagine that it might have been a beautiful city once—So when I remembered that, I thought only one destructive fire. Only one. The

Turin and Westbeth are still in place. Our old home in Claremont is still standing, I'm told.

I must be trying to say something else. Odd that I should have stumbled on that fire when I was on my way home with every intention of writing you. For slowly (I am a slow person, really) I have been turning our deep affection for each other this way and that, looking at it. We tend to frolic a little in each other's company; we get such enjoyment out of seeing things together and talking about them and exchanging news and gossip and just being together a bit in the old way. If you and Carole broke up, I imagine you'd start to miss each other the minute you separated, the minute one of you moved out. As for me, I have a good job I can't easily replace. Let us keep peace.

I have one more memory that just came floating in again. I mean, of a place we lived together. Remember our apartment on Maryland Avenue in Chicago? We lived on the top floor. I drove down there recently with an old friend and was tooling through the neighborhood and there was that building, still in pretty good shape. They had bulldozed right up to the southern brick wall, razing everything for blocks south of it and laying out tennis courts and parking lots and icky little malls and god knows what, but there was our old apartment with young people living in it and sun shining in the windows and a plant or two on the sills and kids playing hopscotch out front and everybody was black or Hispanic and/or a student, busy, normal, a bit down-at-the-heels, but living their lives. The wrecking ball had stopped at the southern wall and they'd put up a neat fence, planted shrubs and a few spindly trees. A metaphor? We can be close without any more damage.

My father wrote back a few days later. *My life is pretty full of activities I like, and am still pretty good at.* He told her he was writing a new book to accompany a museum exhibition at the San Jose Museum of Art he was curating on Nathan Oliveira. *One of the artists from the* New Images of Man *show—remember? Only at the end did he say, Want to see you as much as possible. In the late 60s I had this feeling of terrible guilt. Now it is a sense of great loss, privation!—Perhaps we should talk more. Just to know.* A few months later he flew back East to see her.

I have no idea what happened during that visit. I suspect my mother was careful not to upset me. But I know something final must have been said, or reached or felt, in that meeting. For she called me on the phone soon afterward and told me what she needed to do.

And so I found myself in the spring of 1997, a few weeks before I was due to give birth, driving with my mother out to the tip of Long Island to our old summerhouse on Ferry Road. In the backseat of her car, swaddled in towels like a newborn baby, was the tombstone she'd stolen the day my father moved out of our home. Jemima Payne, Mr. Payne's second wife whom my mother had seized because she couldn't seize Norma. *I wanted to leave Mr. Payne with his first wife, alone and intact, the better to work out their marriage problems in eternity.* Now, after thirty-two years, my mother was finally ready to return the stone to its rightful place. I wasn't thrilled with sneaking into a graveyard that my mother had once desecrated, but I knew, from listening to their taping, how long and uncomfortably the past had haunted her.

It was pouring rain. Pulling the car over beside the old graveyard on the hill, I said, "I don't remember that tree," pointing at the large oak standing like a sentry in the middle of the stones.

"It was a little tree then," Mom said. "A very little tree."

I grabbed an umbrella from the backseat and my mother and

I lumbered up the slope. She cradled Jemima in her arms; my free hand was wrapped protectively over my huge belly, where my restless baby thumped inside me. Without hesitating, my mother opened the gate and found Mr. Payne and the first Mrs. Payne and beside them the ruined remains of the base of Jemima's stone. Gingerly, she set her fragment down beside them. It fit like the last piece of a puzzle.

The rain beat down and my mother and I huddled together underneath my umbrella. Unlike the other stones, Jemima's was untouched by weather and time.

"Look." My mother's pale skin glowed in the thunderstorm. "I preserved her."

MY PARENTS NEVER published their writing project. As my mother admitted, she was slow. When she became ill and I discovered the box of the tapes in the old trunk in her attic, I also found a thirty-page document. An accumulation of anecdotes from her journals and letters, which, after reading through them, I know was her beginning. It was titled *Entering History*. I don't think she ever used the material she'd gathered from the tapes. My mother never entered history, and I'm not sure that's what she wanted. Maybe she just needed the opportunity to say her piece and to roam once again with my father through museums. Art, particularly expressionist and abstraction, which placed such a value on the viewer's presence, was the medium for my parents, the meeting place where electricity ran between them while they looked, shared, spoke and sometimes touched, as if painting were the channel of raw feeling, the agent of their love. *We tend to frolic a little in each other's company; we get such enjoyment out of seeing things together.* Of course, none of us knew that by the end of the taping Alzheimer's already had begun to carve out hollow caves in my mother's memory.

After she relinquished my father and the stone that had weighted her to him, she was less interested in the taping project. She had another dream to accomplish that was more important to her, a monograph and exhibition of Greek-American artists. All the time she had been interviewing Dad, she had also been quietly going around and interviewing every Greek-American artist she could contact—from Lynda Benglis to Lucas Samaras, and even her old friend Theodoros Stamos, with whom she had kept in touch after the Rothko trial when he'd returned impoverished to Greece—was represented. My father agreed to help her.

"What's so important about Greek-American art?" Carole called and asked me two years later in 1999 when my father flew out to attend the opening of their show at the Queens Museum of Art. "Who cares?"

Carole was right. There was nothing terribly special about modern Greek-American art. My mother had simply wanted to research art connected to her heritage, and my father had wanted to help. These were the works of fellow immigrants, after all. People like him who had made the transition from a familiar world to an unfamiliar one. That was the long and short of it.

The Queens Museum of Art was located at the site of the old World's Fair, which had once promised to last a millennium but had closed after only two years, in 1965, the same year my parents divorced. At the end of the evening, after my father spoke about my mother's determined hard work and lauded the Greek-Americans as the inheritors of "an almost insurmountable tradition of classical antiquity," after my mother had been toasted and then had led a procession of these same artists in a Greek line dance to bazooka music, I wandered outside with my parents, my husband and our two-year-old son, Theo. It was a balmy night in early October, an Indian summer night, the warm thaw between first frost and long winter. My mother, in a wide colorful skirt, sallied forth toward the base of *The Unisphere*. This was the world's largest globe, a stainless steel representation of the planet that I hadn't seen since I was a small child and that now, somehow, rising up twelve stories high like a great scaffolding, singular and stately and without the crowds that had once flocked to the fair to see it, was even more grand. The elegant bare bones of a dream.

"*Peace Through Understanding*." My mother read the dedication out loud, turned to my father and laughed. "That's us, Pete. That's us."

I did not have the marriage my parents had. I did not have the understanding of a mind and heart so dissimilar to mine. Some vital glue between my husband and me was missing. He was a kind man, but not verbal. I doubt he understood me, either, for he was always asking me to be a different kind of mother, less attached to my child, a different kind of wife, the kind who ironed his sheets. I tried, but our marriage lasted only seven years.

By then my mother's mind had unraveled, too. It was 2005 and I was forty-seven years old and in the midst of my second divorce when my mother underwent a series of tests and was diagnosed with midstage Alzheimer's disease. She couldn't remember the names of vegetables in the grocery store, not even the place where I sent her taxes (the IRS). Her mail was *important paper*; the bank was the place where *money lived*. Though she could remember that she'd been a writer, she'd forgotten the title of any story she'd ever written. Pictures came to life. William Jefferson Clinton stepped off the cover of *Time* magazine with a bag of lobster for my mother's dinner; my father in his dark suit sailed off a photograph and in the door from Venice. Worse, she escaped from her house whenever her aide went to the bathroom, bolting out the front door. When she went to live in the nursing home, my father told me, "I want to come and see her."

When I drove him to the nursing home to see my mother, my father sat beside me with his beret pulled down over his forehead. I could tell he was worried. He was a man far better at beginnings than endings. My usually chatty father looked out the window and spoke only once, to ask me to stop so he could buy her some flowers. Walking through the corridors of her nursing home, he shook. It must not have been easy for him to see so many women wrinkled and slumped over in wheelchairs so far that their heads nearly rested in their laps. My father carried his bouquet of yellow lilies in front of him like a flag.

We found my mother inside her room sitting in her embroidered armchair, staring out the window. I'd done my best to make the room familiar for her, bringing in a few of her Early American antiques and family photographs. I'd wanted to hang some of her pictures on the walls, but I was warned that they might be stolen.

Her hair was parted down the middle and pushed behind her ears. Hardly gray at eighty, she looked young, as if Alzheimer's, in wiping out the pathways of memory, had erased age, too. She no longer resembled the wild, unhinged woman in her portrait, but, instead, what I imagined the first version of the painting must have looked like, before Appel caught her on the brink of her divorce, gazing out at her own uncertain future.

Two turquoise stones set in silver dangled from her ears. When my mother turned to greet us, my father's face lit up with a big, goofy grin. For a long moment my parents stared at each other. Then my father blinked in disbelief, and I knew he had seen the vacant, passive look in my mother's eyes. It was clear she didn't know him and was no longer waiting for his return.

I'd watched my mother's memory fade, but this lack of recognition was such a shock—she'd been talking about him only a few days earlier—that I sank onto her bed. Her yearning for him was over. I was the only one left clinging to the ghost ship of their relationship.

In the nursing home, at the end of my mother's life, my father's smile faded. Still, he rallied. He'd come such a long way to see her; all the way across his life for one final meeting. Doffing his beret, he bowed and presented my mother with her flowers. She bent her head and smelled the lilies. "You're a nice man," she said. Then she reached out a long hand, the one that had once worn his ring, and offered him the only other chair in the room.

My father sat down.

"I'm Peter," he said, extending his own hand toward hers.

Chapter 20

In the five years following my parents' final goodbye, I built a life with my son, cared for my mother and wrote and published essays on both Alzheimer's and art. Tanya and I divvied up her art collection; I kept the Carracci *Madonna and Child*. I didn't regret selling my mother's art. Relinquishing even her furious portrait felt like I was seeding bits of my mother, sharing her and my heritage with the world.

Traveling to the booming art fairs, I picked up a few pieces, resold some, kept the ones that spoke to me personally. Often these were self-portraits, a form of visual memoir merging self-scrutiny within the larger context of history. Where the artist literally steps into the frame by holding up a mirror. One, a painting by an Iranian-American artist named Taravat Talepasand that depicted her self-portrait within a Persian myth, inspired me to write an article discussing Talepasand's exploration of gender, desire and taboo, for the cultural arts magazine *Art Papers*. On my father's advice, I enlarged my scope to discuss the problems facing women artists in a society where their images had been erased from public view. Along the way, I introduced my father to the work being done by Middle Eastern women artists like Shirin Neshat and Shadi Ghadirian.

I was a single mother with a child, and I wanted to write. The sale of my mother's art had allowed for this. I won a few grants, and I began to feel validated in my writing, though pained that my mother would never know, for she barely recognized me.

One night in 2009, I saw Christopher Rothko at an opening of a show by a mutual friend, Yigal Ozeri. It was the first time I'd seen him since we were children. He had long since abandoned the diminutive Topher in favor of the adult Christopher. I asked him if he recalled visiting us in Berkeley or the walk in the redwood forest we'd taken together. "Gaby," he said, holding his plastic wineglass with the same long, elegant fingers of his father, "I can't remember anything that happened before I was fourteen years old." The trauma of his parents' deaths and the aftermath sat silently between us. Then he told me he had recently edited a book of his father's writings. *The Artist's Reality*, Christopher stated, was part of the legacy he and Kate wanted to share with the public.

Whenever my father came to New York, I traveled in from Long Island to meet him and together we roamed the galleries and museums. Dad was now in his eighties and a professor emeritus at Berkeley. He was on the board of the Neue Gallerie, a museum conceived by Serge Sabarsky and Ronald Lauder and devoted to early twentieth century German and Austrian art, a specialty my father had almost singlehandedly introduced to America. In London, the Tate Modern established a permanent room on the second floor devoted to many of the artists my father had included in his *New Images of Man* show at MoMA in 1959. Paul Karlstrom, an editor for the Smithsonian's Archives of American Art, was compiling a biography of my father's professional life. Dad had published another book in 2006 titled *Art of Engagement* that focused on the art of social and political causes, reaching back to the Beat generation, through free speech, civil rights, Vietnam and feminism. His book ended with an ode to a sustainable earth and a discussion of the visual artists who were calling attention to the environmental challenges humankind and the planet faced. My father believed that a work of art, whether figurative, abstract or environmental, should transcend private feeling and express something of value to mankind.

One of the artists in this last section of *Art of Engagement* was Agnes Denes.

When I'd moved back to New York in 1986 and was scrounging around looking for work, Dad suggested I go over and meet his friend Agnes Denes. Agnes must have been in her late sixties then, still beautiful, with a head of rich chestnut hair. She was the first environmental artist to synthesize land and performance art. She was kooky and stubborn and sometimes too esoteric for me to understand, especially when she talked about mathematics in an accent that had been flavored by her journey as a child from Hungary to Sweden and eventually to New York. All Agnes wanted to do was roll out of bed and make art. She was also impossible to work for, and she could hardly afford to pay me. We became friends instead.

Agnes was famous for a project she'd done in 1982 when she'd planted art in New York: *Wheatfield—A Confrontation*. She'd sown and tended two acres of golden wheat in the heart of Manhattan's Financial District, then harvested it into eleven thousand

Wheatfield—A Confrontation
Agnes Denes, 1982

pounds, feeding the hay to horses and sending the grain to travel globally in a show. The Bauhaus dream of an art that could save mankind was still alive. The piece had an actual, living cycle. More importantly, Agnes said, the piece caused people to really notice the space, to become involved with it, to care. The day the wheat was harvested, stockbrokers left the trading floor, came outside and wept.

This was the type of art that had begun to interest me in my writing, and I credit my father, in part, for his introduction. Not just to Agnes, but to the idea that the role of art was bigger than viewing an object on a wall. Bigger than communing between two people. The idea that art could encompass all of us. Ever since *Running Fence* I had loved art that unfolded like an adventure. Maybe that love went all the way back to my time at Westbeth—I've often thought of the building as one huge collective art project.

My own personal history with art had shaped a bias that would be expressed in the art that I began to write about in 2010. The art of experience, usually installation pieces like *Big Bambú* by the Starn twins that rose atop the Metropolitan Museum like the scaffolding for a new city. Or Doug Wheeler's *Infinity Space*, where Wheeler, a light and space artist, beveled the walls of a room so there were no edges, no horizon, only luminous light. Taking off my shoes, I stepped across a threshold and entered a space that was as airy as a cloud. This was art I could climb inside, crossing through the permeable boundary that separated me from another's imagination. This was art that allowed me to finally step off the sidelines and enter the picture.

Agnes had taken this idea of a direct encounter with the art and, in her case, with the land, a step further, toward the creation of an art form akin to redemption.

At Agnes's gallery in Chelsea—the new art Mecca after SoHo became too expensive—I saw a piece my father had written about in his book. A project that Agnes herself had often spoken about and that she finally realized in 1996. It was called *Tree Mountain—A Living Time Capsule*. Conceived by Agnes in 1992, it was a man-made mountain on the site of an old gravel quarry in Finland, and Agnes planted it with eleven thousand Finnish pine trees in an intricate mathematical pattern. This was eco-art in the truest sense of the term, a land reclamation project dedicated to humanity and to the natural environment. *Tree Mountain* had no life span; or rather its life span was unknown, projected into the future. This was what my father called "the art of engagement."

"This is art with life-enhancing power," my father had said of Agnes's *Tree Mountain*. It wasn't lost on me that this comment was from the man who had tried to poison the *Liquidambar* tree.

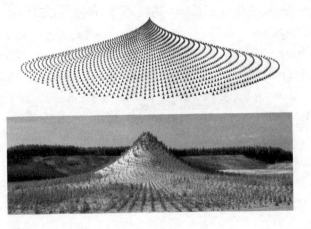

Tree Mountain—A Living Time Capsule—11,000 Trees, 11,000 People, 400 Years
Agnes Denes, 1992-96

Look at the hand of man [or in this case a woman] *on the landscape.* Like an iconographer I had mapped out my father's parts, but they did not add up to his whole. Do any of ours? Do the tributaries create the mainstream, or does the mainstream branch out into tributaries?

My father couldn't make art but he could ferret it out, dredge it from the deep unknown waters offshore and haul it to land. He could sing its praises and honor it. He could place it in history. My father scorned critics who broke art down into individual components, instead of experiencing it as a totality. Art required empathetic involvement, my father often said. His desire was to show how an artist engaged with politics, culture, history and even the natural environment of his own times. But standing looking at the circle of trees, I understood that for my father art had been more than a quest to be heard and seen. By his seeking to have the work of the periphery accepted and appreciated, art had become my father's path to assimilation. Art was his salvation. No coincidence, then, that my father loved the work of Max Beckmann. When my father looked at a Beckmann self-portrait, he saw a man who was placing himself squarely in history and, like him, had risen out of rubble and made an offering. Beckmann wrote: *Perhaps we can find ourselves, see ourselves in a work of art . . . ultimately, all seeking and aspiration ends in finding yourself, your real self of which your present self is only a weak reflection.* This seeking, Beckmann said, was the same whether it was exterior space or interior space. Like love, it was a spiritual endeavor, even while weighted with tragic gravitas.

EPILOGUE

New York, January 2010

On the eve of my father's ninety-first birthday, I met him at the Guggenheim to see the Wassily Kandinksy show. The great Russian pioneer of abstraction, the man who had metamorphosed from painting jewellike folktale paintings with color reminiscent of Monet, through German Expressionism, and finally to geometric abstractions. Kandinsky was one of the heroes from my father's childhood. "He taught at the Bauhaus," my father said.

"You told me that when I was little," I replied.

As we climbed the Guggenheim's ramp, following Kandinsky's momentous career, my father lingered in front of his favorite paintings, sighing with pleasure. He had to rest often. Age was creeping up on him.

And so we moved upward from bench to bench, snaillike, contemplating the pictures as we went. In front of an early Blue Rider painting, the colors as brilliant as stained glass, my father reminded me that for Kandinsky color was meant to trigger emotion. Blue was the color of the spirit, the spirit racing through art toward the future.

A few steps farther, my father stopped abruptly and sucked in his breath. "This is the first abstract painting ever painted," he said. "I saw an early Degenerate Art show right before I left Germany. I saw Kandinsky. I saw Beckmann. This painting is nearly a hundred years old, older than me." He chuckled and turned to me and asked, "I'm not that old, am I? I don't feel old. I still feel young. This painting doesn't feel old. But this is the moment art transformed and a new reality was born. You can see it happening. All the swirling energy, art on the move."

Picture with Circle
Wassily Kandinsky, 1911

Together we gazed at the canvas of dancing colors in quiet amazement and my father said wistfully, "I don't want it to end."

"What, Dad?"

"The curtain coming down."

At the top of the museum we looked down through the open rotunda, the view affording us a glimpse all the way back to Kandinsky's beginning. Here my father asked about his grandson. "How's the boy?" When my son Theo was born, my father christened him *the Boy*. The moniker had shaped Theo. At thirteen, he took art classes and painted brilliant-colored expressionist heads. I flipped open my cell phone and showed my father an image. "The boy's very good," my father praised. Then my father asked, "And what about you? What are you doing?"

I was working on the seedlings of this memoir then, and I knew already that it would not only be my father's story, but mine as well. "I'm writing," I said.

Later that night we went down to SoHo, to the old loft that Christo still lived in. Jeanne-Claude had died a few months earlier, but Christo, surrounded by an entourage of helpers, all of whom seemed to be nephews of either him or Jeanne-Claude, was genial, though sad. "Professore, I lost her," he said to my father when they embraced. "I always thought I would go first." It was hard to imagine Christo without Jeanne-Claude, and indeed he kept her in the room, bringing her into conversation—"Jeanne-Claude would say . . ."—at almost every turn in the discussion. Their son Cyril Christo was married and had a son. I was happy to learn that, like his parents, Cyril and his wife worked as a team. They had just done a book of photographs of endangered elephants. The loft was smaller than I'd remembered, with simple modern furniture. Wrapped items sat on pedestals or hung on

Dad and me.

the walls. Some were mysterious, their contents densely veiled by fabric and twine, forever unknowable. Others, like the partially wrapped telephone near the front door, easy to decipher.

At the end of the evening when we left, Christo walked us out into the hall to say goodbye. I hugged him and then descended ahead of my father, down the long flight of steep cement stairs to the street level below. I wasn't thinking of how my father would manage the climb down those hard, dangerous steps, but when I reached the bottom I turned and saw my dad looking at the narrow but long sheer flight with trepidation. "Professore," Christo said. "I have an idea." From under the banister he unfolded a strange wooden and metal contraption. "We used this for Jeanne-Claude." It was a chairlift.

"Oh, no," my father said, embarrassed.

But Christo insisted. "You will see." Sitting my father down in the seat, Christo pulled out long cloth ties and belts. First he strapped Dad into the chair, then he slowly began to wind the ties around him. When he was done, my father's torso was wrapped like a package, like a gift, like a Christo. My father laughed, his eyes lit up like birthday candles.

Then Christo stepped back and pressed a switch and sent my father—a man wrapped up in art—down to the ground, to earth, where I waited to unwrap him.

ACKNOWLEDGMENTS

I want to thank my agent, Susan Golomb, for making this journey possible.

I am grateful to the many people at W. W. Norton for their expertise, guidance and support, especially Jill Bialosky, Rebecca Schultz and Elizabeth Riley.

Additional thanks to readers of this manuscript for their encouragement and criticism at various stages in the process, in particular: Angela Himsel, Elise Zealand, Adelaide Mestre, Sara Selz, Tajlei Levis and Victoria Rowan.

For advice and counsel, I thank Thomas Selz.

For patience in answering all my questions and for letting me share their stories, special thanks are due to my father, Peter Selz, and my sister, Tanya Nicole Selz.

To my mother, Thalia Selz, I wish you were here. Thank you for writing your beautiful journals.

I could not have written this book without the love of my son, Theo Mync.

I wouldn't have written this book without the inspiration of artists.

AUTHOR'S NOTES ON SOURCES
AND PERMISSIONS

This is a memoir anchored by historical research. Throughout this manuscript I have quoted extensively from my mother's journals, my parents' letters and tapes they made together in the 1990s. I have also relied on memory, my journals, conversations with my father and my sister and talks with my mother before she became ill. I have consulted the interviews my father made for the Smithsonian Archives of American Art and the Museum of Modern Art archives.

Notes

p. 26 Peter Selz, "Degenerate Art Reconstructed," *Arts* magazine, September 1991. | **p. 26** Max Beckmann quote from a letter to his first wife Minna, from the front of World War I, June 8, 1915. | **p. 29** Rainer Maria Rilke, "Solemn Hour," in *Twice a Year*, ed. Dorothy Norman. Double Volume III–IV. Spring–Summer 1942/Fall–Winter 1942, p. 104. | **p. 32** *Beowulf*, line 455. | **p. 47** Peter Selz, *German Expressionist Painting* (Berkeley: University of California Press,1957), p. 17. | **p. 49** Joe Alex Morris, *Nelson Rockefeller: A Biography* (New York: Harper, 1960), pp. 42–43. | **p. 53** Peter Selz, *Seven Decades, 1895–1964, Crosscurrents in Modern Art* (New York: Public Education Association, 1966). |

p. 54 Harold Rosenberg, *"The American Action Painters," Art News*, 1952. | **p. 54** Jackson Pollock, application for Guggenheim fellowship, 1947. | **p. 57** Peter Selz, *German Expressionist Painting* (Berkeley: University of California Press, 1957), Introduction, pp 4–5. | **p. 78** Aline B. Saarinen, "'New Images of Man'— Are They!" *New York Times Magazine*, September 27, 1959, pp. 18–19. | **p. 80** Willem de Kooning, "The Renaissance and Order," (lecture) 1950. Published as "The Renaissance and Order," *Trans/formation* 1:2 (1951). | **p. 83** Calvin Tomkins *The Bride and the Bachelors* (Viking, 1965) p. 173. | **p. 96** Mark Rothko in a personal statement for an exhibition in 1945, published in David Porter's *Personal Statement: A Painting Prophecy*, 1950 (Washington, D.C.: Gallery Press, 1950). | **p. 106** Peter Selz, *The Work of Jean Dubuffet* (New York: Museum of Modern Art, 1962), p. 19. | **p. 109** Peter Selz, *Emile Nolde* (New York: Museum of Modern Art, 1963), p. 196. | **p. 119** Andy Warhol interview with Gretchen Berg in *East Village Other*, 1966. | **p. 124** Peter Selz, *Max Beckmann* (New York: Museum of Modern Art, 1964), p. 97. | **p. 135** Peter Selz, *Alberto Giacometti* (New York: Museum of Modern Art, 1965), p. 8. | **p. 147** Peter Selz, *Directions in Kinetic Sculpture* (Berkeley: University of California Press, 1966), p. 3. | **p. 149** George Rickey, Introduction, *Directions in Kinetic Sculpture* (Berkeley: University of California Press, 1966), p. 15. | **p. 151** Peter Selz, *Seven Decades, 1895–1965, Crosscurrents of Modern Art* (New York: New York Public Education Association, 1966). | **p. 151** Calvin Trillin, The Talk of the Town, *The New Yorker*, May 7, 1966, p. 37. | **p. 163** Willoughby Sharp originated the Air Art Show at Arts Council, YM/YWHA, Philadelphia, PA. Dad saw it and brought it to Berkeley. | **p. 165** Peter Selz, *Funk* (Berkeley: University of California Press, 1967), p. 3. | **p. 203** Patricia Bosworth, *Diane Arbus: A Biography* (New York: W. W. Norton, 2005), p. 309. | **p. 219** Edith Evans Asbury, "Rothko Art, Mostly Unseen, Is Ensnarled in Web of Intricate Suits," the *New York Times*, June 9, 1974. | **p. 220** Edith Evans Asbury, "Baffled as Ever, Rothko Court to Reopen," *New York Times*, August 5, 1974. | **p. 267** Peter Selz, *Art in Our Times*, (New York: Harry N. Abrams, 1981), p. 6. | **p. 284** Derived from *The Real Mother Goose* (Chicago: Rand McNally & Company, 1944), p. 47. | **p. 294** Peter Selz, *Beyond the Mainstream* (United Kingdom: Cambridge University Press, 1997), p. 4. | **p. 318** Peter Selz, "Eduardo Chillida: Sculpture in the Public Domain," *Beyond the Mainstream: Essays on Modern and Contemporary Art* (Cambridge:

Cambridge University Press, 1997), p. 141. | **p. 340** Max Beckmann, "Letters to a Woman Painter," in *Theories and Documents of Contemporary Art: A Sourcebook of Artists' Writings* (Berkeley: University of California Press, 1996), pp. 180–183.

Images and Epigraph Quotes

Front of Book: Mark Rothko quote © 2013 Kate Rothko Prizel & Christopher Rothko/Artists Rights Society (ARS), New York. Alfred Stieglitz quote © 2013 Georgia O'Keeffe Museum/Artists Rights Society (ARS), New York.

Prologue: Karel Appel, *Portrait of a Woman* (Thalia Selz, 1963). © 2013 Artists Rights Society (ARS), New York/ c/o Pictoright Amsterdam.

Part One: Jean Tinguely © 2013 Artists Rights Society (ARS), New York/ ADAGP, Paris. Alberto Giacometti quote © 2013 Alberto Giacometti Estate/ Licensed by VAGA and ARS, New York, NY.

Chapter 1: Photo of Drey family home in Munich courtesy of Gabrielle Selz. Rainer Maria Rilke quote from *The Grave Hour*, translated by Peter Selz in "Twice A Year," 1942. Max Beckmann, *Large Self-Portrait* (1919). © 2013 Artists Rights Scoeity (ARS), New York/VG Bild-Kunst, Bonn. Photo of Peter Selz and Thalia Cheronis courtesy of Gabrielle Selz. **Chapter 2:** Philip Guston working on a mural for the Federal Art Project, February 1939/David Robbins, photographer. Federal Art Project, Photographic Division collection, Archives of American Art, Smithsonian Institution. Jackson Pollock, *Mural* (1943), © 2013 The Pollock-Krasner Foundation/Artists Rights Society (ARS), New York. Image courtesy of: The University of Iowa Museum of Art, Gift of Peggy Guggenheim, 1959. Photo of Max Weber, Jackson Pollock and Peter Selz courtesy of Gabrielle Selz. **Chapter 3:** Photo of Peter Selz, MoMA Press Release courtesy of Gabrielle Selz. Willem de Kooning, *Woman and Bicycle* (1952–1953), © 2013 The Willem de Kooning Foundation/Artists Rights Society (ARS), New York. Photo of Thalia Selz at Party, © Terry Lee Schutte, 1963. **Chapter 4:** Jean Tinguely, *Homage to New York* (1960), © 2013 Artists Rights Society (ARS), New York/ADAGP, Paris © Estate of David Gahr. **Chapter 5:** Mark Rothko, *Red on Maroon* (1959) © 2013 Kate Rothko Prizel and Christopher Rothko/Artists Rights Society (ARS), New York. Photo of Peter and

Thalia Selz in Venice courtesy of Gabrielle Selz. **Chapter 6:** Jean Dubuffet, *à Peter Selz* © 2013 Artists Rights Society (ARS), New York / ADAGP, Paris. Photo of Mark and Christopher Rothko © Peter Selz. Photo of Tanya and Gaby Selz © Peter Selz. **Chapter 7:** Max Beckmann, *The Argonauts* (1949–50), © 2013 Artists Rights Society (ARS), New York/VG Bild-Kunst, Bonn. Dad in front of Max Beckmann, Departures at MoMA opening, © 2013 Artists Rights Society (ARS), New York/VG Bild-Kunst, Bonn, Photo with permission of Martin P. Lazarus. Photo by Stephen Shore of Andy Warhol, Sam Green, Marcel Duchamp, Cordier Ekstrom Gallery, 1965–1967, Black and white photograph, 12.75 × 19 inches. Courtesy 303 Gallery, New York. **Chapter 8:** Alberto Giacometti, *Walking Man I*, 1960. Bronze, 180.5 × 27 × 97 cm. Cast 1981, edition Fondation Alberto et Annette Giacometti. Collection Alberto and Annette Giacometti, Paris, inv. 1994-0186 (AGD 322) ©2013 Alberto Giacometti Estate / Licensed by VAGA and ARS, New York, NY, 2013.

Part Two: George Rickey quote © Estate of George Rickey/Licensed by VAGA, New York, NY. Published in *Directions in Kinetic Sculpture*, Introduction by George Rickey. Diane Arbus quote courtesy of Diane Arbus Estate.

Chapter 9: George Rickey, *Two Lines—Temporal 1* (1964), © Estate of George Rickey/Licensed by VAGA, New York, NY. Photo of Dad in front of Len Lye, *Fountain* (1967), courtesy of the Len Lye Foundation. Family photo courtesy of Gabrielle Selz. **Chapter 10:** Bruce Conner, *WEDNESDAY* (1960). Mixed media, 78 × 16.5 × 21 in. © 2013 Conner Family Trust, San Francisco/Artists Rights Society (ARS), New York. Image courtesy of Fine Art Museums of San Francisco. Gift of Bruce and Jean Conner and Peter and Carole Selz, 189.189. Photo of Dad with Warhol, *Silver Clouds* (1968), © 2013 the Andy Warhol Foundation for the Visual Arts, Inc./Artists Rights Society (ARS), New York. Photo of Gaby Selz courtesy of Peter Selz. **Chapter 11:** Photo of Westbeth Couryard, 1970, © Leonard Freed; Big Yellow W courtesy of Gabrielle Selz; Photo of Diane Arbus with Marvin Israel at Westbeth taken by Cosmos Andrew Sarchiapone, 1970, courtesy of the Estate of Cosmos Andrew Sarchiapone; Photo of Anna Halprin Dancers performing *Parades and Changes*, 1970, courtesy of Anna Halprin. **Chapter 12:** Harold Paris, *Homage to Boccioni #5* (1971), © the Harold Paris Trust, photo courtesy of Kevan Jenson. Photo of Dad marrying Dolores Yonkers, 1972 courtesy of Tanya Nicole Selz.

Part Three: Jean-Claude and Christo quote courtesy of Christo. Cindy Sherman quote courtesy of artist and Metro Pictures.

Chapter 13: Photos of *Running Fence* installation by Gabrielle Selz with permission of use from Christo. **Chapter 14:** Sam Francis, *Iris* 1965/67, acrylic on canvas, 89.5 × 71 in. and Sam Francis, *Iris* (1965/67), acrylic on canvas, 89.5 × 71 inches, collection of Dr. Peter Selz, © 2013 Sam Francis Foundation, California/Artists Rights Society (ARS), NY; photo by Brian Forrest, Santa Monica. Sam Francis, *Ski Painting* (1967), Naibara, Japan, © 2013 Sam Francis Foundation, California/Artists Rights Society (ARS), NY. **Chapter 15:** Richard Diebenkorn, *Woman in a Window* (1957), oil on canvas, 59 × 56 inches (149.9 × 142.2 cm), Estate #1225, ©the Richard Diebenkorn Foundation. **Chapter 16:** Cindy Sherman, *Untitled Film Still #21* (1977), courtesy of Metro Pictures, 519 West 24th Street, NYC 10011. Photo of Dad in his office by Bill Knowland, courtesy of the *Oakland Tribune*. **Chapter 17:** Jacques Villon and Marcell Duchamp, *The Bride* (1934), collection of Gabrielle Selz, © 2013 Artists Rights Socitey (ARS), New York/ ADAGP, Paris. **Chapter 18:** Carolee Schneemann, *Up to and Including Her Limits* (1973), courtesy of Carolee Schneemann photo by Henrik Gaard.

Part Four: Agnes Denes quote courtesy of Agnes Denes.

Chapter 19: Andy Warhol, *Camouflage Self-Portrait* (1986), © 2013 the Andy Warhol Foundation for the Visual Arts, Inc./Artists Rights Society (ARS), New York. **Chapter 20:** Agnes Denes, *Wheatfield—A Confrontation* (1982), and Agnes Denes, *Tree Mountain—A Living Time Capsule—11,000 Trees, 11,000 People, 400 Years*, courtesy of Agnes Denes.

Epilogue: Wassily Kandinsky, *Picture with Circle* (1911), © 2013 Artists Rights Society (ARS), New York/ADAGP, Paris. Photo of Peter and Gabrielle Selz by Nan Phelps Photography.

Please refer to gabrielleselz.com for more information on the artists and links to their work.

ABOUT THE AUTHOR

Gabrielle Selz has published in magazines and newspapers including *More* magazine, the *New York Times*, *Newsday*, and *Fiction*. She writes regularly on art for the *Huffington Post*. She lives in Southampton, New York. For more information, please visit gabrielleselz.com.